The University of Iowa Guide to Campus Architecture

SECOND EDITION

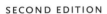

A Bur Oak Book

T0108616

The University of Iowa Guide to Campus Architecture

SECOND EDITION

JOHN BELDON SCOTT

and RODNEY P. LEHNERTZ

with the assistance of

CAROLINE CASEY

Published for the Office of the President

by the University of Iowa Press

University of Iowa Press, Iowa City 52242
Copyright © 2016 by the University of Iowa Press
www.uiowa.edu/uiowapress
All rights reserved
Printed in the United States of America
Design by Richard Hendel

The University of Iowa Press is a member of Green Press
Initiative and is committed to preserving natural resources.

Printed on acid-free paper

Library of Congress Cataloging-in-Publication Data
Names: Scott, John Beldon, 1946– author. | Lehnertz,
    Rodney P., author.
Title: The University of Iowa guide to campus architecture /
    John Beldon Scott and Rodney P. Lehnertz.
Description: Second edition. | Iowa City : University of
    Iowa Press, 2016.
Identifiers: LCCN 2016009157 | ISBN 978-1-60938-459-3 (pbk)
    | ISBN 978-1-60938-460-9 (ebk)
Subjects: LCSH: University of Iowa—Buildings. | University
    of Iowa—Buildings—Pictorial works. | Architecture—
    Iowa—Iowa City. | Architecture—Iowa—Iowa City—
    Pictorial works. | BISAC: ARCHITECTURE / General.
Classification: LCC LD2569 .S36 2016 |
    DDC 378.777/655—dc23
LC record available at https://lccn.loc.gov/2016009157

FOR MICHAEL NEW

We shape our buildings; thereafter they shape us.
—*Winston Churchill*

Contents

Foreword

LYNETTE L. MARSHALL, PRESIDENT AND CEO

THE UNIVERSITY OF IOWA FOUNDATION

If you venture to the fourth floor of the Levitt Center for University Advancement—home of the University of Iowa Foundation and the University of Iowa Alumni Association—you'll find that world-renowned architect Charles Gwathmey incorporated an interesting design feature. When you look through one of his signature twelve-inch-square blocks, you have a perfectly framed view of Frank Gehry's Iowa Advanced Technology Laboratories building in the distance.

That perfect view of Iowa is something Michael J. New, to whom this book is dedicated, was so passionate about preserving. Michael, my predecessor, worked for the University of Iowa Foundation for more than thirty years, serving as president and CEO from 1998 to 2005. He was, perhaps, most publicly well known for leading the University of Iowa to the successful $1.06 billion conclusion of the *Good. Better. Best. IOWA.* campaign. But among his family, friends, colleagues, and donors, he will be most remembered as a warm, witty, sincere, and intelligent man with a deep and abiding passion for his family and his university. Michael died in 2006, just after celebrating that $1 billion milestone, and in the years since his death, his legacy continues to have a deep impact on our work at the UI Foundation.

Michael believed wholeheartedly that the people who love this great institution will help those who come after them and that if you ask our alumni and friends to give back, they will respond in ways you never imagined. I have had the privilege to witness and help facilitate many of these transformational gifts, which bolster student scholarship, speed research, and help keep the University at the forefront of education and discovery. Our donors are changing the face of our campus, especially now, as we continue to build for future generations.

As you navigate the pages of this architectural guide to the University, you'll learn many interesting facts about our beautiful campus. For me, Gwathmey's "perfect view" represents what our donors, collectively, give to Iowa and our students—a perfect view of a brighter future.

To learn more about influential Iowans and donors who are honored with named facilities on campus, please visit www.facilities .uiowa.edu/named-buildings.

A Tradition of Excellence

DAVID J. SKORTON, PRESIDENT (2002–2006)

The University of Iowa has a rich, proud tradition of excellence in education, of distinction and achievement in research, scholarship, and creative activity, of generous service, and of athletic success. Yet none of this tradition would be possible without a distinguished physical campus. In terms of architectural integrity, intellectual inspiration, and cutting-edge function, the University of Iowa boasts an outstanding—and stylistically diverse—ensemble of buildings and public art of which we can all be proud.

We chose the Old Capitol dome as our University symbol, and with good reason. The Pentacrest buildings, topped by this sentinel dome over Iowa's first state capitol, are a classic of campus planning and architecture that commands immediate attention.

As our campus has grown and changed over the years, we have been proud to add many magnificent buildings to our home on both sides of the Iowa River. This tradition of excellence and innovation continues with such buildings as the Iowa Advanced Technology Laboratories, the Levitt Center for University Advancement, and Art Building West, all designed by major architects engaging the most visionary principles of contemporary design. At the same time, buildings such as the Blank Honors Center, the Pomerantz Center, and the Adler Journalism and Mass Communication Building combine up-to-date design with the highest levels of technology and function to serve our faculty, staff, students, alumni, friends, and the public.

Beyond simply providing necessary housing for our educational, research, service, and other activities, our campus architecture exemplifies the attention to good design that demonstrates the UI's historic commitment to the arts. Such beauty and elegance play important roles in our sense of place that sustain faculty, staff, and student recruitment, retention, success, and pride.

Please enjoy this campus guidebook, and please make yourself at home on our campus.

Acknowledgments

Such a comprehensive undertaking as a guidebook must be a collaborative project at many levels, and as authors, therefore, we are indebted to a number of individuals who have contributed in diverse and significant ways. We thank Jennifer Salvo for the months she spent in the University Archives retrieving the architectural history of the UI and searching out detailed answers to our nearly endless list of questions. Gwynne Rohner Dilbeck worked tirelessly and thoughtfully on the checklist of buildings, which is the factual basis of the individual building narratives. She also edited the text entries and campus maps. Steven Addy devoted long, expert hours to organizing and editing the photographs, almost all of which have been newly made specifically for this project. Eric Dean and Joseph Montez provided additional expert assistance with photographs for the second edition. Warren Staal added some touches to the photographs just as the manuscript was going to press. Shawn Albaugh Kleppe has been an ever-present organizational, logistical, and editorial force throughout the entire life of this enterprise. Jay Geisen designed the maps with expertise and patience. Kirk Banks updated the building and architect lists. Caroline Casey contributed significantly, assisting us ably by writing initial drafts of the individual entries and by providing editorial advice on the entire manuscript. We thank John Kimmich-Javier for his expert photographs of some key campus buildings.

We also acknowledge the encouragement and material support of former President David J. Skorton, who conceived this project; President Emeritus Willard L. Boyd, who was a key player in a good portion of the architectural history presented here and who also has collaborated in this project even beyond his insightful introduction to the book; Michael New, former director of the UI Foundation, whom we acknowledge for his early faith in this project, which he generously backed from the beginning; Donald Guckert, director of Facilities Management, who made available to us the essential resources of his organization; Linda Maxson, former dean of the College of Liberal Arts and Sciences, who contributed strategic encouragement; and Dorothy Johnson, former director of the School of Art and Art History, who funded much of the research and editorial staffing for the book. Barbara Burlison Mooney provided invaluable counsel on the history of architecture. Pamela Trimpe helped with the list of sculptures. We also thank the staff of the UI Press for their flexibility and patience along the sometimes difficult road to publication.

Colleagues all over campus responded generously to our requests for information concerning the buildings that they know and love, thereby greatly enriching the guidebook entries. We thank each of them.

All photographs are by John Beldon Scott except the following: Steven Addy (page 95); Peter Alexander, UI Relations (page 140); BNIM, Des Moines (pages 39, 81); Creative Media Group, UIHC (colorplate 5; page 207); Eric Dean (colorplate 9; pages 82, 124, 147, 226); Foster + Partners, London, UK (colorplate 15); Wayne Johnson, Main Street Studio (colorplate 12; page 237); John Kimmich-Javier (colorplates 3, 19; pages ii, 6, 33, 85, 176, 177, 198); Tom Langdon, UI Foundation (colorplates 21, 23); Kirk Murray, UI Strategic Communications (colorplates 11, 14, 17, 24; pages 4, 5); Lawrence Nowlan, Windsor, Vermont (page 220); OPN Architects, Cedar Rapids (pages 113, 182 bottom); Rohrbach Associates, Iowa City (page 62); UI Center for Media Production, Photo Service (page 106); University of Iowa Archives (pages 37, 50, 93, 94, 119, 166, 169 top, 219 top, 241); the UI Museum of Art (colorplate 16); and Dave VanDonselaar, Dale Photographics (page 32).

The publication of this book was made possible in part by a generous gift from Forest D. Jones and Marda Higdon Jones.

This book is dedicated to Michael New, whose work and passion for the University of Iowa leave a legacy that includes many of the buildings we celebrate. We will always be indebted to Michael for all he has meant to the University and the community.

An Introduction to UI Campus Architecture

WILLARD L. BOYD

PROFESSOR OF LAW & PRESIDENT EMERITUS

I have long asserted that people, not structures, make a great university. However, great structures inspire and enable great things to happen in a university. As John Beldon Scott and Rodney Lehnertz have said of the Old Capitol, "In choosing the Greek Revival style of Iowa's first capitol, our forebears sought to connect what was then a still rather rugged land to ancient Athenian democracy. It's easy to imagine how impressive those austere but solid-looking Doric columns must have appeared when most of the population lived in unornamented one-story dwellings. The noble architecture made a clear statement about the just government to which Iowans aspired." A commitment to "noble architecture" makes a clear statement about the academic excellence to which the University continually aspires.

We are indebted to the University leaders of the late nineteenth and early twentieth centuries who had a vision for the Pentacrest as the core of the campus both academically and visually. In the years that followed, the University did not have the financial wherewithal for a built environment worthy of the excellence of its programs. The agricultural depression of the 1920s, the economic depression of the 1930s, and the "pay-as-you-go" policy of the University and the state in the 1950s resulted in a severely underbuilt university. Nevertheless, financial and programmatic resourcefulness responded to some crucially needed buildings. It is amazing that the University of Iowa did not have a freestanding library until the early 1950s, when the current Main Library was built in sections over a decade or more. Previously, it had been located in Macbride Hall along with an auditorium that also served as the University's performing arts venue, as well as a lecture hall. The entrepreneurship of William R. Boyd (no relation), chair of the Finance Committee of the State of Iowa Board of Education, led to Iowa accepting the challenge grant of the Rockefeller Foundation to build a new hospital and medical school on the west side of the river. Wisconsin had previously declined the Rockefeller offer on the grounds that it was tainted money.

At midcentury, President Virgil Hancher first articulated a vision of a physical Iowa Center for the Arts. His successor, Howard Bowen, and Frank Seiberling, director of the School of Art and Art History, felt that vision should be both aesthetically and functionally compelling. In the late 1960s, at Seiberling's prodding, President Bowen persuaded the state Board of Regents to engage in an architectural seminar of several days. As a result, the Regents authorized the universities to engage architects from across the country in joint ventures with Iowa architects. The first was Max Abramovitz of New York City, who became the architect of the Iowa Center for the Arts. His firm had designed the United Nations building and some of Lincoln Center. A disciple of Mies van der Rohe, Abramovitz designed Hancher Auditorium, Voxman Music Building, an addition to the School of Art and Art History, and the Museum of Art. His minimalist approach gave Iowa an inspiring yet functional campus, including one of the finest university art museum buildings in the nation, because he sublimated his architectural ego in order to provide a superb exhibition space for visual artists.

In 2008 the Center for the Arts was ravaged by a five-hundred-year flood. Hancher Auditorium and the Voxman Music Building were destroyed. A new music building has been constructed at the south end of the campus near where the new Museum of Art will be located. The result is that the arts will anchor both the north and south ends of the campus, welcoming visitors and increasing student access to the arts.

The second architect retained in the 1960s was Walter Netsch of Chicago, who had designed the chapel at the Air Force Academy and the initial campus of the University of Illinois at Chicago. His first University of Iowa commission was the Biological Sciences Building (now the Bowen Science Building), which was financed in part by a National Science Foundation Center of Excellence Award. Netsch's challenge was to nestle that vast building into a scenic ravine without overwhelming the environment. A feature of both the Biological Sciences Building and the Hardin Library for the Health Sciences (also designed by Netsch) is an internal passageway for pedestrians to use during inclement weather. Netsch also designed the Lindquist Center on the east campus.

In the early 1980s, Gunnar Birkerts designed the circular College of Law Building (now the Boyd Law Building). The center core of the building has a silver dome reminiscent of both the Old Capitol dome and the top of an Iowa farm silo. In the following years, a number of buildings that are outstanding in both form and function have been created.

Wisely, the University gives attention to sensitive remodeling of such older buildings as Schaeffer Hall. The second half of the twentieth century also brought concern for landscaping in terms of both plantings and preservation of green space such as Hubbard Park and Richard E. Gibson Square. This landscaping commitment is wonderfully represented on the Medical Campus with the relocation of Newton Road, which has created both a green pedestrian campus and the opportunity to view from the north Netsch's contemporary Gothic design of the Hardin Library for the Health Sciences. The University's major commitment to art in public places enhances both the interior of these buildings and their settings with work by well-known local and national artists.

The financing of University buildings became more varied and complex in the second half of the twentieth century, thus enabling the University to provide facilities needed for excellence. Dormitories and academic and support buildings could be funded by bonding secured by fees and earnings. The State of Iowa provided a capital building program, and federal funds have been available for specific facilities.

In the 1920s, private fundraising made possible the first section of the Iowa Memorial Union and the building of Kinnick Stadium. Yet the first major capital fundraising project of the University of Iowa Foundation (established in 1956) was the campaign to build the Museum of Art, followed by a series of successful private fundraising efforts to assist in the construction of many crucial University buildings.

A signal event of the 1970s and beyond has been the rebuilding, conceived by John Colloton, of the University of Iowa Hospitals and Clinics. Both its design and its financing are exceptional. Financed from earnings and private gifts, UIHC is horizontally and architecturally congruent with the growing health sciences campus of striking buildings. In 2016, an impressive vertical Children's Hospital was opened and will be followed by two additional buildings.

UIHC is also a unique center of the visual and performing arts. In preserving the 1920s Gothic Tower, a visual arts gallery was established at its internal base. This blossomed into Project Art, which incorporates original visual art in every part of the complex, along with a venue for the performing arts.

In addition to UIHC, the west campus is the site of extraordinary new facilities for the University's health colleges. Nowhere is this more visible than looking west from Old Capitol where once the Gothic Tower stood alone on the west campus skyline.

People make buildings. Dedicated committees oversee campus and building planning and construction. A variety of professional offices in the University's Office of the Vice President for Finance and Operations arrange financing and directly supervise every detail of construction and maintenance. With the increasing sophistication of academic programs and related technology, both the construction and operation of buildings have become extraordinarily complex. In the 1950s, the built campus was the responsibility of the small Office of the University Architect, headed by George Horner and Richard Jordison, and the Department of Buildings and Grounds. To meet the monumental challenges of a large and complex campus, there emerged a comprehensive and able Facilities Services Group (now known as Facilities Management) under the leadership of Richard Gibson. Structures are not only well built but also exceedingly well maintained by a variety of user-oriented staff across the campus.

The Iowa campus presents a panorama of diverse and significant architecture of changing eras. The University's entry into the twenty-first century is marked by the coming to fruition of a number of exciting new buildings that inspire and serve us. We continue to rethink the uses to which existing buildings can be put for new times. For example, the Old Capitol also serves as a public exhibition venue for the humanities.

President Walter Jessup said that education is Iowa's never-ending frontier. Now more than ever the University is committed to being on the frontier of educational excellence that will require pioneering and inspiring architecture.

A Diversity of Styles
The History of UI Campus Architecture

Some American university campuses are characterized by a consciously conceived and carefully guarded uniformity of architectural style. These are most typically neo-Gothic or neo-Classical and on the model of Oxford and Cambridge or Thomas Jefferson's University of Virginia. There are also a few instances of Colonial and Romanesque Revival and at least one major example of Spanish Colonial. There are even new campuses built entirely in the 1960s and 1970s in a consistent Modernist stylistic idiom. The campus of the University of Iowa is not like any of these. But what may sometimes seem an almost confusing assemblage of styles actually was generated by assumptions, usually unarticulated, that reveal a fairly consistent vitality and logic to the stylistic evolution of UI buildings and planning principles.

The initial impression of uniformity presented by the Greek Revival Old Capitol (1842) and the four symmetrically disposed Proudfoot and Bird Beaux-Arts buildings of the Pentacrest (1902, 1908, 1912, 1924) dissipates the farther one moves away from that historic center of the UI campus, although the oldest and closest buildings to the Pentacrest display an effort to maintain the Beaux-Arts model of Classical Revival design. The Sciences Library (1902), Biology Building and Seamans Center for the Engineering Arts and Sciences (1905), and Gilmore Hall (1910) show this. But even as the Pentacrest buildings themselves were still ongoing projects, that uniformity of style was evolving into something else. The President's Residence (1908) and Currier Residence Hall (1914), at some distance from the Pentacrest, opted for Colonial Revival, as did Stuit Hall (1918). But even nearby buildings such as Halsey Hall (1915), Trowbridge Hall (1918), Chemistry Building (1922), and the Iowa Memorial Union (1925) tempered the classical vocabulary of the Pentacrest buildings, displaying a gradual move away from that rigorous high-style formality. The shift in these buildings from Indiana limestone to the more vernacular red brick with limestone trim was a marker for the turn away from absolute fidelity to consistency of style. In particular, Halsey's shedding of the classical orders, Trowbridge's introduction of the more up-to-date Chicago window, and Chemistry's use of steel industrial windows indicate a tension between the past and the present—and a hint of things to come.

Just at this historical moment when intimations of contemporary design were showing up on the Main Campus, the move of the medical and hospital departments to the bluffs on the west side of the Iowa River produced a surprising evolutionary loop. The planners of the Medical Campus had, by the mid 1910s, imposed a uniform style on the designs Proudfoot and Bird were charged with producing for this grandest architectural undertaking in the history of the UI. Westlawn, Children's Hospital (razed, 1999 and 2003), and the Medical Education Building, all completed in 1919, were in a neo-Medieval mode, mostly Tudor Revival. Medical Laboratories (1927), in full-blown Tudor Revival, and General Hospital (1928), in Collegiate Gothic, would seem at first glance an emphatic rejection of Pentacrest Classicism. But this ostensible stylistic shift also had its own coherent logic. One historical style, Beaux-Arts Classicism, would now be complemented with another, neo-Gothic. The Gothic orientation of the Near West, Athletics, Medical, and UIHC campuses was a forceful and successful effort to declare a uniform aesthetic. Even the Field House (1927) and Kinnick Stadium (1929) with their spur buttresses, heraldic shields, and corbelled balconies contain medieval references. Hillcrest Residence Hall, on the highest campus bluff, was the last UI building with any historicizing detail. It opened in 1939, ninety-seven years after Old Capitol. We can therefore think of two distinct UI campuses, one Classic and one Gothic, one Jeffersonian and one Oxbridge. But it would be just as correct to see one historical-revival campus that embraces both styles and spans the entire first century of UI campus architecture.

Within four years of General Hospital's spectacular neo-Gothic statement, George Horner's Mechanical Engineering Building (1932; now Seamans Center for the Engineering Arts and Sciences) recommenced the evolutionary march of contemporary design on the UI campus. This unassuming building holds the distinction of being the first nonhistoricizing design on the UI campus. Its Moderne motifs at the entrance are a completely contemporary reference. Horner's Arts Campus, which was taking shape just at this time (Theatre Building, 1936; Art Building, 1936; Iowa Memorial Union Pedestrian Bridge, 1936), is transitional, straddling both the past and the present. Renaissance arches (Art Building), Streamline Moderne verticals (Theatre Building), and Art Deco detailing (IMU Pedestrian Bridge) coexist. But the way to the future is sufficiently clear even in these ambivalent designs. Horner's utilitarian South Quadrangle (1942), the earliest UI campus building that is completely shorn of ornamental embellishment, is a modest but noteworthy milestone.

With the Communications Center (1951), International Style Modernism debuted on the UI campus. Its Brutalist concrete grid façade emphatically rejected all historicizing detail and pointed the way to the machine aesthetic of standardization that triumphed in the subsequent post–World War II era: Burge Residence Hall (1959), Van Allen Hall (1964), Phillips Hall (1965), and the English-Philosophy Building (1966). In a noteworthy example of historical symmetry, the design firm of the Communications Center (Brooks Borg, Architects-Engineers) was the successor firm to the venerable Proudfoot and Bird, the designers of the Pentacrest.

Under the leadership of President Howard Bowen, an accelerated trajectory toward contemporary design was initiated by the Board of Regents' 1965 decision to offer Iowa architectural firms the option of partnering with design firms from anywhere in the nation. The commissioning of Max Abramovitz, one of the most prominent architects of the time, to design the former Museum of Art (1969) was the first fruit of this new progressivism in architectural thinking. Three new Abramovitz buildings (former Voxman Music Building, 1971, razed 2013; Clapp Recital Hall, 1971, razed 2013; and Hancher Auditorium, 1972, razed 2013) soon put the UI campus in the mainstream of architectural design. These three connected buildings, with their unwavering worship of the Modern, introduced a sophistication to the UI campus that had not been reached by their Modernist predecessors.

If Abramovitz's Arts Campus buildings brought the UI to a new level of contemporary design, it was a series of three radical buildings by Walter Netsch (Bowen Science Building, 1972; Lindquist Center, 1973; and Hardin Library for the Health Sciences, 1974) that pushed the UI to the very edge of contemporary architecture. The application of Netsch's own Field Theory of design made these buildings not only stylistically advanced but also experimental in their methodology. This progressive, even venturesome, initiative of President Willard Boyd's administration marks an apogee of contemporary design in the history of UI campus architecture, one that would be matched only in the early twenty-first century. That legacy has made possible other well-designed buildings (Carver-Hawkeye Arena, 1983; Boyd Law Building, 1986; Levitt Center for University Advancement, 1998; the Medical Education and Research Facility, 2002; Pappajohn Biomedical Discovery Building, 2014; and Hancher Auditorium, 2016) and has even cleared the way for exceptionally progressive designs like Frank Gehry's Iowa Advanced Technology Laboratories (1992) and Steven Holl's Art Building West (2006) and Visual Arts Building (2016), projects that put the UI at the forefront of world architecture.

Notwithstanding its apparent variety of styles, at few moments in its evolutionary development has UI campus architecture failed to build on its own diverse stylistic momentum. The march away from the Pentacrest was never a total rejection, and Frank Lloyd Wright's stern admonition to forget about Old Capitol and the Pentacrest was never entirely heeded. There is a long succession of campus designs that look back even as the stylistic trajectory propelled administrators and architects ever forward. Without Old Capitol's noble dome we cannot have General Hospital's Gothic Tower or Boyd Law Building's dome, perched on the Gothic West Campus but visible from the Main Campus. Even the Modernist façades of the English-Philosophy Building and south extension of the Main Library (1971) reference the proud columnar profiles of the Pentacrest, just as the rotundas of the Levitt Center and the Adler Journalism Building (2005) recall the west façades of Schaeffer and Macbride Halls. On the West Campus the projecting white triangles of Hardin Library, the vent towers of Bowen Science, and the dynamic atrium of the Medical Education and Research Facility, all Modern and Postmodern, pay their respects to the totemic image of General Hospital's Gothic Tower. The UI, with its educational commitment to the arts and creative imagination, manifests itself in this innovative legacy of diversity within continuity, and that is the premise of this guidebook.

Iowa River Floods: 1993, 2008

During the summer of 1993, the University of Iowa and residents and business owners along the Iowa River basin suffered through the worst flood in memory, ending a local sense of security that had existed since completion of the Coralville Reservoir and Dam in the late 1950s. Damage to the campus reached $6 million, and there were months of programmatic disruptions on campus and throughout a good part of the state.

Even as eastern Iowa emerged from a long, cold, and snowy winter in 2008, and even as record rain events hit the Iowa River watershed in March, April, and May, many felt 1993 would maintain the distinction "as bad as it could get." In May 2008 the University unveiled its flood emergency plan and proactively assembled sandbag walls, which would protect the campus from this newest flood threat, even if water levels approached the extremes reached in 1993. Small pockets of enthusiastic and confident volunteers worked together to accomplish the plan. Then came June.

Forecasts continued to worsen, and saturated landscapes from southern Minnesota to the Mississippi River offered no relief for those within the Iowa and Cedar River Valleys. Projections began to threaten those historic 1993 flood levels; the unthinkable was suddenly and quickly approaching. Completed sandbag walls were rebuilt to two and three times their original heights. Dozens of rain-soaked volunteers grew to hundreds and then thousands. The campus and the community became as one and fought tirelessly against the unrelenting wave of worsening news. On the afternoon of June 12, 2008, the campus and its community lost the battle. After a hot and sunny morning that saw as many as 3,000 volunteers covering the campus riverbanks, one last severe thunderstorm scattered even the heartiest of workers, and then it ravaged the county. The makeshift walls, some more than ten feet high, were overtopped, and much of the campus was inundated. A day later, vigilant workers at the campus's sole power plant were forced to evacuate when water inside the building reached twenty-two feet. The campus went dark. The University of Iowa had experienced a flood event with river flows through the heart of its campus that were 40 percent higher than the record flood experienced in 1993. The eastern half of Iowa had endured the fifth worst natural disaster in U.S. history.

Two days later UI President Sally Mason, facing a local and national rush of media, stated that the campus would find a way to reopen for limited summer sessions within ten days and would recover in time to welcome a record number of Iowa students in August. This declaration was challenged by the realization that, in order to bring reservoir water back to safe levels, outflow from the dam would keep the campus flooded for another month. Cleanup and emergency recovery efforts were extreme, and while many people remained displaced by floodwaters that had closed one-sixth of the campus, President Mason's promise was realized.

Over the next eight years, University officials worked with state legislators, Iowa Homeland Security, and the Federal Emergency Management Agency (FEMA) to assess, negotiate, plan for, and finally execute the physical recovery and protection of more than twenty major buildings affected by the flood. FEMA review of the campus ultimately resulted in replacement of the programs hosted by the original Art Building (1936) and the Hancher-Voxman-Clapp complex (1971 and 1972). These efforts have produced three replacement facilities, which are highlighted within this revised edition. Each represents a rebirth of the arts programs that suffered direct hits in 2008.

Many surviving buildings along the Iowa River were also affected by the flood, but coordination with FEMA historic-building experts ensured that protection from future flood risks would not come at the cost of notable and historic architecture. Buildings were repaired, and students returned.

After eight years and damages totaling nearly $800 million, the University of Iowa emerged from the disaster of 2008 with memorable tales of and lessons in perseverance. Programs poignantly affected by the event, including the School of Art and Art History and the School of Music, survived difficulties that rested on the resilient shoulders of students, faculty, and staff alike. The result of this resolve, and the combination of state and federal support, revealed a campus that serves as both a warning and a model for protection against natural disasters, as well as a testament to the University of Iowa's continued commitment to the architecture that has become so central to its mission and heritage.

How to Use This Guide

This guidebook aims at several audiences. Its primary readership is an educated public consisting of students, parents, alumni, and other nonspecialists who have an interest in the UI campus and its architecture or a desire to recall years spent on the campus frequenting its many historic and high-design buildings. This reader may skim through the book, sampling the short entries on individual buildings of particular interest. A secondary audience is made up of architecture enthusiasts, both professional and amateur, who seek a more detailed understanding of how architectural design shaped the UI campus over time. This reader may choose to devote more attention to the analytical components of the volume, such as President Emeritus Willard L. Boyd's reminiscence of his long personal involvement with UI campus architecture, the historical essay on the stylistic diversity of our campus architecture, or the biography of University architect George Horner. A new component to this second edition is the essay on the flood of 2008 and its transformative consequences

At the back of this book is an alphabetized list of extant campus buildings, providing the building name, any major additions and renovations, design architect or architectural firm and the associated Iowa firm, date completed or occupied, and campus zone; we have omitted purely utilitarian structures. Two other lists are organized by architects and building completion or occupancy dates. A final list provides information about notable sculptures, mostly funded by the Art in State Buildings Program. In these lists, buildings and sculptures indicated in bold are featured in the body of the guide. And, because architecture cannot be fully analyzed without occasional use of technical vocabulary, we also append a glossary of terms and the major trends of nineteenth- and twentieth-century architecture.

The complete campus map with its list of building abbreviations that follows this essay will aid the reader with an overview of the layout of the campus and its buildings. Each chapter is preceded by a detailed map of that particular campus zone. The names of buildings discussed in that chapter are spelled out on the map, whereas other buildings are designated only by their official abbreviations.

There are a total of 102 entries, 11 of which are introductions to campus zones and 91 of which are devoted to the explication of buildings. This is not the totality of campus architecture, but it does comprise most major buildings. Individual buildings are grouped in campus zones and within each zone the sequence of buildings follows the logical order of a campus visit. Each building entry consists of at least two pages, one page with a photograph and a text page consisting of two, or occasionally more, paragraphs. The first paragraph contains information about the building's history and its function. Subsequent paragraphs point to observable architectural features and note the building's place in UI campus architecture and its sources in the history of architectural design. Buildings of exceptional merit and interest are given fuller discussion in four-page entries.

Mindful that the names of architectural firms change over time, we have attempted always to refer to the moniker applicable at the date of building completion. For example, the firm established by William T. Proudfoot and George W. Bird in Des Moines in 1895 and originally known as Proudfoot and Bird has, over the decades, changed frequently and radically. The reader will therefore encounter a variety of names for this and some other firms. For the sake of consistency, when referring to the names of firms, we have used "and" in the text and "&" in the lists at the back.

The intent of this guidebook is both to illustrate and to celebrate the rich and diverse architecture of the University of Iowa campus. The individual entries grow from one another and display the common thread of innovative architectural development marking the structures that constitute our campus.

MAP OF UNIVERSITY OF IOWA CAMPUS

AB	Art Building
ABW	Art Building West
AJB	Adler Journalism Building
B	Burge Residence Hall
BASE	Duane Banks Baseball Stadium
BB	Biology Building
BBE	Biology Building East
BCSB	Becker Communication Studies Building
BELL	Bedell Entrepreneurship Learning Laboratory
BH	Bowman House
BHC	Blank Honors Center
BLB	Boyd Law Building
BSB	Bowen Science Building
BT	Boyd Tower
C	Currier Residence Hall
CALH	Calvin Hall
CB	Chemistry Building
CBRB	Carver Biomedical Research Building
CC	Communications Center
CDD	Center for Disabilities & Development
CHA	Carver-Hawkeye Arena
CHST	111 Church Street
CMAB	College of Medicine Administration Building
CMF	Cambus Maintenance Facility
CPHB	College of Public Health Building
CRWC	Campus Recreation & Wellness Center
D	Daum Residence Hall
DC	Danforth Chapel
DH	Dey House
DSB	Dental Science Building
EMRB	Eckstein Medical Research Building
EPB	English-Philosophy Building
ERF	Engineering Research Facility
FH	Field House
GALC	Gerdin Athletic Learning Center
GH	General Hospital
GILH	Gilmore Hall
GSL	Glenn Schaeffer Library
H	Hillcrest Residence Hall
HA	Hancher Auditorium
HFPC	Stew and LeNore Hansen Football Performance Center
HH	Halsey Hall
HLEA	Hydraulics East Annex
HLHS	Hardin Library for the Health Sciences
HLMA	Hydraulics Model Annex
HOPE	Hope Lodge
HPR1	Hospital Parking Ramp 1
HPR2	Hospital Parking Ramp 2
HPR3	Hospital Parking Ramp 3
HWTA	Hydraulics Wind Tunnel Annex
IATL	Iowa Advanced Technology Laboratories
IMU	Iowa Memorial Union
IMUR	Iowa Memorial Union Parking Ramp
JAB	Jacobson Athletic Building
JB	Jefferson Building
JCP	Colloton Pavilion
JH	Jessup Hall
JPP	Pappajohn Pavilion
KH	Kuhl House
KS	Kinnick Stadium
LC	Lindquist Center
LCUA	Levitt Center for University Advancement
LIB	Main Library
LSHS	Lagoon Shelter House
MAPF	Melrose Avenue Parking Facility
MEB	Medical Education Building
MERF	Medical Education Research Facility
MH	Macbride Hall
ML	Medical Laboratories
MLH	MacLean Hall
MRC	Medical Research Center
MRF	Medical Research Facility
MSRH	Madison Street Residence Hall
MSSB	Madison Street Services Building
MW	Music West – aka Museum of Art
NB	Nursing Building
NCP	North Campus Parking
NH	North Hall
NRP	Newton Road Parking Ramp
OC	Old Capitol
P	Petersen Residence Hall
PARK	Parklawn Residence Hall
PBB	Pappajohn Business Building
PBDB	Pappajohn Biomedical Discovery Building
PC	Pomerantz Center
PFP	Pomerantz Family Pavilion
PH	Phillips Hall
PHAR	Pharmacy Building
PP	Power Plant
PR	President's Residence
Q	Quadrangle Residence Hall
R	Rienow Residence Hall
RB	Recreation Building
RCP	Carver Pavilion
RMCD	Ronald McDonald House
S	Slater Residence Hall
SC	Seamans Center for the Engineering Arts & Sciences
SFCH	University of Iowa Stead Family Children's Hospital
SH	Schaeffer Hall
SHC	Wendell Johnson Speech & Hearing Center
SHL	Stanley Hydraulics Laboratory
SHSE	Shambaugh House
SL	Sciences Library
SLP	Spence Laboratories of Psychology
SQ	South Quadrangle
SSH	Seashore Hall
STAN	Stanley Residence Hall
STH	Stuit Hall
SW	South Wing
TB	Theatre Building
TH	Trowbridge Hall
UCC	University Capitol Centre
USB	University Services Building
VAB	Visual Arts Building
VAN	Van Allen Hall
VOX	Voxman Music Building
WCTC	West Campus Transportation Center
WL	Westlawn
WP	Water Plant

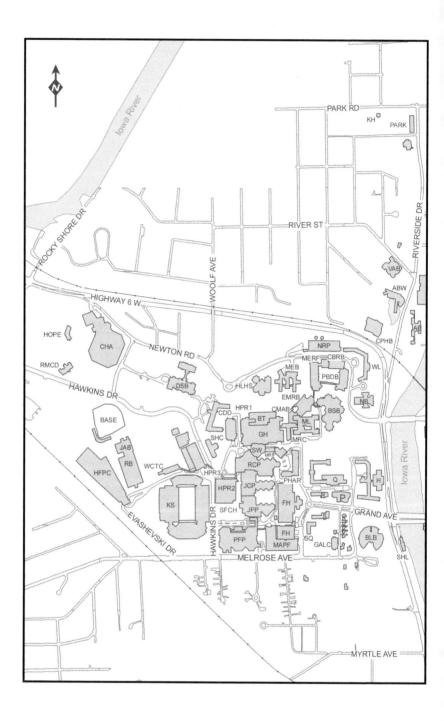

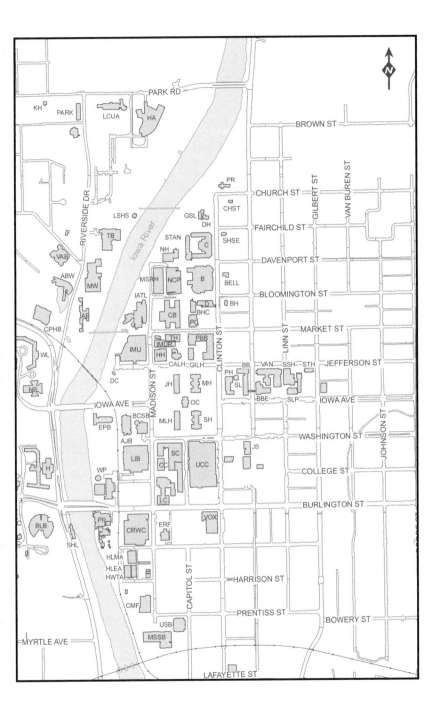

The
University
of Iowa
Guide to
Campus
Architecture

SECOND EDITION

Pentacrest

In its first decades, the University of Iowa grew up according to the needs of students and the demands of building an institution of higher learning in what was still, in many ways, a frontier town. Italianate and Second Empire style brick buildings sprang up next to the state's original capitol building, mostly on a north-south axis. As the nineteenth century came to a close, the decision to construct a major new Classical building adjacent to Old Capitol made a decisive break with that tradition, initiating a new era of campus planning that took shape over the span of a quarter of a century and the administrations of four University presidents. For the first time, designs were chosen based on their stylistic resonance with the Greek Revival Old Capitol and on how they could summon a sense of the University as a center of scholarship and learning. As new buildings of Bedford limestone went up, the older, more informal structures burned down, were torn down, or (in one instance) were moved away.

Today's Pentacrest, four monumental halls organized on diagonal axes around the Old Capitol, did not take definitive shape until the last remnant of its nineteenth-century brick buildings was razed in 1975. Pentacrest, meaning "five on a place of prominence," got its designation from a 1924 naming contest sponsored by the *Daily Iowan*, right after the completion of Jessup Hall, the last of the four new buildings. This name was suggested by Emerson A. Plank (D.D.S., 1929) of Independence, Iowa, who later said that he coined the term because he wanted it to "recall the Old World." Plank's idea was an endorsement of the original concept behind Old Capitol and the Pentacrest, which aimed at continuity and expression of the shared cultural values of Western civilization, as understood at the time.

The Pentacrest, however, is more than the mere sum of its individual buildings. It exemplifies the City Beautiful Movement of the 1890s, which looked to the urban planning principles first formulated in the Italian Renaissance and then spectacularly realized in the

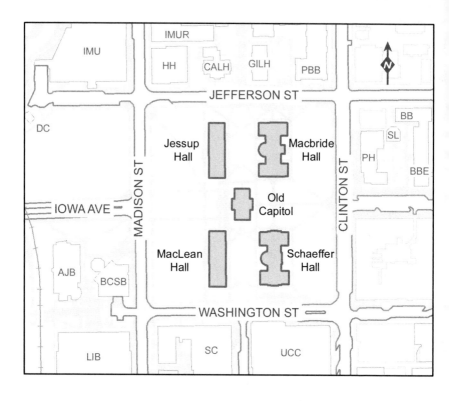

symmetrical disposition of buildings at world's fairs and expositions. The Paris Exposition Universelle of 1889, with the Eiffel Tower as its centerpiece, and, above all, Chicago's World's Columbian Exposition of 1893, with its unrestrained commitment to Beaux-Arts Classicism, were decisive for the thinking that produced the Pentacrest. A premium on axial relationships had already been established by Leander Judson's 1839 grid plan of Iowa City, which created a broad boulevard, Iowa Avenue, connecting the territorial capitol with the projected governor's mansion eight blocks to the east. Although the latter component was not to be realized, the axial thoroughfare ensured that the Old Capitol, once transferred to the University, would be the centerpiece around which other buildings would develop and that the campus would have an inextricable link to its host city.

The ideal, rigidly symmetrical plan of the Pentacrest was probably the idea of Henry Van Brunt, partner in the Kansas City firm of Van Brunt and Howe, chosen by President Charles A. Schaeffer (1887–1898) and the Board of Regents to select the architect of the new Collegiate Hall (later, Schaeffer Hall) to be erected near Old Capitol. Van Brunt worked in a succession of late nineteenth-century styles, from Gothic to Classical, and had designed institutional and campus buildings in the East, notably Harvard's Memorial Hall (1878), but, as one of the lead architects of the Chicago Exposition, by the 1890s he was a fully committed proponent of the triumphant Beaux-Arts Classicism exemplified by that impressive ensemble of buildings known as the Great White City. He was also a theoretician, and his advocacy of the Classical Revival style predisposed him to select the design submitted by the young Des Moines architects Proudfoot and Bird. It was the beginning of a long relationship with the University that continues in recent design work by Proudfoot and Bird's successor firm, Brooks Borg Skiles. It was, however, Van Brunt's idea that created the momentum for an ideal planning scheme that came to fruition in the fully realized five-building central campus complex known as the Pentacrest.

Pentacrest, aerial view. A classic example of Beaux-Arts planning, the Pentacrest is on the National Register of Historic Places. This architectural image of the UI campus is based on the symmetrical planning principles of the ideal Italian Renaissance city. The four major buildings added to Old Capitol to form the

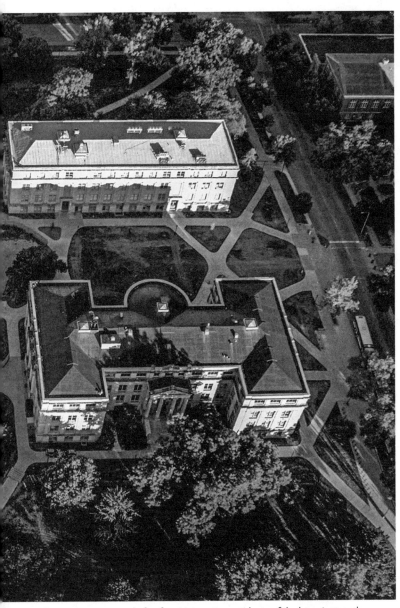

Pentacrest are named after four University presidents of the late nineteenth
and early twentieth centuries under whose administrations the modern
University of Iowa was shaped.

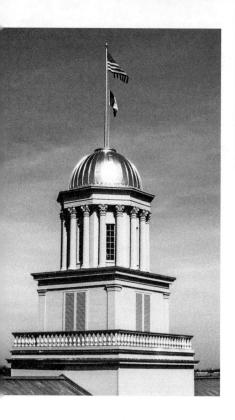

Old Capitol, 1842

ARCHITECT:

JOHN FRANCIS RAGUE,

SPRINGFIELD, ILLINOIS

PREVIOUS NAME:

CENTRAL HALL

Old Capitol's original louvered bell housing, lantern (cupola), and dome.

Old Capitol's history began as the seat of the territorial government of Iowa. It became the University's first permanent building in 1857 when the state legislature moved to Des Moines. In addition to being the administrative center of the University, at various times it was also the home of the law school, the library, a museum, a dormitory, and even a gymnasium. The story of Old Capitol intersects with some of the most defining moments in the nation's history. Abraham Lincoln was eulogized on its steps on April 19, 1865. A hundred years later, another moment of turmoil—the protests over the Vietnam War—engulfed Old Capitol. It is the heart of the University, its pivot, and the image conjured up when remembering the high bluffs and city above the Iowa River.

Despite Old Capitol's popularity, it has had its detractors. In 1939, the rabidly anticlassicist Frank Lloyd Wright famously called the building his least favorite on campus, adding, "all of your buildings are very bad . . . and they are destructive of me and my work." He advised the University to "forget your sentimentality for Old Capitol else you are doomed to destruction." Wright was advocating for contemporary design. Yet Old Capitol remains the focus of collective memory and the point of departure for architecture on campus, having inspired the Beaux-Arts Classicism of the Pentacrest buildings, the dome of Boyd Law Building, and the axes along which the various campuses are organized. Old Capitol itself has also been refined and redefined over the years, with a near total rehabilitation from 1921 to 1924 that added the west portico, an element included in the original design but never built. Owing to a lack of space, and after 110 years and fifteen University presidents, the Office of the President was moved in 1970 from its location in the southeast corner of the first floor to Jessup Hall. Old Capitol was rededicated as part of the 1976 Bicentennial celebrations, this time restored to its original character as territorial seat and home of state government. The 2006 renovation, made more extensive than originally planned by a November 20, 2001, fire that destroyed the lantern (cupola) and dome, has even more fully revived the building's nineteenth-century character.

A late example of Greek Revival architecture, Old Capitol reiterates on a more modest scale the state capitol in Springfield, Illinois (also designed by Rague), and a distinguished succession of state capitols (Ohio, Tennessee) going all the way back to Thomas Jefferson's Virginia state capitol at Richmond (1799). The walls of Old Capitol are composed of porous Iowa limestone, giving the building a rough-hewn quality. The portico columns, pediment, bell housing, and lantern (cupola) were all wood painted to imitate stone. Owing to its prominent porticoes, Old Capitol is a Doric building. This choice was both symbolic and aesthetic—the fluted Greek Doric order, and its associations with the Parthenon and Athenian democracy, conveys efficiency, modesty, and good government. The façade walls are articulated with the even sparer Doric pilasters. Frugality and moral rectitude are the order here, relieved only by the Corinthian capitals of the lantern columns, modeled on the Choragic Monument of Lysicrates, a fourth-century BCE work in Athens. The gilded dome captures the

The elegant fluted Corinthian columns of the second-floor interior, with capitals based on those of the Choragic Monument of Lysicrates, Athens.

sun to become the focal point of the building and the entire campus. The results of the 2006 project are also visible in the detailed work done to restore Old Capitol with greater historical accuracy. Because no drawings existed from the building's construction, architectural historians pieced plans together from fragments. Some changes were made—the original wood-shingled roof, which had been replaced first with slate, then with asphalt shingles, was restored with standing-seam metal cladding—but Old Capitol today is as close to its original design as it has been since the nineteenth century (colorplate 2). Inside, the inversely rotated stairway has been retained (colorplate 3) and the building's bell—destroyed in the fire—has been replaced by one from the same period. The new interior color scheme, more in keeping with the mid-nineteenth century, has also been introduced; in place of sober white walls from the 1970s, Old Capitol is warmed by lavender, rose, and azure hues. Burnished and reopened in May 2006, it again greets visitors and looks westward across Iowa, as it has since 1842. As a "nationally important example of Greek Revival architecture," Old Capitol has been designated a National Historic Landmark.

Schaeffer Hall, 1902

ARCHITECT: PROUDFOOT AND BIRD, DES MOINES, IOWA

PREVIOUS NAME: COLLEGIATE HALL

The notion of the Pentacrest began with Charles A. Schaeffer, the University of Iowa's seventh president (1887–1898). As part of a larger agenda to invest in the facilities and faculty necessary to make the University a national institution, Schaeffer brought in Henry Van Brunt, one of the architects of the 1893 World's Columbian Exposition in Chicago, to judge a competition for the design of a new academic hall. Proudfoot and Bird's winning entry began their long service as the University's architects of choice and introduced a dignified Beaux-Arts Classicism that would become synonymous with the Pentacrest. Despite Schaeffer's untimely death, a construction fire, and conflicts between the architects and contractors, the doors to Schaeffer Hall finally opened on January 23, 1902, providing a permanent and modern location for the College of Liberal Arts and Sciences (CLAS), which was then known as the Collegiate Department. The College has called Schaeffer Hall home ever since, and the building underwent a complete renovation in 1998, marking a century since construction began on the original building. CLAS is the largest of the UI's 11 colleges and comprises the core of the University with 18,000 students, 700 faculty, and 38 departments (six of which rank in the top ten nationally). As such, it is appropriate that, at the corner of Clinton and Washington Streets, it occupies the "cornerstone" position of the UI campus. Schaeffer Hall is the oldest University classroom building still in use for instruction.

Schaeffer Hall's design signals a decision to define and ennoble the center of campus. By choosing to build in Bedford limestone instead of the more traditional red brick, on a monumental scale, and in the Classical tradition, the University lent Schaeffer Hall a distinction appropriate to its setting and to its potential importance in the life of the institution. On the east façade, a portico greets downtown Iowa City, and the frieze of the pediment, reading "Liberal Arts," promi-

Schaeffer Hall architecturally embodies the University's early aspiration to be a major institution of higher learning and to project a national image of scholarship and culture.

nently announces the building's purpose. While the design is sympathetic to Old Capitol, the choice to move up one order, from wooden Doric to monolithic limestone Ionic columns, also expresses the transition from the older structure's Greek notions of good government to Schaeffer's Renaissance ideals of education and culture. Referencing Old Capitol's Doric prototype, the decorated pediment, ornamental globes, and horizontal scrolls mounting up to the now-removed central flagpole freight Schaeffer with a sense of grandeur that amplifies the building's message that art and science are essential to a democracy. The narrow end façades repeat the portico motif of the east front but with engaged rather than free-standing columns and without a pediment, which might compete with Old Capitol's venerable image.

Garlands of fruit
and vegetables
surround this
fertility goddess (or
personification of
Iowa), whose hair
resembles the roots
of the flanking
corn stalks. The
goddess's left eye
looks upward to the
sky, while her right
eye stares straight
ahead.

The west (rear)
façade of Schaeffer
Hall, with its
powerful rotunda
projecting from a
great recess, traces
its ancestry back to
the Italian Baroque.

The model is Ange-Jacques Gabriel's façade of the Petit Trianon at Versailles. On its west or rear façade Schaeffer Hall trades the rectilinear for curvilinear forms with a powerfully projecting rotunda that unexpectedly introduces baroque drama in place of the relatively restrained classicism of the east front.

Macbride Hall, 1908

ARCHITECT: PROUDFOOT AND BIRD, DES MOINES, IOWA

PREVIOUS NAME: HALL OF NATURAL SCIENCE

The commitment to erect a quartet of monumental buildings around Old Capitol was furthered by President George E. MacLean (1899–1911), who saw it as an effort to compose a formal university campus and to express better the academic aspirations of a modern institution of higher learning at the turn of the twentieth century. Macbride Hall, named for Thomas Huston Macbride, eleventh president of the University of Iowa, is perhaps the clearest example of this determination; construction could not begin until Calvin Hall had been moved off the Pentacrest and across Jefferson Street to the north. Once completed, Macbride stood as a testament to the University's place as an outpost of civilization on the prairie, and it marked a continued determination to remake the architectural image of the University on a grander and more ordered scale—one that embodied MacLean's

Macbride Hall's proud portico references Old Capitol and balances with that of Schaeffer Hall.

Interior Doric columns echo the exterior. Faux-marble painting was applied to the brick-core columns to create a convincing visual effect of red-veined marble.

conception of the civilizing role of the modern university. The building houses the largest classroom on campus, as well as the Museum of Natural History—the oldest existing university museum west of the Mississippi. For more than four decades, the building was also the home of the University's library. Built in the basement with exposed interior columns instead of walls, to accommodate the ever-increasing collection, the library still became so short of space that the floor was eventually lowered to house even more books.

While Macbride Hall resembles Schaeffer Hall in plan and elevation, significant variations between the buildings prevent the uniformity of the Pentacrest from becoming tiresome. Both have projecting Ionic porticoes in recessed central sections flanked by two wings, and prominent rotundas grace the west side of each building. Macbride's portico is shallower, however, and its cornice is topped with ornamental urns, not globes, as seen at Schaeffer Hall. The façade is also less severe than Schaeffer's, with channeled limestone and sculpted reliefs above the windows. The freestanding columns of the east portico become engaged columns on the north and south end façades and pilasters on the west face of the building. The rotunda, like Schaef-

Limestone bas-reliefs above Macbride's main floor windows form a sculpted classified encyclopedia of the earth's fauna, among them a walrus head flanked by garlands and seals.

fer's, is reminiscent of the Italian Baroque, creating a play of light and shadow that adds to the building's visual power and interest.

The Pentacrest buildings are meant to be seen in the round, and Macbride Hall is a particularly good example. The harmonious proportions, portico, and rotunda are all evident at a quick glance, but a closer look reveals extravagantly carved panels on the first-floor windows of the wings and end façades. The creatures in these relief sculptures are grouped by species, each having an animal at the center and related creatures forming the swags. The program was developed by famed zoologist and conservationist William Temple Hornaday and sculpted by Sinclair Shearer of Perth, Scotland. Charles Nutting, professor of zoology, arranged the groups in the correct relationship. All of the vertebrate classes are included. The field of the pediment represents a buffalo, moose, and elk. Like the animals in the window panels, these three have been included because of scientific, not just decorative, interest; they are the largest mammals indigenous to North America. Walking the perimeter of Macbride Hall, "reading" them, one can find a hawk, turkey, snapping turtle, llama, stingray, eagle, and walrus. The ornamental urns at attic level on the end façades are studded with three human heads each, representing different racial types—all related to the anthropological study of humankind appropriate to "natural science" as understood at the turn of the twentieth century. The mosaic Great Seal of the University welcomes visitors just inside the main portal (colorplate 1).

MacLean Hall, 1912

ARCHITECT: PROUDFOOT, BIRD AND RAWSON,

DES MOINES, IOWA

PREVIOUS NAME: PHYSICS BUILDING

The presidency of George E. MacLean (1899–1911) saw the University of Iowa's most expansive growth to date. A frenzy of construction was initiated after a 1901 fire that destroyed the Medical Building and South Hall and damaged the under-construction Schaeffer Hall—all on the Pentacrest. MacLean Hall, built on the former site of South

The two-dimensional pilaster treatment of MacLean's east and end façades switches on the west to engaged columns, thereby providing a more prominent elevation as seen from a distance.

The names of venerated scientists grace the Classical frieze of MacLean Hall.

Hall, was intended to replace classroom and laboratory space lost in that blaze. The project stalled almost before it began, however, when a trove of human bones was discovered during excavation. Further examination revealed that the bones were refuse from South Hall's anatomical laboratory, and President MacLean ordered them quietly disposed of so that construction might resume. The Cockroft-Walton "atom smasher" was installed here in 1938.

Marching along MacLean's frieze are the names of noted scientists including Franklin, Newton, Galileo, and Archimedes. This design feature recalls the practice of inscribing names of great artists on the exterior of museums, as was done on the 1893 Art Institute of Chicago, and points to the faculties of physics and engineering that originally occupied the building. The west entry includes ornate pentaglobed lamps that reference the five structures of the Pentacrest and the dominance of the Ionic order on the post–Old Capitol buildings. The lamps are creative variations of the Ionic order column and add interest to this "rear" view. MacLean's interior is also worth a visit; just inside the west portal an ornate, curved staircase connects the main and lower levels.

Jessup Hall, 1924

ARCHITECT: PROUDFOOT, BIRD AND RAWSON,

DES MOINES, IOWA

PREVIOUS NAME: UNIVERSITY HALL

Jessup Hall originally housed the Departments of Education, Commerce, and English. When the latter moved to the English-Philosophy Building in 1970, President Willard L. Boyd transferred his office from Old Capitol to the more spacious vacated administrative suite, which was a model of Spartan frugality. The standard office desk, linoleum

On the end façades, Jessup's projecting columns and Michelangelesque scrolls at the attic level surpass in ornamentation the comparable, but more two-dimensional, end façades of MacLean Hall.

Jessup Hall completed the monumental five-building plan for the Pentacrest and gave a finished shape to the architectural center of the campus. Its design contains numerous subtle variations from its pendant on the south, MacLean Hall.

floor, and throw rug were alleviated only by a painting borrowed from the Museum of Art. In addition to the Office of the President, Jessup now also houses the Office of the Executive Vice President and Provost. Its current name honors one of the University's most visionary leaders, Walter Jessup. The twelfth president of the University of Iowa (1916–1934), Jessup presided over the grandest building campaign in University history, including the completion of the Pentacrest buildings and the campus's westward expansion across the Iowa River.

Reflecting the creative variation on the Ionic order seen throughout the Pentacrest, Jessup Hall defines an internal campus green with Macbride Hall and provides a harmonious finale for the Beaux-Arts Classicism of the four buildings flanking Old Capitol. On its east face, a simple design with two-story-high pilasters contrasts with the drama of Macbride's facing rotunda, while nodding at ancient imperial Roman architecture with the geometric grillwork above the two entrances. The north and south end façades present a more ornamented style than the adjacent MacLean Hall, replacing that building's pilasters with engaged columns and powerful Michelangelesque scrolls (consoles) visually buttressing the attic level. Deeply carved horizontal channels at foundation level and columns on the west façade make a strong impression, nicely recapitulating MacLean's west façade and enframing Old Capitol as viewed from the river valley approach. The lamps flanking the west entrance also repeat those in a comparable position on MacLean. They are five-globed fantasies on the Ionic column, the dominant motif of the Proudfoot and Bird Pentacrest buildings. The attention given to all four sides of Jessup is consistent with the overall design of the Pentacrest.

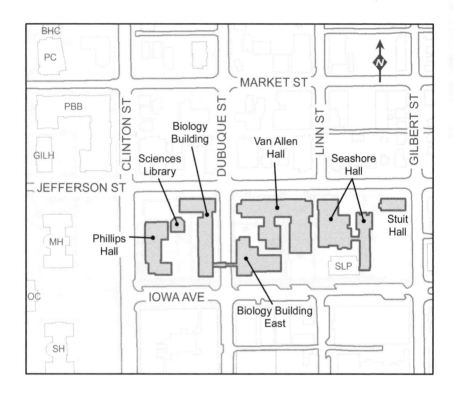

Iowa Avenue Campus

The Iowa Avenue Campus, a one-by-three-block peninsula extending from the Pentacrest into downtown, is an example of University facilities penetrating the city's residential and commercial neighborhoods. Devoted to the sciences (with the exception of Phillips Hall), these buildings function as an eastward spur of the liberal arts campus.

If the Iowa Avenue Campus is a departure from the campus core and its prevailing architecture, its function and history are more intimately tied to the University than most. The first classes ever taught at the University of Iowa were held in an Italianate building (Mechanics' Academy) that once stood near the corner of Iowa and Linn Streets, and a remnant of the first general hospital (Seashore Hall) survives on that site today. Modernizations and expansions of the facilities devoted to science are abundant here, and future planning efforts will continue to explore the long-term development possibilities of this prominent campus zone.

Phillips Hall, 1965

ARCHITECT: WOODBURN O'NEIL ARCHITECTS

AND ENGINEERS, WEST DES MOINES, IOWA

Constructed on the former site of Iowa City's second Universalist Church building, Phillips Hall was built to house the College of Business Administration. Since its founding in 1921, the then College of Commerce had vastly outstripped the facilities available in its first home, Jessup Hall. The move across Clinton Street provided a more functional facility until growth forced yet another relocation, this time to the newly built John Pappajohn Business Building in 1993. Phillips

Standardization was the dominant concept in the Modernist design of Phillips Hall.

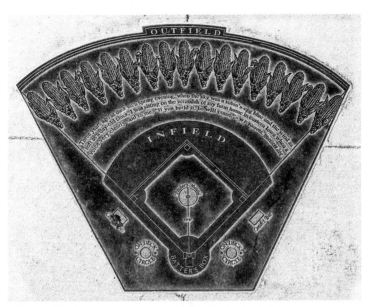

"If you build it, he will come."—W. P. Kinsella, *Shoeless Joe* (1982). Iowa Avenue's Literary Walk refers to the works of authors who gained for Iowa City the designation of a UNESCO City of Literature in 2008.

Hall was named after Chester A. Phillips, the college's first dean and a leader in the field of money and banking. It now contains foreign language and literature departments within the College of Liberal Arts and Sciences.

Campus lore once held that the west façade, with its rows of deeply punched windows, was meant to be a play on the then-common computer punchcards, but this seems to be an idea born of the popular imagination rather than an intended design concept. The building does, however, reference Modernism's valorization of standardized forms and the machine aesthetic. The windows evoke the sun baffles of Le Corbusier, specifically his Unité d'Habitation in Marseilles (1946–1952). The external grid, with recessed windows, has the practical benefit of protecting the interior from direct sunlight. The design also makes visible a functional separation; classrooms and faculty offices are in the main block, while the large lecture hall is in a single-story wing to the south.

Phillips Hall's location also marks the beginning of the Iowa Avenue Literary Walk, a joint University/Iowa City project designed by Gregg LeFevre and opened in 2001. Forty-nine bronze panels embedded in the sidewalk celebrate, in image and quotation, writers connected to the University or state: Marvin Bell, Frank Conroy, John Irving, Flannery O'Connor, Jane Smiley, Kurt Vonnegut, and Tennessee Williams, among others, can be found in the sidewalk-mounted plaques. Many of the authors are graduates or former faculty of the famed Iowa Writers' Workshop.

Sciences Library, 1902

ARCHITECT: PROUDFOOT AND BIRD, DES MOINES, IOWA

PREVIOUS NAMES: HALL OF ANATOMY,

BIOLOGICAL SCIENCES LIBRARY

When the Medical Department was still located on the Iowa Avenue Campus, this building was an anatomical theater. The entire second floor was taken up with this function. Medical students sat in

The Sciences Library was originally an anatomical theater.

semicircular bleachers, with the instructor and cadaver in the arena below.

Only the second Beaux-Arts style structure, after Schaeffer Hall, to be erected on the UI campus, the building indicates an intention to establish that architectural style as the dominant aesthetic of the campus, not only on the Pentacrest but also beyond. The continuation of the Ionic order also reflects Schaeffer. Reprogrammed as the Biological Sciences Library in 2004, the building was originally conceived as the center of a larger complex that would form a court, but of that plan only the Biology Building on Jefferson Street was ever built. The rear wall of the building is canted from both corners so that the semicircular raised seating of the anatomical theater is expressed on the exterior. Decorative elements, such as the use of quoins to extend the channeled rustication of the base upward, become more expressive as they rise. At the broad entrance bay, pairs of flanking Ionic pilasters on the second and third levels give distinction to the cubelike edifice, and floral swags swing from the volutes of the capitals. The library's most ornate touch, a palmette above the cornice, crowns this diminutive building neatly tucked away near the heart of campus. The open area in front has now been redeveloped as a peaceful enclave adjacent to the bustle of downtown Iowa City.

Biology Building, 1905

ARCHITECT: PROUDFOOT AND BIRD, DES MOINES, IOWA

PREVIOUS NAMES: MEDICAL LABORATORY (1905),

ZOOLOGY BUILDING (1927)

Originally a laboratory component of the College of Medicine, the Biology Building stands on the former site of Close Hall, which had been the University of Iowa's first gymnasium. The additions of 1965 and 1971, undertaken at the behest of the chairs of Zoology, Botany, and Microbiology to accommodate the University's growing student population and commitment to the sciences, have been matched by the latest renovation (2004), which encompassed the entire biology complex: Biology Building, Sciences Library, Biology Building East, and the provocative Biology Bridge. The project added thirteen state-

The Beaux-Arts Classicism of the 1905 Biology Building contrasts strongly with the standardized grid of its Modernist wing of 60 years later, but each represents architecturally the scientific thinking of its time—one with literal depictions of scientific instruments, the other with metaphoric allusion to scientific method.

of-the-art laboratories and upgraded existing laboratories, classrooms, and offices.

Erected three years after the Sciences Library (as the Hall of Anatomy), the Biology Building shares that earlier structure's Beaux-Arts Classicism, its fondness for Ionic pilasters with swags at the volutes, and its channeled rustication and prominent keystones above the ground-floor windows. Additions of 1965 and 1971 obscure much of the original structure, but the entrances facing Iowa Avenue and Jefferson Street remain, and, along with them, the building's detailing. Above the cornice, a crest with the eagle from the University of Iowa seal interrupts the parapet. In the frieze a bas-relief of scientific

An eagle flanked with scientific instruments, and with Ionic capitals below, reveals the Biology Building's original function as a medical laboratory and the Beaux-Arts style of the Pentacrest.

instruments informs visitors of the building's use. The calibrated beakers and microscopes refer to its original function as a medical laboratory. In the flanking Modernist addition, the repetitious standardized geometry, similar to that of nearby Phillips Hall, architecturally announces the exactitude of scientific procedure, as did the artfully sculpted beakers on the original building.

Biology Bridge, 2000

ARTIST: SIAH ARMAJANI, MINNEAPOLIS, MINNESOTA

The bridge connecting the Biology Building and Biology Building East is a work of art as well as architecture. The designer, sculptor Siah Armajani, is known for his bridge projects, including the torch, tower, and bridge in Atlanta for the 1996 Olympics and the tower and bridge on Staten Island's North Shore Esplanade. An interesting design challenge, as it connects two very different architectures while passing over a main entry route to Iowa City (Dubuque Street), the bridge was considered by Armajani mostly in isolation, a conscious and radical noncontextualism. While it created some controversy during the design phase and immediately following its construction, the bridge has now become a conversation piece and is recognized as a gateway to downtown Iowa City. The artist named his work *A Bridge for Iowa*.

The historicizing allusions and emphatic asymmetry of the bridge typify Postmodern design and complement the dynamic composition

The Biology Bridge spans Dubuque Street and connects the Biology Building with Biology Building East.

DNA and Darwin come together in the Biology Bridge interior. Inlay in the floor quotes Walt Whitman: "I believe a leaf of grass is no less than the journey work of the stars."

of the new Biology Building East while rejecting the standardized geometry of the Modernist wing of the Biology Building it connects. The guiding motif, Iowa's covered bridges, is conveyed by the exposed diagonal truss work, while the ornamental webbing below alludes to the now almost as rare iron truss bridges. But the arched upper half of the design unmistakably references Venice's famed Bridge of Sighs. Iowa's bridge, however, metaphorically connects the campus to the city, and campus and city to the state. Some viewers may see in it a reference to *The Bridges of Madison County* and the popular film based on Robert James Waller's novel. On the interior, perforated panels in the ceiling allow light to filter from above, and the space is warmed by the stained glass in the windows and skylights. Quotations from Charles Darwin and Walt Whitman run along the walls and floor. Also on the floor, a strand of DNA in terrazzo connects the two buildings and contains an error that biology students are now challenged to discover.

Biology Building East, 2000

ARCHITECT: BROOKS BORG SKILES ARCHITECTURE

ENGINEERING, DES MOINES, IOWA

Housing classrooms and research facilities, Biology Building East, popularly known as Biology East, was the first part of a two-phase construction and renovation effort to upgrade the complex of biology buildings fronting Jefferson and Dubuque Streets and Iowa Avenue. It emphasizes state-of-the-art technology for both teaching and research. Biology East accommodates electron microscopy and other sophisticated technologies together with the traditional greenhouses occupying the roof.

This fourth component of the biology complex is connected to the Biology Building by a pedestrian bridge over Dubuque Street. If Phillips Hall and the Biology Building's Dubuque Street wing architecturally represented the leap across Clinton Street, the Postmodernism of Biology Building East announces its distance from those buildings as well. Having moved farther from the Old Capitol in space and time, there is a departure from both Classicism and Modernism, manifested in new materials and the introduction of a more varied palette of colors. Biology East is composed of raw concrete, brown brick, white metal cladding, red stone, and a variety of glass—including green-tinted glass and glass block—that express the function of each part of the building and the heterogeneity of its urban context. Glass curtain walls front Iowa Avenue and are echoed by the exposed rooftop greenhouse. The building's entrance responds to the corner of Iowa Avenue and Dubuque Street with a Postmodern complexity of intersecting planes emerging from the simply framed south façade. The recess at the corner shades the entrance, leaving the white-paneled second and third stories floating above.

In its asymmetrical composition and in its variety of construction materials, Biology Building East illustrates the Postmodern freedom from Modernist design principles.

Seashore Hall, 1899

ARCHITECT: JOSSELYN AND TAYLOR, CEDAR RAPIDS, IOWA

PREVIOUS NAMES: UNIVERSITY HOSPITAL, EAST HALL

Seashore Hall (as University Hospital) was preceded on this site by the Mechanics' Academy building, where a small, 20-bed hospital was installed in 1873. This facility was jointly operated by the University's Medical Department faculty and the Sisters of Mercy (from Davenport) until the sisters transferred off campus to found their own hospital. The University of Iowa Hospitals and Clinics, however, dates its foundation from 1898 and the construction of University Hospital, which began as a 65-bed unit designed for both patients and clinical instruction. President Charles A. Schaeffer (1887–1898) led the way in advocating for this project, which was funded with a one-tenth mill tax approved by the state legislature to pay for needed University buildings. The original building was expanded twice before the entire hospital operation was moved to the new General Hospital on the west side of the Iowa River in 1928. In its definitive form as a hospital, achieved in 1915, University Hospital had patient wards, private rooms, clinics, and a surgical theater and accommodated a total of 350 beds. In 1930 it was remodeled as a research building and renamed East Hall; psychology and journalism became the major occupants. In 1981 the building was renamed after psychologist Carl Seashore, dean of the Graduate College.

The building history of Seashore Hall is a complicated one. The original all-brick, stripped-down, Beaux-Arts building of 1899 faced Jefferson Street rather than Iowa Avenue and was constructed on a red-brick base with buff-colored walls and an argyle pattern in red and beige brick on the top two floors, which were devoted to the surgical theater. An entrance with a monumental arched opening at the top of a flight of steps projected from the main block, and a wing on one side jutted back toward Iowa Avenue, making for an asymmetrical plan. In 1908 Proudfoot, Bird and Rawson were brought in to add a matching wing to the east and reorient the central block toward Iowa Avenue

An archival photograph of the 1920s shows Seashore Hall
(University Hospital) in its definitive form.

An archival photograph of circa 1900 shows the original
Seashore Hall facing Jefferson Street.

by adding a porch and main entrance. In 1915 two large multistoried additions topped with solaria, picturesque elevator towers, and red-clay-tiled gambrel roofs were built between the projecting wings and Jefferson Street, again based on a Proudfoot, Bird and Rawson design. This is the definitive view of University Hospital seen in the archival photograph. The bifurcation of the hospital reflects the arrangement of the sexes into separate wards. The additions provided the appearance of symmetry that, at least for the forward-projecting wings, suggests Gabriel's Cour Royale at Versailles as the prototype—a typical reference for architects working in a Beaux-Arts style and implied already in the Josselyn and Taylor design. In 1968 Spence Psychology Laboratories were placed in front of the central block, and the pedimented façade of the right wing was masked with a Modernist entrance. In 2000 the southwest wing on the left was razed because of failing structure.

Stuit Hall, 1918

ARCHITECT: PROUDFOOT, BIRD AND RAWSON,

DES MOINES, IOWA

PREVIOUS NAMES: ISOLATION HOSPITAL, OLD MUSIC BUILDING

The Isolation Hospital was built at the corner of Jefferson and Gilbert Streets just to the northeast of University Hospital, separate from but within easy communication of the main building. The function of this facility moved with the rest of the medical units to the west campus in 1928. After that the building was converted for use by the Department of Music, and a Georgian Revival rehearsal

The middle sections of the horizontal windows on the second and third floors originally had French doors providing access to open-air porches, now removed. Roundheaded dormer windows with keystones and interlaced pane membering add an unanticipated refinement.

hall, designed by George Horner, was added to the south end of the building in 1931 (razed, 1988). After the Voxman Music Building was completed in 1971, the School of Music vacated the building, which then received the designation of Old Music Building. It was used for graduate painting studios until 1999. After a thorough restoration to house the Psychology Clinic, it opened in 2010 and functions as the training center for doctoral students in the Department of Psychological and Brain Sciences. The building is named in honor of Dewey Stuit, dean of the College of Liberal Arts and Sciences from 1947 to 1977.

The red-brick foundation level and buff-colored upper stories retain the exterior color and materials of the adjacent Seashore Hall (University Hospital) complex. The Georgian Revival only suggested in the original main building is fully embraced here. Elegantly detailed dormers and the mutules under the cornice of the third floor reinforce the stylistic orientation. While in use as an isolation ward, the building's south façade was completely faced with tiers of wooden porches, which allowed patients to follow a fresh-air regimen. The balconies were later removed as the function of the building changed. On the rear Jefferson Street façade a gambrel-roofed central bay projects above the cornice and, at the top, displays a Palladian window, the unique example on the UI campus.

Van Allen Hall, 1964

ARCHITECT: DURRANT GROUP, DUBUQUE, IOWA

PREVIOUS NAME: PHYSICS RESEARCH CENTER

One of twenty buildings completed during the presidency of Howard R. Bowen (1964–1969), Van Allen Hall is a manifestation of both Bowen's strong support of the sciences and the critical importance of its namesake's work. James A. Van Allen, a native Iowan, earned his Ph.D. at the University of Iowa and taught in the physics department for decades. Using rocket-launched balloons as early satellites, Van Allen discovered high densities of radiation in the Earth's upper atmo-

The monolithic south façade of Van Allen Hall seems to float above the slab-roof-covered auditorium.

sphere, a phenomenon now known as the Van Allen Belts. His findings earned him the May 4, 1958, cover of *Time* magazine, a National Medal of Science, and membership in the National Academy of Science. Van Allen Hall continues to house the physics and astronomy faculty from which he retired in 1986.

James Van Allen's space-age research finds expression in the architecture of Van Allen Hall. Its Modernist concrete façade is adamantly antitraditional and anticlassical, rejecting the ornamentation of the campus's Beaux-Arts buildings and replacing it with a spare machine aesthetic. Curtain walls, standardization, and a quasi-modular design make for a building that was not only economical to construct but also in sympathy with the collaborative spirit of the scientists and NASA engineers working inside. Functionality and productivity are key contributors to the design intent. The Brutalist ferro-concrete canopies supported on center piers at the west entrance express the malleability and strength of modern materials. An observatory is visible above the roofline, and the building's auditorium—a single-story, slab-roof-covered auditorium attached to a multi-use, multistory structure—makes Van Allen visually consistent with other buildings on the Iowa Avenue Campus.

Main Campus North

Growing northward along the bluffs of the Iowa River, the University of Iowa gradually integrated itself into the original residential neighborhoods of Iowa City. In addition to several important academic facilities, Main Campus North includes the Dey House and the Shambaugh House, two of the University of Iowa's most significant historic homes and anchors of the University's famed writing community. Another home, the President's Residence at 102 Church Street, acts as a gateway to the campus and caps the stretch of University buildings along Clinton Street. The area also contains the first dormitory and is one of two centers for on-campus residence life, sheltering approximately 5,000 students in total. Student foot traffic, moving south from residence halls to academic buildings, gives shape to another noteworthy feature of this campus: the T. Anne Cleary Walkway. Named after a beloved administrator, the walkway traverses what once was a stretch of Capitol Street to provide convenient, safe, and attractive passage to pedestrians.

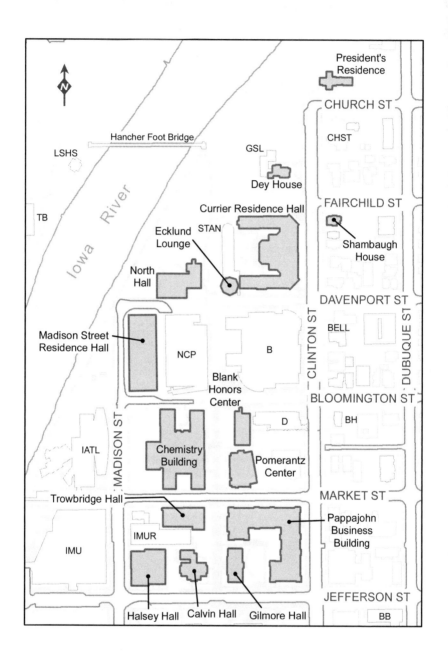

President's
Residence

CHURCH ST

CHST

Hancher Foot Bridge

LSHS

GSL

Dey House

Iowa River

FAIRCHILD ST

TB

Currier Residence Hall

Ecklund STAN
Lounge

Shambaugh
House

North
Hall

DAVENPORT ST

Madison Street
Residence Hall

NCP

B

BELL

CLINTON ST

DUBUQUE ST

Blank
Honors
Center

BLOOMINGTON ST

MADISON ST

D

BH

IATL

Chemistry
Building

Pomerantz
Center

MARKET ST

Trowbridge Hall

Pappajohn
Business
Building

IMUR

IMU

JEFFERSON ST

Halsey Hall Calvin Hall Gilmore Hall

BB

Halsey Hall, 1915

ARCHITECT: PROUDFOOT, BIRD AND RAWSON,

DES MOINES, IOWA

PREVIOUS NAME: WOMEN'S GYMNASIUM

Before the construction of Halsey Hall, the women's gymnasium had been confined to a small space in the basement of Schaeffer Hall known as the Crypt. With a new building and the advent of Elizabeth Halsey as director of women's physical education (a post she held from 1924 until 1956), the athletic life of female students at the University of Iowa was transformed. Once restricted to gymnastics, dance, and hygiene, women were able now to participate more fully in the sporting activities previously available only to men. The building, which now houses the Department of Dance, a Recreation Services satellite (Fitness East), and other fitness facilities, has also achieved a

The pedimented gable of Halsey Hall suggests a Classical building
in brick but without columns or pilasters.

measure of fame as an exterior shot for the 1980s television sitcom *Coach*, the title character of which was loosely based on former UI football coach Hayden Fry.

The building's origins as a gymnasium appear carved in limestone on the lintel above the front entrance. Although suggestive of Beaux-Arts Classicism, its almost all-brick, less-ornamented, utilitarian character separates it from the more formal buildings rising on the nearby Pentacrest. With its faint classical echoes (portal consoles, pilaster bands, roof-cornice corbels, and pediment), Halsey might be thought of as a temple to the body, in contrast with those nearby porticoed temples to the mind. Situated on the slope of the bluff marked by Jefferson Street, the ground falls away, creating a basement level and allowing for a south façade with a pronounced podium and temple front. Halsey also has some of the most accomplished brickwork on campus. Panels of diagonally laid bricks with central diamonds are repeated beneath the ample second-floor gym windows flanked by brick pilaster bands. Halsey is the best example on campus of the bricklaying technique known as Flemish Bond, which alternates along each course between headers and stretchers.

Calvin Hall, 1885

ARCHITECT: R. S. FINKBINE, DES MOINES, IOWA

PREVIOUS NAME: SCIENCE HALL

Originally located on the Pentacrest, Calvin Hall is best known for its dramatic relocation in 1905. When Macbride Hall displaced it from the Pentacrest, it also took over its core functions. In a bold decision for the time, the teaching of science was not interrupted during relocation, with classes continuing to be taught in Calvin while it was moved across Jefferson Street at a rate of two feet per day. More than 1,000 screw jacks and an army of horses kept the building level and usable during this 105-foot trek to the north. Calvin Hall was eventually renamed after a distinguished faculty member who taught there—Samuel Calvin, a geologist and curator of the Museum of Natural History. Today, it contains a variety of student services offices. A boulder beneath the south façade commemorates the 1855 decision

Except for Old Capitol, Calvin Hall is the oldest
University building in continuous use.

to admit women on the same basis as men; Iowa was the first state university west of the Mississippi River to do so.

A major factor behind the decision to move Calvin Hall was its Italianate red-brick exterior, which was out of place on the developing Pentacrest. The resources expended in that transfer illustrate the University's commitment to campus architecture; not only did the administration carry through the plan for a limestone Beaux-Arts Classicism theme for the buildings surrounding the Old Capitol, it also recognized the worth of Calvin Hall and expended the resources needed to retain the older structure. The building is the oldest University building, excepting Old Capitol, and the best example of the buildings that once populated the Pentacrest. Today, Calvin Hall stands as the sole surviving relic of the red-brick campus that once was.

Calvin bears some curious ornamentation, including the three terra-cotta reliefs above the second-story porch: two spirals that flank a head in profile wearing a liberty cap (a pointed headpiece symbolic of the struggle for political liberty). Rising even further, the building is topped by a wide frieze, cornice, and gabled mansard roof.

Gilmore Hall, 1910

ARCHITECT: PROUDFOOT AND BIRD, DES MOINES, IOWA

PREVIOUS NAME: HALL OF LAW

Built to house the College of Law, Gilmore Hall provided that faculty a suitable space after years of overcrowding in the Old Capitol. It was eventually renamed after Eugene A. Gilmore, dean of the College of Law, who went on to become president of the University of Iowa (1934–1940). During his administration the University suffered drops in enrollment and resources due to the Great Depression. Gilmore was known for his efforts to press forward with a plan for expansion

Gilmore Hall recapitulates the Beaux-Arts Classicism of the Pentacrest buildings.

The prestigious former law library, seen in this archival photograph of 1924, suggests with its use of the more austere Doric order of columns an effort to recall the virtues of Athenian democracy and well-ordered society as seen in Old Capitol.

of both student body and facilities and for projecting an aura of optimism and growth that belied the troubled academic and economic climate of that era. Gilmore Hall now houses critical University administrative functions, including the offices of the Dean of the Graduate College. The Department of Religious Studies occupies the top floor.

The building is the earliest surviving classroom building originally located north of the Pentacrest and indicates an intention to continue with the limestone Beaux-Arts Classicism of Schaeffer Hall, which was the only one of the projected Pentacrest buildings completed at the time. Gilmore Hall's use of limestone and the Ionic order attaches authority to the building and makes clear the importance of the program housed there. Approached from the west, today it seems a continuation of the quartet of Beaux-Arts buildings across Jefferson Street to the south. Originally, Gilmore's engaged columns, massing, and horizontal lines of rustication portended the end façades of Macbride and Jessup. A line of brackets beneath the roofline visually supports the cornice while drawing attention to the high windows shared by the building's third and fourth floors. Once an elegant, Doric-columned law library, that space has been split into two levels to provide for additional offices. Also inside, an ornate and noteworthy entry stair has been partially restored. Gilmore Hall's over-scaled ground floor indicates that the design anticipated a future extension to the north, which would have restored classical proportions.

John Pappajohn Business Building, 1993

ARCHITECT: ARCHITECTURAL RESOURCES, CAMBRIDGE,
MASSACHUSETTS / NEUMANN MONSON ARCHITECTS,
IOWA CITY, IOWA
PREVIOUS NAME: PAPPAJOHN BUSINESS
ADMINISTRATION BUILDING

Nodding to the Beaux-Arts Classicism of the Pentacrest (and Gilmore Hall),
the architects designed the John Pappajohn Business Building as a Postmodern
temple of commerce.

The John Pappajohn Business Building architecturally embodies the study of business at the University of Iowa. Founded as the College of Commerce, the Tippie College of Business has outgrown a succession of homes, most recently Phillips Hall. Pappajohn Business Building also houses several related endeavors, including the Pappajohn Entrepreneurial Center and the Small Business Development Center. These affiliated bodies work locally and regionally to assist Iowa-based enterprises.

When the UI's College of Business moved from Phillips Hall, a rigorously Modernist building that consciously rejected the traditional Beaux-Arts Classicism of the Pentacrest, its new home would, by contrast, strive for a historicizing Postmodernism in sympathy with that older style. But the new building reimagines the Classicism of the Pentacrest and its neighbor, Gilmore Hall, through a contemporary lens. A commanding edifice of aggregate stone, the structure refers to the legacy of Proudfoot and Bird while enjoying the freedom and stylistic diversity of Postmodernism. It strays from both the rules and ornaments of classical design as well as Modernism's taboos against historical references. While alluding to the Pentacrest, the pedimented entrance porticoes with their paired column shafts at the entrances stand forward of the glass curtain walls, completely detached from the main body of the building. And they are self-consciously unclassical in their lack of ornament and in their top-heavy proportions, seeming instead to make a statement about the a-tectonic nature of classical forms. With Pappajohn's denuded classicism, even the capitals are uncarved. The obsessive rectilinear geometry and prefabricated components, however, still pay homage to Modernism's machine aesthetic. Temple fronts with truncated pagoda-like towers rise above the cornice at the juncture of the south and west wings as well as at their midpoints. Abundant clusters of dollar-bill-green square cubes form shade canopies over the tables on the exposed courtyard terrace. Pappajohn's faux classicism also references iconic financial institutions like the New York Stock Exchange.

Trowbridge Hall, 1918

ARCHITECT: PROUDFOOT, BIRD AND RAWSON,

DES MOINES, IOWA

PREVIOUS NAME: DENTISTRY BUILDING

Trowbridge originally housed dental science, which had moved from its first home (in Old Dental Building, razed in 1975) on the Pentacrest. With the relocation of the health sciences to the new Medical Campus on the western bluffs of the Iowa River, Trowbridge was freed up and reprogrammed for the Department of Geology in 1973. It was also named after Arthur C. Trowbridge, a longtime geology professor at the University.

Like other buildings on Main Campus North, Trowbridge Hall is faced in Flemish Bond brick with limestone detailing. While giving up the more noble (and expensive) materials of the Pentacrest, Trow-

Trowbridge Hall reveals a determination to continue the Beaux-Arts Classicism of the Pentacrest even in brick. Here, however, Proudfoot and Bird begin to introduce a freer use of the vocabulary of classical design.

bridge maintains the same Beaux-Arts stylistic orientation, as the Classical detailing shows. This is also apparent in the monumental scale of the brick-faced Doric pilasters paired at the entrance. These dominant verticals add visual power to the façade, but the shift down to Doric from the elegant Ionic used in all the preceding Beaux-Arts campus buildings indicates a more modest architectural image. There are, however, a few oddities about the design that need explanation. The unclassical asymmetry of the façade, with the entrance offset to the left, could be accounted for by an intended south wing with an equal number of bays to the left, which would have balanced the composition. The other unusual feature, the horizontal windows squeezed between the pilasters of the second and third floors, is perhaps a concession to contemporary design of the day. The famous three-sectioned Chicago window, already popularized by Louis Sullivan (Carson-Pirie-Scott Department Store) and introduced to Iowa City on the 1904 Carnegie Public Library, seems to have made an impact here. It can be seen in the recessed third-floor window of the entrance bay and all along the north flank, which marked the earliest hint of Modernism on the UI campus.

Pomerantz Center, 2005

ARCHITECT: SAVAGE-VER PLOEG AND ASSOCIATES,

WEST DES MOINES, IOWA

Named for Marvin A. Pomerantz, a 1952 graduate of the University of Iowa and a member of the University of Iowa Foundation Board of Directors, the Pomerantz Center functions as a hub for University outreach activities, including the Admission Visitors Center, Academic Advising Center, Alumni Career Exchange, Executive MBA Program,

The design of the Pomerantz Center expresses the outward corporate look of the offices and programs it houses.

MBA Career Services, and the Marvin A. and Rose Lee Pomerantz Career Center. The facility also includes a 400-seat auditorium.

The Pomerantz Center's activities focus mainly on the University's external constituency, a purpose that is expressed in its design, which is emphatically polished and more corporate than its traditionally academic surroundings. Composed of glass, stone, and white metal panels, with pilotis and sun baffles to the west, the building self-consciously rejects the Classicism of the Pentacrest and even the scraped Classicism of the John Pappajohn Business Building. Instead, the metal panels and sun baffles create a visual connection to the Levitt Center for University Advancement. Another vivid visual statement is made by the tapering 1950s retro glass entry atrium, which addresses the corner of Market Street and the T. Anne Cleary Walkway and recalls corporate office architecture.

A bronze bas-relief monument at the southeast corner of the Pomerantz Center marks the former site of the Iowa Child Welfare Research Station. Established in 1917, this research unit pioneered the study of normative child development. The sculpture represents a classically draped man and woman holding a scallop shell from which a small stream of water originally poured. A bird descends to drink from the shell, no doubt a punning allusion to Bird T. Baldwin, first director of the Research Station, in whose honor the fountain was originally erected near this site in 1928. The frog, fish, duck, and turtle that once perched on the edge of the wading pool have since vanished, along with the pool itself.

Chemistry Building, 1922

ARCHITECT: PROUDFOOT, BIRD AND RAWSON,

DES MOINES, IOWA

PREVIOUS NAME: CHEMISTRY-BOTANY-PHARMACY BUILDING

World War I inspired a great interest in the study of chemistry, and enrollment in the subject doubled between 1917 and 1921. By the mid-1920s, the department had the largest staff and most course offerings of any on campus, a popularity that prompted the University of Iowa to consolidate its resources into a single facility. Before that time, laboratories and classrooms had been scattered around campus; some were even located in a former mess hall. Walter Jessup, the University's president at the time, included the new facility in a broad program of construction that gave the campus east of the Iowa River much of the appearance it has today.

As this building boom, and the focus of campus architecture, moved away from the Pentacrest, there was a growing desire to express that transition architecturally, even while maintaining the same Beaux-Arts Classicism style. The Chemistry Building (colorplate 7), composed of brick with limestone detailing, effectively represents that initial shift. The stonework—at the entrance, around the windows, and in quoining—recalls the Pentacrest, but the brick walls represent the shift to a more economical material. Classical ornament nevertheless remains important. The columns framing the entrance bay are a Corinthian variant (capitals with acanthus leaves below and palm above) that recall the first-century BCE Tower of the Winds in Athens. The industrial windows reflect the utility of chemistry as a field of study.

The Chemistry Building combines classical formality (columns, portico, pediments, quoins) with industrial-duty steel windows.

Blank Honors Center, 2003

ARCHITECT: HLKB ARCHITECTURE, DES MOINES, IOWA

Named for Myron and Jacqueline N. Blank of Des Moines, the Blank Honors Center is home to the University Honors Program and the Connie Belin and Jacqueline N. Blank Center for Gifted Education, which honors the work of Connie Belin, an Iowa educator and former member of the State Board of Regents. The building houses classrooms, offices, gathering spaces, and a food service area, as well as special meeting rooms devoted to the honors program. A connecting bridge links the center with the honors floor of the adjacent residence hall, Daum Hall.

A dark, monolithic glass-and-steel box, the building's neo-Miesian aspects recall the International style. The machine aesthetic is everywhere in evidence, contrasting the simplicity of its design with the complexity of the program and the architect's environment-friendly concept. (The Blank Honors Center is one of the first University buildings to incorporate aspects of "green architecture.") The west-facing façade has a double-glazed curtain wall whose outermost screen functions as a filter reducing the effect of the afternoon sun without the use of solar baffles. An aura of monumentality is achieved by a massive stone wall, which dominates the north elevation and rises above the roofline, laterally bisecting the building. The presence of this sheer masonry backdrop, the façade screen, and the absence of fuss coalesce in an Honors Center of elegant restraint.

Blank Honors Center aims for simplicity of form through
a neo-Modernist machine aesthetic.

Madison Street Residence Hall, 2017

ARCHITECT: ROHRBACH ASSOCIATES, IOWA CITY, IOWA

The University of Iowa offers two primary on-campus housing neighborhoods, one on the east side of the Iowa River and one on the west. Together they provide housing for nearly every freshman on campus. In 2015 the first new residence hall built on campus in forty-seven years opened within the West Campus neighborhood (Mary Louise Petersen Residence Hall). The combination of a larger student population, evidence that on-campus housing improves student academic and social performance, and the demolition of the Quadrangle Residence Hall led to immediate construction of a second new hall. With recognition that most undergraduate classes are hosted on the east side of the river, the University took advantage of a site that had remained undeveloped since the University purchased it from Iowa City. In the late 1990s the UI and Iowa City arranged for a property

With its three projecting towers, Madison Street Residence Hall makes one of the most powerful impressions of any campus building facing the river (architect's rendering).

swap. East Hall, located at the corner of Iowa Avenue and Gilbert Street, had become obsolete, and the site served as an opportunity for downtown development. At the same time, Iowa City had recently completed a new water treatment facility, allowing for its original water plant facility, at the north end of Madison Street, to shut down. Following the trade, the former water plant remained vacant until the residence hall project began. The site not only affords immediate student access to Madison Street but also offers a main entrance, via a skywalk, onto the bluff and T. Anne Cleary Walkway, making MSRH a new and important part of the East Campus residence hall neighborhood.

Its significant orientation to the Iowa River distinguishes the Madison Street Residence Hall from almost every other building on the East Campus. Starting with Old Capitol and the University buildings of the Pentacrest, façades invariably faced the city. By contrast, MSRH emphatically represents the new thinking of the UI campus master plan, which envisions a turn toward the waterfront as a positive resource and campus amenity. Even nearby IATL, which displays its most spectacular side to the river, nevertheless has the entrance on the south end. Mindful of the potential for flooding at the lower level, the architects raised MSRH on a high podium, with exposed structural pilotis at the southeast entrance corner and a service entrance toward the north. Three monumental blocks project outward and, in their elemental regular geometry, contrast markedly to IATL's fractured riverfront composition. The open courtyards created by the forward wings, with their river-facing floor lounges, provide student residents with the maximum number of views toward the water below. Just as the design turns to the river, the aqua-tinted glazing and window panels bring a bit of the river into the design, while the red-brick facing of the residential blocks references the nearby dormitories of an earlier epoch. MSRH has the further advantage of blocking from view the exposed and utilitarian side of the North Campus Parking ramp and cooling towers.

Ecklund Lounge (in Stanley Residence Hall), 1966

ARCHITECT: ALTFILLISCH, OLSON, GRAY AND THOMPSON,

DECORAH, IOWA

PREVIOUS NAME: STANLEY HALL LOUNGE

The Ecklund Lounge stands at the juncture of Currier Residence
Hall and Stanley Residence Hall, two major residence halls, and is
named after David Ecklund, Associated Residence Halls president in
1978. The lounge was built as a component of Stanley Hall but now
serves both residences. Carrie Stanley was a professor in the University of Iowa's English Department for thirty-four years and founded
the University's Writing Laboratory.

Marking the south end of Stanley Hall, the polygonal structure
consists of a brick podium and curtain wall of dark-tinted glass. A
distinctive serrated cornice lends a sense of playfulness appropriate
to the small structure's social function. The jaunty profile continues

Ecklund Lounge is perhaps the zaniest building on the
UI campus and much enjoyed by students.

The surreal cloud canopy of Ecklund Lounge
dominates the interior.

in the accordion canopy of the exterior stairs, which is a counterpart
to the turquoise-trimmed undulating wave-canopy that once graced
the front of nearby Burge Residence Hall (removed 2004) and the
zigzag canopy at Daum Residence Hall (both were also designed by
Altfillisch). The tiny interior is one of the most unusual to be found
anywhere on campus. The ceiling follows the ups and downs of the
exterior roofline, but a saucerlike indoor awning supported on pilotis
and with a light-admitting oculus in the center fills the space. Like
something from a dream or perhaps a 1950s science fiction movie,
this strange and unanticipated object resolves the angular profile of
the exterior into a soft-edged expanding cloud. Whether this bizarre
shape was designed for its acoustical properties is unknown, but the
fantasy world conjured by Ecklund Lounge provides an ideal respite
for students seeking refuge from the busy campus outside.

North Hall, 1925

ARCHITECT: PROUDFOOT, BIRD AND RAWSON,

DES MOINES, IOWA

PREVIOUS NAME: UNIVERSITY HIGH SCHOOL

At the time of North Hall's construction, another building on campus already bore that name. Opened in the 1860s and not demolished until 1949, the previous structure was used as a science facility and library and was located on the Pentacrest. The present North Hall was built to house University High School, an experimental school founded in 1916. Until it closed in 1972, the school's core faculty of graduate students provided an evolving, progressive curriculum to children from Iowa City and its nearby environs. Now home to the School of Social Work, North Hall has a small café, Wild Bill's, that employs and benefits persons with disabilities. The story of Bill Sackter, after whom the café is named, was the subject of a television movie, *Bill*, starring Mickey Rooney.

An unpretentious and relatively utilitarian building, North Hall continues Main Campus North's string of red-brick buildings designed by Proudfoot, Bird and Rawson. With its modest entrance bay and the restriction of detailing to limestone quoins, it is also one of the least ornamented. Both the upper and lower entrances are crowned by plaques announcing the building's former life as a school, and North Hall as a whole has a reticence in keeping with that history. One whimsical and enigmatic touch, a pair of doubled X's, is executed in brickwork on the east façade.

The unusual off-center portal anticipates the addition of three more bays to the left, but this was not realized before the University High School closed in 1972.

Currier Residence Hall, 1914

ARCHITECT: PROUDFOOT, BIRD AND RAWSON,

DES MOINES, IOWA

Currier Residence Hall, the University of Iowa's oldest extant residence hall, was built to address the shortage of housing for female students. It was named after Amos Noyes Currier and his wife, Celia Moore Currier, both fixtures in the Classics Department where Amos held a professorship and Celia was a Latin instructor. During his time at the University, Amos Currier held an array of positions. As a volun-

Currier Hall is the oldest student residence hall on the UI campus.

teer librarian, he organized the University's first card catalog; he also served as the first president of the Iowa chapter of Phi Beta Kappa, was dean of the Collegiate Department (now College of Liberal Arts and Sciences), and served as interim president (1898–1899) between Charles Schaeffer and George MacLean. Currier Hall, home to 168 women in 1914, is today a coeducational residence with renovations that address current student life needs.

This Georgian Revival dormitory is composed of simple brickwork and contrasting limestone detailing. Quoins at its corners and insets above the first- and third-story windows add distinction, as do the brackets under the cornice. Currier was enlarged in 1940, which extended the Clinton Street wing to the north. While the original Parisian-style glass fan-canopy above Currier's main door has been removed, the flanking Doric pilasters and the rooftop balustrade marking the entrance façade remain in place. Behind the balustrade and running along the roofline, pedimented dormers open from students' rooms and create a characteristic neo-Colonial profile. Currier was enlarged several times before it achieved its current U-shaped configuration. The aura of tradition pervades Currier; legend has it that the building is haunted by the ghosts of three residents from the 1930s, adding further luster to this classic residence hall's venerable character.

Shambaugh House, 1900

ARCHITECT: O. H. CARPENTER, IOWA CITY, IOWA

Benjamin F. Shambaugh, professor of political science from 1896 until his death in 1940, was an Iowa native and a University of Iowa graduate. Known around campus as a sharp dresser and the author of *The Campus Course: Approaches in Liberal and Cultural Education*, Shambaugh had a dedication to the intellectual and artistic that still infuses the home his widow, Bertha, bequeathed to the University in 1953. The Shambaugh House, while a private residence, was host to Amelia Earhart and to Roald Amundson, among others, as part of the University Lecture Series, which Benjamin Shambaugh chaired. After becoming University property, the building at 219 Clinton Street housed the Honors Program. In planning for the new Blank Honors Center in 2001, it was determined the home should be moved to its current location, three blocks to the north. The Shambaugh House now welcomes visitors again as the home of the International Writing Program.

When Shambaugh decided to build his home, he requested a design that was "substantial, but not ostentatious." Completed at a cost of $1,620, the Queen Anne–style house is, nevertheless, notable for its ornamentation, including finial-topped balustrades, Ionic colonnettes supporting the front porch, a scallop shell in the front gable, and an elliptical window on what is now the south side. Renovations in the 1940s had obscured or removed much of this decorative work, and cast iron had replaced the front porch colonnettes. Before the building was moved to its current location in January 2002, it enjoyed a renovation that restored much of the house to its original state. The attention to woodwork continues inside with fine finishes in the public spaces of the first floor.

Shambaugh House, in its classic Queen Anne style,
now hosts the International Writing Program.

Dey House, 1857, and
Glenn Schaeffer Library and Archives, 2006

ARCHITECT: UNKNOWN (1857)

OPN ARCHITECTS, CEDAR RAPIDS, IOWA (2006)

The Dey House, home to the Iowa Writers' Workshop, is one of several historic homes adapted for reuse as academic or administrative space by the University. Peter A. Dey, who brought the railroad to Iowa City in 1855, had commissioned the house to convince his fiancée to move west from New York City and join him here. The University purchased the house in 1949, but the Writers' Workshop has only been in the house since 1997. Prior to that, the Workshop occupied many settings, finding its first home in a barracks on the banks of the Iowa River in 1936. Through the years, noted writers, including Frank Conroy, John Irving, Flannery O'Connor, Philip Roth, Jane Smiley, Kurt Vonnegut, and Marilynne Robinson, have participated in the Writers' Workshop as both students and faculty. Today, the house represents the core of a writer's community, making Iowa City an epicenter for top writing talent.

Facing Clinton Street, the Italianate design is fronted by a porch with clusters of four colonnettes that splinter the light, creating a lively pattern of shade on the building's eastern face. Above, a hip roof

Dey House is home to the Iowa Writers' Workshop.

The restraint of the façade design of the Glenn Schaeffer Library and Archives of the Iowa Writers' Workshop respects the historic integrity of Dey House. The addition opens expansively at the back to allow Workshop faculty and students views of nature displayed on the slope of the bluff (colorplate 12).

with cast iron fretwork and widow's walk supports Dey's contention that, although Iowa City was far west of New York, it was not lacking in civilization. The Dey House has been expanded since its original construction, most notably with the addition of an ornate hall and staircase in the 1870s. While respecting the original house as the front door to the Writers' Workshop, the 2006 addition nearly doubled the programmed square footage.

The Glenn Schaeffer Library wing is pulled back from Clinton Street, creating a backdrop for the original structure. Its quiet street front, however, transitions to an expressive, contemporary Prairie Style Revival that takes maximum advantage of its setting above the Iowa River Valley (colorplate 12). The use of natural materials and the expansive glass facing west are anchored by a limestone base that grows from the natural bluff. Clerestory windows and shed roofs suggest a visual pun on the literary workshop concept. The main spaces inside the addition are a large, vaulted-ceiling library and public reading room where the more than four thousand volumes written by Workshop graduates and faculty are on display. The room is named in memoriam to Frank Conroy, the Workshop's director from 1987 to 2005.

President's Residence, 1908

ARCHITECT: PROUDFOOT AND BIRD, DES MOINES, IOWA

The residence was first occupied by President George E. MacLean and contains a third-floor ballroom (though difficult to access and seldom, if ever, actually used for public functions), second-floor private quarters, and a first floor made public for receptions, fund-raising, and other outreach efforts. Those public areas greet as many as 200 University advancement events each year. The State Board of Regents requires that the University president live in the facility.

Due to such heavy use and decades of administrative reluctance to update the house, by 2002 the building was in dire need of significant rehabilitation. While the University presidency was vacant prior to the selection of David J. Skorton as president, the University, in conjunction with the State Board of Regents, began a comprehensive renovation project that included a garage addition to the east of the original structure, a complete overhaul of the mechanical, plumbing, and electrical systems, and the addition of an elevator to provide for improved accessibility. Major repairs to the kitchen and west and north porches corrected structural concerns and significantly improved the ability to host events. Additional deferred maintenance work was completed in 2016.

Restoring the Georgian Revival home with period-appropriate details was paramount. The residence is a classically detailed structure that at least alludes to the Pentacrest in its use of the Ionic order at the entrance portico. Like those of the Old Capitol, the portico columns are wooden. During the renovation, colonnettes were also added to the west porch, better integrating it with the rest of the house. The addition to the east not only improved access but better balanced the overall massing of the structure. Careful brick selection and detailing helped to match the new to the original. Inside, period light fixtures were chosen for their compatibility with designs popular at the turn of the century, and a humble elegance in finishes was achieved as the house recollects its early years.

The Georgian (Colonial) Revival style of the President's Residence alludes to a more domesticated version of Classicism than does that of the Pentacrest buildings with its references to ancient Greece and Rome.

Main Campus South

With the exception of the original portions of the Seamans Center for the Engineering Arts and Sciences, the campus south of the Pentacrest was not developed until the 1950s. The University of Iowa's original athletic facilities, including a football stadium and armory, were once tucked along this stretch of the Iowa River but have since been replaced by academic buildings. That athletic heritage is resurrected by the Campus Recreation and Wellness Center located at the southwest corner of Burlington and Madison Streets. As a complement to the original Field House on the west side of the river, this facility not only enhances access to recreational and leisure activities on the east side of campus but also strengthens an ill-defined south campus border, giving shape to Gibson Square as a university quad. Farther east and riding the crest of the bluff, the Voxman Music Building brings the arts to downtown and establishes a major campus extension south of Burlington.

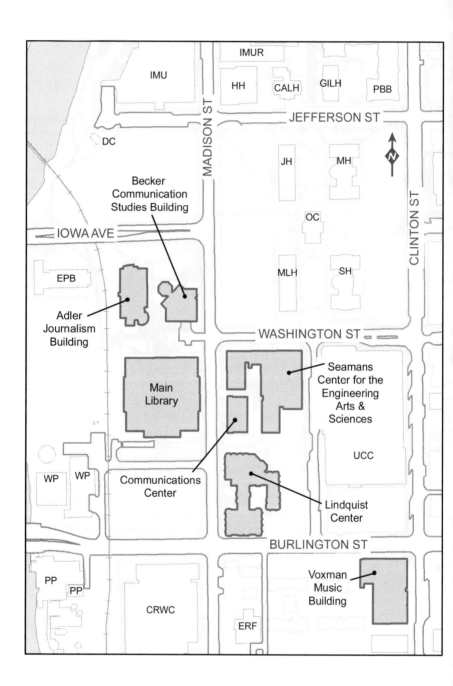

Seamans Center for the Engineering Arts and Sciences, 1905, Seamans Center Addition, 2001, and Seamans Center South Annex Addition, 2018

ARCHITECT: PROUDFOOT AND BIRD, DES MOINES, IOWA (1905)

ANSHEN + ALLEN, LOS ANGELES, CALIFORNIA /

NEUMANN MONSON ARCHITECTS, IOWA CITY, IOWA (2001)

BNIM, DES MOINES, IOWA (2018)

PREVIOUS NAME: ENGINEERING BUILDING

The modest Beaux-Arts façade of the Engineering Building (now the Seamans Center for the Engineering Arts and Sciences) was no competition for Schaeffer Hall across the street, but it does express the ambition of the University to extend the Pentacrest style beyond the new buildings that had only just begun to rise around Old Capitol.

The Engineering Building was the first University structure to jump Washington Street and move south of the Pentacrest. Since that time there have been a total of eight additions to the original building. The three most important of these are Mechanical Engineering,

1932; Electrical Engineering, 1964; a south addition and restructuring of much of the interior, 2001; and the South Annex, 2018. Gary F. Seamans, 1971 graduate of the College of Engineering, and his wife Camille made a major gift to the college, and the entire Engineering Building complex was renamed in their honor.

Originally known as the Engineering Building, the Capitol Street façade of the Seamans Center was the third Beaux-Arts-inspired building on the UI campus designed by Proudfoot and Bird. Only nearby Schaeffer Hall and the Sciences Library (formerly Hall of Anatomy) are older. The design offers a twist to the more correct Classicism seen on the Pentacrest. Horizontal channeling at the entrance on Capitol Street reverses Schaeffer's notions of rustication by placing those elements above, while the podium below is finished smoothly (an arrangement later followed at Macbride). Playful departures, such as the superimposition of orders (Ionic pilasters overlap Doric at the entrance), underscaled capitals, and domestic-looking windows of the central bay are intentional "mistakes" that give the Seamans Center its air of slight irreverence. Ornament, including a proud palmette at the apex of the pediment and wreathed medallions beneath the cornice, adds further embellishment. Note the series of panels above the second-story windows; years from 1906 through 1927, carved engineering instruments, and other details all attach context to the design and communicate what goes on inside to passersby. The modernized addition to the south, constructed in 2001, creates an inviting entrance, which communicates with a spacious new interior while paying homage to the adjacent, original structure by repeating its horizontal banding and stone finish. The South Annex addition, 2018, extends the horizontal sweep of the complex to almost the entire west side of Capitol Street. The white-paneled cladding with its vertical channels nevertheless provides a certain air of Classical articulation, notwithstanding the Postmodern irregular spacing of the fenestration.

Raised on pilotis, the South Annex addition to Seamans Center creates a gateway connecting University Capitol Centre with the campus buildings down the slope of the bluff to the west (architect's rendering).

Voxman Music Building, 2016

ARCHITECT: LMN ARCHITECTS, SEATTLE, WASHINGTON /

NEUMANN MONSON ARCHITECTS, IOWA CITY, IOWA

Following the flood of 2008, the University was forced to find a location for the replacement of the devastated Voxman Music Building (1972); it made a bold strategic decision. A site nearer the center of the undergraduate campus and also in close proximity to the core of downtown Iowa City offered the possibility of extending the arts to more students and to a broader community. Originally, the building was designed to occupy both the east and west sides of Clinton Street with a connecting overhead bridge, but federal restrictions related to funding support eligibility pushed the entire program to the south-

A musical theme animates the façade of Voxman Music Building and its detailing (photo digitally enhanced).

west corner of the intersection. The site constraints resulted in a taller than anticipated building. During foundation excavation, contractors encountered several historic foundations that required investigation. While these finds temporarily slowed the construction work, coordination with the federal government and the state archaeologist resulted in a unique glimpse into the origins of Iowa City. Once that challenge was overcome, work began on the most acoustically complex building on campus. Not only the quality of the sound produced in the rehearsal and performance venues but also the containment of sound in the practice rooms required special attention. After eight years of multiple temporary locations the School of Music once again enjoys a consolidated program, one that has a long-term impact on both students and the surrounding community.

The Voxman Music Building anchors one of the most prominent downtown street corners in Iowa City, and the massing of the volumes reflects that tight urban setting. The Clinton Street main façade expresses the glass-walled public atrium, while the dense block of practice rooms seems to hover high above, an effect achieved by the placement of the vertical supports behind the transparent panels. A welcoming grand staircase positioned at the street corner leads up to the performance halls on the second level, where a monumental amber and gold chandelier (2003) by Dale Chihuly, secured as part of the University's Art in State Buildings program, can be seen. Just at that point the glass façade tilts and expands to provide a porte cochère over the entrance. The bulge is harmoniously emphasized in the articulation of the practice block above, where the size and spacing of the windows first widen and then narrow toward the center, creating a fittingly musical quickening of tempo or even a crescendo as read from left to right. Adding to this visual dynamic, the recessed decorative channeling of the practice rooms fenestration shifts to the left of each individual window. Overall, the viewer is left with the impression of a keyboard in preparation for a musical performance. A red-hued recital hall, looking over Clinton Street, is on view to the left of the glass swell, while the large concert hall on the Burlington Street side projects from the main body of the structure, providing shelter at the sidewalk entrance. The terracotta tile cladding of this expressive volume, with its reticulated surface, adds visual impact, while the lilting pattern of the slit windows and the upturn at the soffit ends may suggest musical scales or, to some, perhaps even a melody. LMN Architects created a series of experiences through a continuous processional pathway that starts at the street level and invites the visitor up and through the various performance, rehearsal, and teaching spaces.

Lindquist Center, 1973

ARCHITECT: WALTER NETSCH OF SKIDMORE
OWINGS AND MERRILL, CHICAGO, ILLINOIS
PREVIOUS NAMES: EDUCATIONAL RESEARCH BUILDING,
LINDQUIST CENTER FOR MEASUREMENT

Lindquist Center is a particularly fitting commemoration of Everet Lindquist's contributions to the University of Iowa. A professor of education, Lindquist developed the Iowa Test series as well as the electronic scoring machine that made it possible. These innovations, used by students nationwide, revolutionized skills testing and secured

The geometry of Walter Netsch's Lindquist Center is expressed on the underside of the bridge connecting the two main wings and in the projecting brick-faced volumes of the superstructure.

Lindquist's place as a leader in the field. He set aside the profits from the Iowa Test for a fund dedicated to capital improvement and education-based research. Those resources were instrumental in the construction of the center that bears his name and has housed the University computer center and College of Education since its opening.

Designed by Walter Netsch, the architect responsible for the University of Illinois-Chicago campus and the Air Force Academy and Chapel in Colorado Springs, the Lindquist Center displays some characteristic features of his academic buildings. Working with Field Theory, a design methodology he pioneered, Netsch created a geometric grid for the floor plan that also informs the elevation of the building. This method reverses the Modernist dictum of "form follows function" (Louis Sullivan), making it instead "function follows form." The program of the building is made to fit into the preconceived geometry of the plan. At Lindquist the basic geometric shape that constitutes the "field" is the octagon/square. This geometry is also expressed on the exterior by projecting or recessed portions of octagons of unequal sides (four short and four long). Application of the Field Theory eliminated the need for interior hallways. Built in north and south phases of earthy brown brick, the main sections of the building are connected by an elevated bridge supported on attenuated pilotis. Incised marks on the building's underside reflect an ideal geometry.

The courtyard of the Lindquist Center hosts one of the most noteworthy works of sculpture on the UI campus, Louise Nevelson's *Voyage* (colorplate 16).

Campus Recreation and Wellness Center, 2010

ARCHITECT: RDG PLANNING AND DESIGN, DES MOINES, IOWA

Since 1927, the University of Iowa had relied on its Field House as the hub of student recreational activities. The building's layout and condition limited its capacity and, furthermore, impeded efforts to accommodate new trends in campus physical recreation. This led to the construction of the new Campus Recreation and Wellness Center (CRWC), which was, nevertheless, conceived to work in tandem with the Field House, which would continue to host many court and intramural sports. The selection of the new CRWC site was based on its proximity to the center of campus and both east and west residence halls. The location also allowed the University to reserve the land to the south for long-term growth. In the midst of construction the 2008 flood ravaged the University and delayed the project, but this afforded an opportunity to incorporate features that will protect it against future flooding.

Exposed vertical supports lend monumentality to the façade of the Campus Recreation and Wellness Center—a calculated response to its more formal academic neighbors. The corner cantilever suggests the energy of the inside activity.

Following concerns that the initially proposed design did not respond sufficiently to the surrounding campus context, the CRWC was the benefactor of a noteworthy on-campus design charrette event. Faculty, staff, and students joined the designers in a discussion that produced a more prominent and welcoming presence at the corner entrance, with a cantilevered third floor, and a north façade more responsive to the grandiloquent statement of the monumental south façade of the Main Library, located directly across Gibson Square. That enhanced grandeur was achieved in particular by the treatment of the row of colossal piers running through all three floors on the Burlington Street front. These are continuously exposed at ground level and intermittently revealed on the second and third floors where the glass curtain wall recedes here and there. Set behind the primary north façade of glass is a core red-brick structure designed to reflect and celebrate the visual authority of the nearby main Power Plant (1928). At night the building is a beacon of youthful, athletic energy as the illuminated interior becomes easily visible from the street and invites passersby to join the healthful activities on display. Upon entering, patrons may admire Gary Drostle's 2010 floor mosaic, *River of Life*. The Native American pattern alludes to the stewardship of the natural environment, just as the meandering river running through (and beyond its bounds) reminds us of the powerful forces that can overwhelm human culture, as occurred in the 2008 flood. A bronze bas-relief sculpture by Lawrence Nowlan celebrates the invention of the butterfly swim stroke at the UI in 1936. The programmatic positioning of the various recreational activities within the building highlights views to and from each other and encourages visitors to participate. The aquatics center, operated in cooperation with the Athletic Department, includes generous natural light from above and a dramatic dive tower structure anchoring its south end.

Gary Drostle's expansive atrium floor mosaic represents metaphors of life and of nature, with particular emphasis on the untamed potential of the nearby river.

Communications Center, 1951

ARCHITECT: BROOKS BORG, ARCHITECTS-ENGINEERS,

DES MOINES, IOWA

The Communications Center, the first permanent classroom building constructed during the expansive post–World War II era, was built to house the School of Journalism and the *Daily Iowan*. Spun off from the Department of English in 1923, Journalism already had distinguished alumni, including George Gallup. Before going on to found his opinion poll, Gallup was also the editor-in-chief of the *Daily Iowan* and, briefly, a member of the faculty. The Communications Center now primarily houses departmental offices.

As the first example of International-style Modernism on the main campus, the Communications Center used its radical design to express the advanced communications technologies originally located inside. Aggressively advancing a machine aesthetic of simple, hard-edged geometries expressed in concrete, the Communications Center disdains traditional ornament in favor of clean horizontal lines and the repetition of standardized forms. The recessed podium, faced in Brutalist concrete panels, emphasizes the forward thrust of the sun baffles of the top two stories, which were referred to as "a distinctive as well as functional feature, providing shade from direct sunlight and reflecting light into the building." It references similar grids developed by Oscar Niemeyer and Le Corbusier for tropical locales. Had the planned fourth floor not fallen victim to the budget, the street façade's lattice would have been still more imposing. The Communications Center's Modernism presages many later campus buildings with standardized façades, including the Center for Disabilities and Development (1954), Burge Residence Hall (1959), Van Allen Hall (1964), and Phillips Hall (1965). It is perhaps fitting that this Modernist design aesthetic was introduced to campus by the successor firm of Proudfoot and Bird, the Des Moines architects who first brought architectural distinction to the University. Historically, this departure represents the University's daring first initiative to engage a cutting-edge mode of mid-twentieth-century architectural style, an approach to progressive design thereafter supported by successive University administrations.

The Communications Center was the first International-style Modernist building on the UI campus.

Main Library, 1951

ARCHITECT: KEFFER AND JONES, DES MOINES, IOWA (1951)

CHARLES RICHARDSON AND ASSOCIATES, DAVENPORT, IOWA

(1961, 1965, 1971)

The first freestanding library at the University of Iowa was a long time coming. Growing from an original selection of fifty books that were sent from New York to Iowa City in 1855 by Amos Dean, first president of the University of Iowa (1855–1859), the collection has frequently exceeded the space available to house it. First kept in a cubicle in the Mechanics' Academy (the first university building), then moved to Old Capitol, Old North Hall (where three-fourths of the volumes were lost in an 1897 fire), Schaeffer Hall, Macbride Hall, and finally the Old Armory, it was not even until additions to the new Main Library were completed in 1971 that there was room enough to accommodate the main collection in a single building. That building provided open stack shelving so students could have direct access to the books and take advantage of the "serendipitous nature" of research and learning, as head librarian Ralph Ellsworth (1943–1958) understood it. The Main Library now serves as the hub of a 4,000,000-volume library system with seven branches across campus and a generous lending policy that extends borrowing privileges to any Iowan with a card from a public library. In 2014 a large section of the main floor was redesigned as a Student Learning Commons with modern technology amenities, group study spaces, varied comfortable seating arrangements, and the Food for Thought Café. This modernization also added a new building entrance along the busy Madison Street façade.

The Main Library, set on a high platform, makes a statement (color-plate 6); the building is both a repository of knowledge and a monument to learning. Visitors approach the south façade via stairs that, along with the scale of the building and its massive slab roof, suggest an impenetrable fortress while at the same time announcing the value of what lies within and the need for protecting it. The vaguely medieval-looking design references multiple architectural sources while under-

The original 1951 Keffer and Jones Main Library north façade was the sole example of Zigzag Moderne on the UI campus. Twenty years later it was masked in a Modernist remake of the library.

mining them with a Modern sensibility. Just below the projecting roof, narrow vertical windows recall the defensive features of a fortified castle, while the powerful plane of the roof itself functions as the capstone. At the entrance, the spaces between the muscular brick piers turn what was solid in classical architecture (paired columns) into voids of tinted glass; and cantilevering at the corners highlights the strength of modern materials. Ornament is banned. The refer-

93

The Romanesque Revival Old Armory (1904), located on the current site of the Philip D. Adler Journalism and Mass Communication Building, did service as the Reserve Library from 1927 to 1951, when the books were transferred to the new building by a human chain of students.

ence to a columnar composition follows the New Formalism phase of Modernism that began in the 1950s with Edward Durell Stone and which was developed further by others, including Max Abramovitz, who would later transform the Arts Campus.

The original 1951 Art Deco–like central section of the north façade was reworked in 1971 to conform to the Modernist aesthetic of the south elevation of the building. Characteristic of post–World War I American Moderne architecture with its streamlined elements, this original design had strong vertical components with limestone detailing projecting above the central block and geometric patterning in the decorative insets over the entrance windows. The Zigzag Moderne panels flanking the now-obscured central block were also censored, but the wings with their horizontally zigzagging window embrasures remain. A set of nine aluminum panels illustrating a humorous view of the history of education and libraries, commissioned from "Ding" Darling, the Pulitzer Prize–winning cartoonist of the *Des Moines Register*, were removed from their mountings above the north façade

Public education and the history of books converge in "Ding" Darling's cartoons that once adorned the main entrance on the library's north façade. Here a caveman, Egyptian, Roman, medieval monk, and Renaissance humanist carry their tomes toward the library portal, while caricatured exemplars of the various disciplines enthusiastically bring forward their stacks of books. The image must have recalled the human chain of students who conveyed books to the new library when it opened in 1951.

entrance doors at the same time and are now displayed inside the building. The sleek aluminum stair railings and the staggered pattern of the cream-and-rose-colored linoleum tiles of the flooring in the original (north) section of the building are surviving remnants of this Moderne design.

Philip D. Adler Journalism and Mass Communication Building, 2005

ARCHITECT: OPN ARCHITECTS, CEDAR RAPIDS, IOWA

Home to the School of Journalism and Mass Communication, the Department of Cinema and Comparative Literature, and the *Daily Iowan*, the Philip D. Adler Journalism and Mass Communication Building establishes a disciplinary quad with the Samuel L. Becker Communication Studies Building. The building is named after Philip David Adler of Davenport, Iowa. While at the University of Iowa in the 1920s, Adler was editor of the *Daily Iowan*, becoming publisher of the *Kewanee Star Courier* after graduation. Taking over as the publisher of the *Davenport Daily Times* in 1949, Adler went on to build a regional newspaper conglomerate.

Intended to define a plaza between the Main Library and the Becker Building, the Adler Building also weaves together all the surrounding brick architectures. The connecting bridge provides interdisciplinary communication between Becker and Adler, and the red-brick square arch under the bridge also helps to restore the visual axis between the Main Library and the Iowa Memorial Union, which had been sacrificed to Becker's octagonal auditorium. The Adler Building is respectful of its visual proximity to the Pentacrest as well. Set back from Iowa Avenue, it leaves open the dramatic upward view from the west. An expressive south façade makes for a memorable pedestrian zone (colorplate 21). Here, the crossbars of the rotunda (typically Postmodern in their ornamental function) contrast with the utter simplicity of Becker. The rotunda itself recalls the projecting west façades of nearby Macbride and Schaeffer Halls. Inside, a three-story brick wall and atrium bisects the building from north to south and separates the more public general assignment spaces to the east from the westward spaces, dedicated to the School of Journalism and Mass Communication.

The Philip D. Adler Journalism and Mass Communication Building occupies the site of the Romanesque Revival Old Armory (1904) and, while rejecting any stylistic references to the past, its rotunda recalls those of the Pentacrest buildings and, more recently, the Levitt Center for University Advancement.

Samuel L. Becker Communication Studies Building, 1984

ARCHITECT: THORSON-BROM-BROSHAR-SNYDER,

WATERLOO, IOWA

PREVIOUS NAME: COMMUNICATION STUDIES BUILDING

Built during the presidency of James O. Freedman (1982–1987), Becker Communication Studies Building was state-of-the-art, from the exterior design to its broadcasting facilities. It was rededicated in 1993 in honor of Samuel L. Becker, distinguished professor emeritus in communication studies.

Becker Communication Studies Building exhibits many of the hallmarks of Late Modernism: shifted-grid plan, stark massing, tinted and mirrored glass, and circular vent openings. The dark glazing of the

The Late Modernist style of the Samuel L. Becker Communication Studies Building expresses the forward-looking character of the discipline it houses.

opposite: David Middlebrook's eroded globe, cubic map, and bouncy spiral, entitled *Small World*, 1986, reiterate the distant reach of communications suggested in the surrounding setting.

window walls of the main level on the street front creates the illusion of a red-brick monolith floating on a white concrete band, an effect similar to that on the International style Communications Center just down the street. Set at a 45-degree angle to the monolithic street-front block, the projecting mirrored auditorium section serves as a transition between two red-brick-clad masses. These large, sharp-edged monochromatic forms are used to create visual interest, but there is also a unique acknowledgment of the adjacent campus setting—the Becker Building's east-facing mirror-glass windows are angled to provide a reflected view of the gilded lantern dome of Old Capitol; thus, the building's design reflects its campus context. In the atrium, a Chinese moon gate, curving stair ramps, and ocean-liner railings all suggest travel and communication with distant places.

River Valley Campus

The River Valley Campus comprises a set of buildings that are varied in appearance and diverse in function but which share a common engagement with the Iowa River. Like many communities, Iowa City can trace its origins to the river that runs through it and can bemoan decades of underappreciation of the waterfront. Once considered a necessity, not an amenity, the Iowa River is now recognized as the defining topographical attribute of both Iowa City and the University. The romance and sweep of the bluffs give the campus much of its aesthetic power and make possible the dramatic views of the Pentacrest from the west. The River Valley Campus, on the river's eastern banks (the exception is the C. Maxwell Stanley Hydraulics Laboratory), takes advantage of this position with a bike and pedestrian path affording casual interaction with the river. The postflood renovation of the Iowa Memorial Union added an extensive terrace overlooking the water, and future campus planning will continue to increase the enjoyment of, and relationship to, the Iowa River.

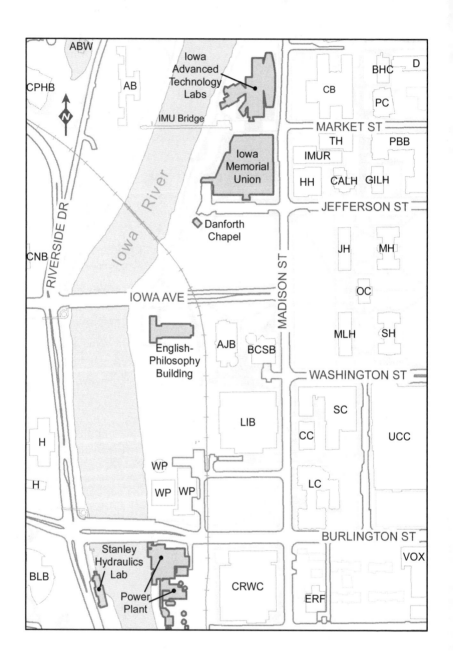

English-Philosophy Building, 1966

ARCHITECT: SASAKI, WALKER AND ASSOCIATES,

WATERTOWN, MASSACHUSETTS / PRALL ARCHITECTS,

DES MOINES, IOWA

The English-Philosophy Building, known on campus as EPB, has been home to these two humanities departments and the Department of Linguistics since its construction and to the Department of Rhetoric since 1970. Begun under President Virgil M. Hancher (1940–1964) and completed under President Howard R. Bowen (1964–1969), EPB was one of many building projects on campus that exhibit a new desire to pursue architecture of current note and merit. Nationally renowned architects took part in a campus building boom, particularly during the Bowen years, and EPB has the distinction of being the first fruit of the University's look beyond the state for high-quality design.

President Bowen had the architects rotate the design of the English-Philosophy Building to provide better views of the Iowa River from the faculty offices.

Notwithstanding its unmistakable Modernist aesthetic of standardized forms, the strong vertical articulation of EPB's river façade conveys intimations of Classicism that reverberate with the Doric-columned portico of Old Capitol located on the distant bluff. The rigor of the design—with symmetry and uniform rectilinear geometry—is characteristically Modernist but employed to invite associations with the buildings of the Pentacrest. Alternating brick and precast concrete elements create a façade of light and dark components, with the vertical stacking of the paired windows suggesting column shafts. The building's horizontal platform and articulated cornice line also gesture at classical forms. After the design phase of EPB was completed, President Bowen asked that the building be rotated to maximize the river views from the faculty office wing, making it the first postwar building to acknowledge the river as a campus amenity. Interestingly, however, the building faces the river but does not engage it, with no pedestrian access on the west side of the building, so that the abstract purity of the Modernist framework remains undisturbed.

Power Plant, 1928

ARCHITECT: PROUDFOOT, RAWSON AND SOUERS,

DES MOINES, IOWA

At 8:00 AM, noon, 1:00 PM, and 5:00 PM, Monday through Saturday, the steam whistle at the University of Iowa's Power Plant blows, punctuating the day. A task performed manually by a member of the staff, the four-times-daily raucous blast has made the plant part of the texture of life in downtown Iowa City. The Power Plant is more than an anchor of the soundscape, however; the facility generates the steam that heats and operates the University on a daily basis. The facility also co-generates about thirty percent of the electric power used on campus. Previously relying on coal, with natural gas as backup, the Power Plant has become a leading example of sustainable operation by introducing the burning of discarded oat hulls, a renewable resource pro-

As an example of functional architecture and potent massing of forms, the Power Plant is the building that some contemporary architects admire the most.

An archival photograph of Proudfoot, Rawson and Souers's original tour de force design reveals the full extent of its inspiration in Romanesque of the early tenth century, as in the abbey church of Saint-Philibert at Tournus, with its classic Westwerk and flanking bell towers.

duced thirty miles north in Cedar Rapids, which now accounts for as much as fourteen percent of the Power Plant's fuel needs. New biofuels, including annually harvested *Miscanthus* and wood chips, continue to increase the sustainable production of steam and power on the campus.

Though utilitarian in nature, the Power Plant is a formidable example of the possibilities when service architecture is conceived with attention to its impact. Renowned architects visiting the University often cite the building as their favorite on campus, recognizing the combination of its powerful massing of volumes and brick detailing. The strength of the Power Plant is in its variegated composition. While the flues and boilers are interesting on their own and grew purely out of necessity, the functional components of the building refine themselves as they near the original structure at Burlington Street. There, the Power Plant recalls the transept of a Romanesque cathedral. The west end of this remaining original part of the building is crowned with a series of blind arches supported on corbels. Lombard bands, typical of the Romanesque style, mark the two slightly projecting bays, each of which also bears the narrow Medieval loophole windows. The Power Plant and the now vanished Old Armory were the only two Medieval Revival buildings to gain a foothold on the east campus.

C. Maxwell Stanley Hydraulics Laboratory, 1928

ARCHITECT: PROUDFOOT, RAWSON AND SOUERS,

DES MOINES, IOWA (NORTH WING) / GEORGE HORNER,

UNIVERSITY OF IOWA (CENTRAL BLOCK AND SOUTH WING, 1933)

PREVIOUS NAME: HYDRAULICS LABORATORY

The C. Maxwell Stanley Hydraulics Laboratory was designed as a wet lab for hydraulic engineering research and teaching. Before its 2002 renovation, it contained scale models of hydraulic structures such as rivers, dams, and culverts. There were also flumes, weighing tanks, measuring basins, and a pump room. The experimental channel that originally fed water from the Iowa River through the subbasement was later converted to a 290-foot-long model ship towing tank. In 2003, the Hydraulics Laboratory was renamed in honor of 1926 engineering graduate C. Maxwell Stanley. The structure is home to

A hybrid of Romanesque Revival wings and a Moderne central block, the C. Maxwell Stanley Hydraulics Laboratory is an architectural curiosity as well as an important monument in the history of hydraulics.

the nationally prominent College of Engineering's Iowa Institute of Hydraulic Research and the Iowa Flood Center.

Much like its Power Plant neighbor, the Stanley Hydraulics Laboratory is of utilitarian design but with reference to architecture of the past. Best seen from the east side of the river, the building is a composite of two distinct styles. Both north and south wings have arched neo-Romanesque windows similar to the contemporaneous Power Plant directly across the river, but the separation between floors can be seen through the glass, demonstrating the non-weight-bearing function of the walls and announcing a modern steel-frame construction. In place of the historical features, the vertical fins of the central block indicate an Art Moderne streamlined effect for the tower. UI architect George Horner's intervention here seems to have been decisive for the stylistic shift in the central tower. This was one of his first designs for the campus. The 2002 renovation, which converted most of the building to office space while maintaining its historic features, also added a walled service unit at the top and a stylistically compatible entrance pavilion on the north façade. The American Society of Civil Engineers has designated the Stanley Hydraulics Laboratory a National Historic Civil Engineering Landmark. It is the oldest university-based research and education hydraulics laboratory in the U.S.

Danforth Chapel, 1952

ARCHITECT: GEORGE HORNER, UNIVERSITY OF IOWA

Constructed with funds from a gift by Mr. and Mrs. William H. Danforth of the Danforth Foundation of St. Louis, the nondenominational chapel occupies a picturesque site on the east bank of the Iowa River. The compact brick and wood-trim building was designed by University architect George Horner to recall St. John's Methodist Episcopal Church (known as the Old Zimmermann Church), an 1874 pioneer church on Morse Road in northeast Johnson County. Diagonally oriented and set against a backdrop of sycamore and pine trees, Danforth Chapel's site also introduces the bucolic setting of St. John's in the middle of campus.

Danforth Chapel's picturesque setting on the banks of the Iowa River is an integral component of its simple design.

Danforth Chapel has load-bearing masonry walls and simple brick detailing, most notably on the east façade. Inside, a plaque reads: "To aspire nobly, to live daringly, to serve humbly." The dilapidated original had been spotted in the early 1930s by Rufus Fitzgerald, director of the School of Fine Arts at the time. Together with Grant Wood, who was then on the faculty, Fitzgerald studied the possibility of moving the church to campus, but that proved too costly. Funding to build a replica of the structure was also delayed, and Wood died long before construction could begin. The painter was to have provided murals for the interior, with the idea that all would be finished in time for the University's centennial in 1947. Had the project been realized according to plan, it would have been a noteworthy testament to Wood's Regionalist vision for contemporary American art and would surely have reminded his students of Giotto's Arena Chapel re-created on the banks of the Iowa River.

Iowa Memorial Union, 1925, Iowa House Addition, 1965, and East Façade / Hubbard Commons Addition, 2007

ARCHITECT: BOYD AND MOORE, DES MOINES, IOWA (1925)

TINSLEY, HIGGINS, LIGHTER & LYON, DES MOINES, IOWA (1965)

BURT, HILL, KOSAR, RITTELMANN ASSOCIATES, BOSTON,

MASSACHUSETTS / OPN ARCHITECTS, CEDAR RAPIDS, IOWA (2007)

With the close of World War I, student unions honoring the veterans of that conflict came into vogue at large midwestern universities. The multifunction building served as a monument to students who had participated in the Civil War, Spanish American War, or World War I. It became the center of social life on campus, a place for students to congregate and engage in extracurricular activities. Over the years, the Union has housed a bowling alley, a nightclub (the Silver

The original 1925 Beaux-Arts façade of the Iowa Memorial Union references the formal Classicism of the Pentacrest but now in less expensive brick. Limestone is used only for the detailing.

The insertion of a three-story addition into what had been an open courtyard in 2007 ties the original 1925 building to the later additions of the south. Vertical elements seen through the slightly curved glass façade sustain the rhythm of the Classical pilasters.

Shadow), and faculty club. The latter organization, the Triangle Club, gave its name—and triangular light fixtures—to what is now the R. Wayne Richey Ballroom. The Main Lounge, host to performances, speeches, and dignitaries over the years (from Frank Lloyd Wright to Vladimir Horowitz and from Martin Luther King, Jr., to Howard Zinn), is still the most popular such venue on campus.

The Union's original building consists of the Main Lounge and the three-story block facing Madison Street. It continues the brick-and-limestone Beaux-Arts Classicism of the nearby Trowbridge Hall (1918) and Chemistry Building (1922). That design included a channeled base on the first floor from which rise Doric pilasters, paired above the entrance portal and in the slightly projecting end wings. Limestone was used as detailing at the entrances, along the frieze, in quoining, and in Doric capitals. Ornate floral carving surrounding the main portal celebrates Iowa's state flower, the wild prairie rose. The original 1925 project envisioned a threefold replication of the extant east façade and a great central pavilion facing south and on axis with the north façade of the Main Library. But that was not to be. Additions of 1955 and 1965 extended the building to the south and west, adding a new main entrance facing south, a hotel (Iowa House), and offices and meeting rooms for administration and student organizations—all in a spare Modernist style of unrelieved functionalism. The win-

An architect's rendering shows the redesign of the IMU riverfront following the 2008 flood. The main building not only is mitigated against future threats from the river but also has a serpentine-walled terrace where students and visitors can enjoy the river as a campus amenity (architect's rendering).

dows of the hotel wing merely puncture the wall—a stark Modernist response to the ornamented Beaux-Arts building it adjoins. The rejection of detailing of any sort and omission even of a cornice impart an austere character. The 2008 flood, which closed the lower level for seven years, forced the addition of a new protective floodwall along the river's edge. The wall and associated terrace respond to the flow of the river and the adjacent exterior amphitheater. While protecting the building from future flood risks, the terrace also invites visitors to engage the river from above.

Iowa Advanced Technology Laboratories, 1992

ARCHITECT: FRANK O. GEHRY, LOS ANGELES, CALIFORNIA / HLKB ARCHITECTURE, DES MOINES, IOWA

President James O. Freedman (1982–1987) sponsored the enterprise to attract laser scientists to campus using a high-design building as a magnet. Today the Iowa Advanced Technology Laboratories building continues to play an important role in the University's pursuit of scientific research. Functioning as a research facility for several University units, the building acts as a cluster site for the applied sciences. The chemistry and physics faculty make use of the space, as do the chemical and biological engineering, civil and environmental engineering, electrical and computer engineering, and mechanical

Monumental forms of the Iowa Advanced Technology Laboratories' east façade blur the lines between architecture and sculpture.

Exploring the aesthetics of light, IATL's atrium skylights and rectilinear service elements constitute a visual essay on light, geometry, and space.

engineering departments. IATL also houses the Center for Global and Regional Environmental Research, the Optical Science and Technology Center, and part of the Center for Computer-Aided Design. This iconic building serves as an incubator of interdisciplinary exchanges among a range of cutting-edge fields while expressing through good contemporary design the dynamic character of initiatives in the applied and theoretical sciences at the University of Iowa.

It could be said that the march to Bilbao began here. Designed by Frank O. Gehry, IATL is an important transitional building in his evolution as an architect, from the fragmented rectilinear compositions of his California phase (Aerospace Museum, Los Angeles, 1981) to the curvilinear extravaganza of the Guggenheim Museum in Bilbao,

Spain (1997). Experientially, IATL is really two buildings, one as seen from the Main Campus North and the other from the Arts Campus and pedestrian bridge over the Iowa River (colorplate 18). The windowless east façade is pure monumental Minimalist sculpture, à la Claes Oldenburg and Carl André—with a copper-clad "fish" (a favorite anti-historicist symbol of Gehry's with overlapping metal plates suggesting fish scales) pushed against a huge Iowa-limestone-faced slab wall. The cladding of the fish contains hints of the irregularly curved surfaces that soon came to dominate Gehry's work. By contrast, the river façade at first appears to be a riot of shattered forms, but, in fact, is organized in three wings (only the foundation of the north and final wing was completed). This spectacular composition is inspired by the stark geometry of Iowa farmscape architecture. Hints of sheds and silos pop up here and there in the ensemble, displaying a Postmodernist fondness for referencing locality, with metal cladding (in this case stainless steel). The burnished exterior skin of the conference room facing southwest is the one concession to irregular curvilinear form on this side of the building.

As the visitor traverses the south plaza in front of the main entrance and continues toward the river, the geometries explode kinetically, fanning out to the dazzled eyes of the passersby. IATL is experiential architecture and negates traditional concepts of what a building should be. When seen from the pedestrian bridge in the late afternoon, the play of light on the metal surfaces animates Gehry's radical design with a constantly shifting configuration of light and shade and a minute-by-minute transition from white, to pink, to red, to gold shimmering across the metal cladding and reflecting on the water's surface. The Iowa Chapter of the American Institute of Architects designated IATL as one of the top one hundred buildings erected in the state in the twentieth century.

Arts Campus

The University of Iowa developed its Arts Campus in response to the notion that the practice of art is essential to the liberal arts education. Influenced by this idea, gained during his studies with John Dewey at Columbia Teachers' College, President Walter A. Jessup (1916–1934) began planning this part of the western campus in the 1920s. Jessup and graduate dean Carl Seashore used funds from the state, the Carnegie and Rockefeller Foundations, and the WPA to reclaim swampland and Hutchinson Quarry on the western banks of the Iowa River. The Arts Campus was originally limited to the Art Building, the Theatre Building, and the IMU Pedestrian Bridge. When sufficient funds were secured, the campus expanded as the Museum of Art (1969) and the early 1970s music and performance complex—Hancher Auditorium, Voxman Music Building, and Clapp Recital Hall—were added (colorplate 11). The Arts Campus not only raised the profile of the performing arts within the University, it also gave architectural form to the "Iowa Idea" that the study and practice of the fine arts should be one. This same impulse later produced the Writers' Workshop and has cemented Iowa's place as a leader in arts education.

Demolition of the Hancher-Voxman-Clapp complex following the flood of 2008 radically changed the Arts Campus. The Voxman Music Building and Clapp Recital Hall were rebuilt in downtown Iowa City (2016), but a new Hancher Auditorium arose, phoenixlike, just to the north of the original site. In visual complement with the Levitt Center, this new performing arts venue anchors the extreme end of the Arts Campus and also forms a welcoming and triumphal formal gateway for visitors arriving from the north.

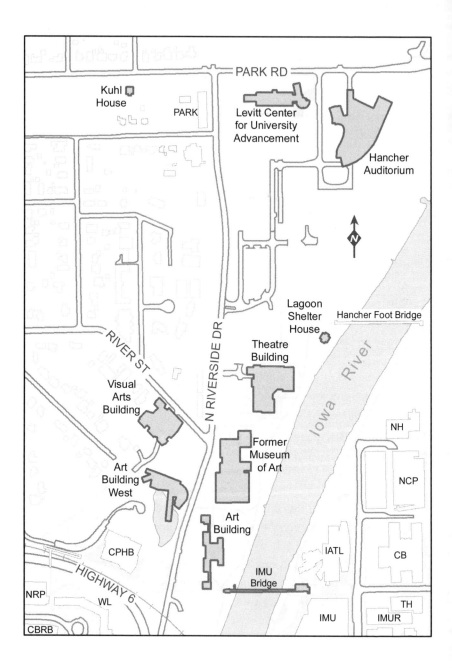

Art Building, 1936

ARCHITECT: GEORGE HORNER, UNIVERSITY OF IOWA

During the Depression-era presidencies of Walter Jessup and Eugene A. Gilmore, the University of Iowa undertook a program of construction aimed to maintain a high level of public education even amid budgetary severity. The Art Building was erected in the midst of these difficulties and demonstrated the University's commitment to the arts. The Art Building housed the School of Art and Art History, created by combining the Department of Graphic and Plastic Arts with the Department of the History and Appreciation of Art. This merger, and the new facility, embodied the innovative "Iowa Idea" of appointing practicing artists to a university faculty and in a liberal arts context and put the University of Iowa on the map. Art historian Lester Longman arrived from Princeton in 1936 and, as the first head of the department, took on the task of uniting the programs under one roof. Grant Wood was already on the faculty, and other established artists such as Stuart Edie and Philip Guston soon followed.

The Art Building, which colonized the swampy west bank of the Iowa River, was made possible by a Civilian Conservation Corps project that ran a stone wall along the water's edge, keeping it at bay. University architect George Horner designed the building after the plan of Palladio's Villa Emo near Venice. By choosing Palladio's farm

An archival photograph of the late 1930s shows the Art Building with the limestone river embankment wall still intact.

villas as his source, Horner implicitly nodded at the importance of agriculture in Iowa. The central block, which would have been a Palladian gentleman's residence, housed the library and study of art history and theory, while the outlying buildings—work areas and storage for farm implements in Palladio's time—are studios for art creation. Grant Wood's Mural Studio occupied the north pavilion beyond the arcaded loggia. The riverfront façade is marked by a monumental limestone frontispiece inscribed with the ancient poet Horace's words ARS LONGA VITA BREVIS EST (Life is short but art endures). The geometric grillwork above the entrance, inspired by Jessup Hall, appropriately references the Pentacrest Classicism.

Studio additions built to the east and south in the 1960s and 1970s were razed following the flood of 2008, thereby restoring the Art Building's original relationship with the river. Although no longer the home of the School of Art and Art History, the Art Building's architectural and heritage value is recognized, and it is to be restored and repurposed.

The triumphal three-arched entrance on Riverside Drive invites passersby to enter the exhibition space at the core of the central block.

1. The mosaic Great Seal of the University of Iowa, with original name and foundation date, adorns the main entrance of Macbride Hall, 1908. The bald eagle, with arrow in its beak and bow and olive branch in its talons, derives from the 1838 Territorial Seal.

2. Old Capitol, 1842, as seen from the east, occupies the crest of the bluff overlooking the Iowa River Valley.

3. The inversely rotated spiral stairs of Old Capitol, covered with a blue-painted dome, lead to the upper floor with the House and Senate chambers.

4. The east façade of Medical Laboratories, 1927, with its pointed-arched portal, two-story bay window, and flanking towers, takes inspiration from Henry VIII's palace at Hampton Court. It exemplifies the original Oxbridge architecture of the Medical Campus.

5. General Hospital's 1928 Gothic Tower, modeled on the tower gate at Magdalen College, Oxford, ranks with Old Capitol, its Pentacrest counterpart, as one of the most prominent skyline features of the UI campus.

6. Main Library's 1971 south façade, facing Richard E. Gibson Square, provides a monumental entrance to the University's central collection of books.

7. Peter Randall-Page's *Ridge and Furrow* (2011), a massive granite boulder from Cornwall, UK, located on T. Anne Cleary Walkway, has become a campus talisman. Students rub "Brain" with the hope it will bring good luck on exams. The Classical façade of the Chemistry Building provides the setting for many of those tests.

8. The Dental Science Building, with its raw concrete exterior surfaces, glass-walled courtyard, and monumentally projecting pavilions, exemplifies 1970s contemporary design on the Medical Campus.

9. Hancher Auditorium's sweeping curves and powerful cantilevers suggest the creative dynamism of the performing arts and serve metaphorically to represent a resurgent commitment to the arts following the 2008 flood, which destroyed the auditorium's predecessor (photo digitally enhanced).

10. The tiered "opera house" seating of Hancher Auditorium provides maximal sightlines and proximity to the stage from all seats. The dynamic LED lighting design by Francesca Bettridge of New York reminds patrons of Hancher's tradition of commissioning new works of ballet (architect's rendering).

11. An aerial view shows the expanding wedge of the Arts Campus defined by the Iowa River below and the rising bluff at the top. Hancher Auditorium, Voxman Music Building, and Clapp Recital Hall formed a single complex (razed, 2013), with the red brick Theatre Building at the upper left. Hancher-Voxman-Clapp was a powerful restatement of the UI's commitment to the arts, first articulated architecturally in the 1930s, but the tripartite ensemble of buildings fell victim to the flood of 2008.

12. The Glenn Schaeffer Library addition to the Writers' Workshop Dey House takes advantage of its setting high on the bluff overlooking the Iowa River Valley.

13. Hardin Library for the Health Sciences, 1974, has distinctive pyramidal skylights and prominent inverted triangles. The design methodology applied, known as Field Theory, was developed by architect Walter Netsch and emphasizes floor plan grid over façade elevation.

14. Black and old gold are the dominant colors on game day at historic Kinnick Stadium. The great arched openings of the south end reference the Roman Colosseum.

15. The unusual elliptical shape of the University of Iowa Stead Family Children's Hospital tower rises above nearby Kinnick Stadium (architect's rendering).

16. *Voyage* (1975), a thirty-foot work in black-painted Cor-ten steel by Louise Nevelson, stands in the Lindquist Center courtyard. It was the first sculpture purchased with funds provided by the Art in State Buildings Program initiated in 1978. One-half of one percent of the total cost of state building projects is devoted to the inclusion of the fine arts.

17. The radial plan of Boyd Law Building, 1986, makes it unique on the UI campus; the central dome references Old Capitol.

18. Iowa Advanced Technology Laboratories, river façade, 1992, unfolds a composition of fragmented volumes referencing the geometry of the Iowa farmscape.

19. The light-filled rotunda of the Levitt Center for University Advancement, 1998, with its expansive volumes and sweeping stair ramps, accommodates public receptions and the display of art.

20. The asymmetrical volumes and upward mounting acute angles of the copper-clad
Medical Education and Research Facility, 2002, make it a leading exponent
of Postmodernism on the Medical Campus.

21. Sculptor James Sanborn's *Iacto* ("to broadcast"), 2004, a large cylinder punched with historical quotations in eight languages, stands in front of the rotunda of the Philip D. Adler Journalism and Mass Communication Building.

22. Susan Chrysler White's 2012 *Flash Point* mural in the West Campus Transportation Center demonstrates the relationship between architectural space and the visual arts. Flat surfaces and empty spaces have been transformed to enliven the daily routines of commuters.

23. With its trapezoidal forms, the red-painted atrium stair of Art Building West, 2006, also functions as a monumental sculpture in the angular style of Russian Constructivism.

24. The Arts Campus during the flood of June 2008.

Art Building West, 2006

ARCHITECT: STEVEN HOLL ARCHITECTS, NEW YORK, NEW YORK /

HLKB ARCHITECTS, DES MOINES, IOWA

One of the foremost examples of contemporary architecture on campus, this building renews the University's commitment to the "Iowa Idea" of linking humanists and artists. Space for the studio and academic study of art has been reconsolidated here, making up for decades of splintering in various places around campus.

The site on Hutchinson Quarry Pond, recommended by Steven Holl for its visual appeal, creates an informal quad for the school.

The dramatic cantilever projects over Hutchinson Quarry Pond
in a synthesis of art and nature.

The prismatic skylight, inspired by Russian Constructivism,
illuminates the atrium stair.

That relationship is reinforced by the choice of a weathering Cor-ten
steel facing that reflects the red brick of George Horner's original Art
Building. Because this building had to be a work of art itself, Holl
sought inspiration in Pablo Picasso's 1912 sculpture, *Guitar* (Museum
of Modern Art, New York). The conceit is visible in the cantilevered
wing—the instrument's fret board—and its curved east façade—the
soundbox. The dynamic forms of Art Building West engage and ener-
gize the lagoon, weaving it into the life of the campus and encouraging people to linger by the water and adjacent limestone bluff. Art and
nature merge sympathetically.

Designing around the school's artistic needs, as well as those of the
site, led Holl to create a building of custom exteriors. Channel glass
along the north façade and sawtooth skylighting maximize valuable
northern light for studios and are examples of the unique glazing of
Holl's design. The cantilever tilts upward dramatically, while inside,
the extreme projecting end houses the Art Library's imposing two-
story reading room. Art Building West plays with a certain fuzziness,

allowing walls and exposed-steel structure to exist independently and different planes to project and intersect in unanticipated ways. Employing a concept he designated "horizontal porosity," Holl opens up interior walls unexpectedly to bring light to the innermost spaces of the building. In the atrium, a seemingly self-supporting steel stair evokes the revolutionary early twentieth-century style of Russian Constructivism and acts as a floating piece of sculpture in this community space (colorplate 23). Turquoise wall accents reference the watery setting while also recalling the distant days of High Modernism and the International style.

Visual Arts Building, 2016

ARCHITECT: STEVEN HOLL ARCHITECTS, NEW YORK, NEW YORK /
BNIM, DES MOINES, IOWA

Following the flood of 2008, FEMA supported replacement of the original Art Building. Steven Holl was selected to create a building that would sit next to his first UI design, the internationally awarded Art Building West (2006). While the site selected for the project afforded important adjacency and an elevation free of future flood risks, it also forced the 126,000 square feet of art studio and art history classroom space into a confined footprint. This presented a significant challenge because of the need to distribute natural light in the art studio spaces

Channel glass recesses excavated into the main façade wall of the Visual Arts Building bring light deep into the public spaces of the interior, while Rheinzink screening filters the light entering the studios through the square windows of varying sizes and asymmetrical distribution (photo digitally enhanced).

Diagonally positioned through the core of the building, a four-story sculpted-concrete atrium provides circulation into and throughout the building. Ramps and stairs encircling the skylighted open space allow for easy movement from floor to floor to encourage interdisciplinary exchange among the media-based studios (photo digitally enhanced).

throughout the four-story structure. A skylighted interior atrium and innovative glazing methods overcame this difficulty. This campus location near the epicenter of the flood now provides the opportunity to experience Steven Holl designs that display the development of his architecture over a ten-year span. In the 1930s the School of Art and Art History advanced the art world as the first university program to unite the study of art history and studio arts. After eight years of temporary facilities those innovative "Iowa Idea" roots have been reestablished.

Like the adjacent Art Building West, also designed by Steven Holl, the Visual Arts Building is a work of art at the forefront of contemporary design, one intended to stimulate the creative potential of student-artists. Its reinforced concrete structure, vertical light shafts, and perforated screening comprise a yang to ABW's earlier yin (exposed steel structure, horizontally introduced lighting, and opaque cladding). Both facilities acknowledge the primacy of light in the creation of art:

the earlier building is horizontally porous, whereas the newer design is vertically permeable. Innovative structural and mechanical systems were applied in the VAB, including a bubble-deck with radiant heating/cooling floor plates. The exterior composition is organized as four stacked and shifted tectonic plates with exposed channel glass light wells—excavated into the façades and vertically staggered—that further illuminate the core of the interior. A Fibonacci sequence generates the varied proportions of the irregular window distribution and adds historical and whimsical interest. Rheinzink screens on the east and south façades serve as sunshades during the day but display the window pattern at night, while solid zinc panels sheathe the street and rear façades. The ramped, four-story atrium runs diagonally through the building, encouraging interaction among the various media studios while also connecting ABW and the campus beyond to the residential neighborhood on the bluff. A sedum-planted green roof and an outdoor sculpture platform surround the studio art penthouse and gallery on the fifth-floor terrace. The monumental "I" projecting at the southeast corner is a happy, if unintended, consequence of the design process.

Former Museum of Art, 1969

ARCHITECT: MAX ABRAMOVITZ OF HARRISON AND
ABRAMOVITZ, NEW YORK, NEW YORK / NEUMANN MONSON
ARCHITECTS, IOWA CITY, IOWA

When Owen and Leone Elliott decided to share their collection of contemporary art with the University, they made a proper home for it a condition of the gift. The opportunity to acquire more than seventy paintings by such artists as Matisse, Kandinsky, and Munch prompted

The closed, self-contained pavilion opens up on the riverfront to provide views of the water and the eastside campus beyond. The supine profile and regular rhythm of the structural membering and the fenestration express a common orientation to mid-twentieth-century simplicity and abstraction.

the University of Iowa Foundation to undertake its first fund-raising drive. The resulting Museum of Art was also home to the work of many other major modern artists. Jackson Pollock's large *Mural*, a gift from Peggy Guggenheim in 1948, hung there, as did a Robert Motherwell painting commissioned by the museum for the central sculpture court. UI faculty member Grant Wood's autumnal *Plaid Sweater* is also in the collection. The African art holdings are among the most extensive in an American university and were donated by Maxwell and Elizabeth Stanley of Muscatine, longtime supporters of the University.

The former Museum of Art was one of the first campus buildings to result from the State Board of Regents' 1965 decision to hold an open selection process that allowed Iowa architectural firms to partner with top design firms all across the nation. Le Corbusier, perhaps the most influential architect of the twentieth century, was initially considered for the project, but the commission ultimately fell to a less radical designer. Max Abramovitz designed the exterior walls of prefabricated aggregate concrete panels, complemented with a glass curtain wall that opens up the building toward the river. The purity of exterior composition owes its formal characteristics to Mies van der Rohe's 1950 Farnsworth House, located on a riverside site in the country west of Chicago. Rising on a low, recessed podium and capped with standardized sections of cornice forming a prominent slab roof, the Museum of Art is an uncompromisingly reductive Modernist structure, reflecting the dictums of abstraction that held sway in all the visual arts at that time. Inside, the textured concrete elements of the central sculpture court are hallmarks of Brutalism.

In advance of the 2008 flood, the collection was removed and has been temporarily stored and displayed in several remote locations. Current planning and design will result in the return of the entire collection to the campus. The former museum building has been restored and will be reprogrammed.

The Brutalist sculpture court with sunburst oculus and clerestory lighting was designed for Pollock's *Mural* (1943) and Motherwell's *Elegy for the Spanish Republic* (1965–1975).

Theatre Building, 1936, and Addition, 1985

ARCHITECT: GEORGE HORNER, UNIVERSITY OF IOWA (1936)

MAX ABRAMOVITZ OF ABRAMOVITZ-HARRIS-KINGSLAND,

NEW YORK, NEW YORK / NEUMANN MONSON ARCHITECTS,

IOWA CITY, IOWA (1985)

The University of Iowa's reputation as a home for creative faculty and students is supported by the Department of Theatre Arts. By 1937, the "Iowa Idea" had made its way to Tom Williams, an aspiring playwright and transfer student a year short of a degree. He enrolled at the University, earning his B.A. in 1938, and soon thereafter picked up the moniker "Tennessee." Since then, graduates have gone on to many distinctions in film, television, and theatre. Alumni include Mary Beth Hurt and Gene Wilder, who (as Jerry Silberman) graduated from the University in 1955.

The Theatre Building, part of the UI's mid-Depression construction boom, is a testament to intra-University collaboration. George Horner's design benefited from the input of Arnold S. Gillette, who taught set design and construction at the University for more than forty years and championed a thirty-six-foot revolving stage within a stage, one of the first of its kind. This theatre, later named after E. C. Mabie (the guiding force in the department's earliest days), is articulated on the river façade and fly loft by a series of vertical fins typical of the streamlined mode of the Moderne style. (Horner had already used them on the Stanley Hydraulics Laboratory just downstream.) A 1985 renovation added to the old building the David L. Thayer Theatre (named for another emeritus faculty member) and Theatre B. The Modernist addition, red brick with a cornice of limestone detailing, echoes the stepped massing of the original Moderne-style structure, now shorn of all ornament. The white aggregate cladding of the new office wing serves as a visual podium for the theatre blocks rising above and sympathetically continues the extensive row of square-framed windows Abramovitz had designed for the nearby Voxman

Moderne meets Modern at the Theatre Building complex.

Music Building (razed, 2013) fourteen years earlier. A tinted-glass atrium on the building's river side provides access to all three stages.

Lagoon Shelter House, 1939

ARCHITECT: GEORGE HORNER, UNIVERSITY OF IOWA

A Works Progress Administration project, the Lagoon Shelter House was designed by University architect George Horner. The small riverside structure was sited well north of the then new Theatre Building in an undeveloped area of the Arts Campus adjacent to the University Skating Lagoon. What remains of the depression that once contained the lagoon is still visible in front of the Shelter House. The small interior housed a concession where skaters could buy candy and coffee. Two exterior fireplaces provided warmth for skaters' hands and feet. In season, floodlights illuminated the lagoon at night, and phonograph music was played on a speaker system for the enjoyment of skaters. During the two seasons the Lagoon Shelter House served its original function, there was an annual ice carnival. Owing to the unpredictability of the weather, the ice skating facility was not cost effective and was converted to a canoe house for the Department of Physical Education. The structure is now informally known as the Canoe House but functions as a rustic events venue.

Constructed of local limestone and rough-hewn timbers, this picturesque building has a homey appeal. It epitomizes the architectural concept of rustication, which here is a chief design feature and in harmony with the originally primitive setting. Exposed wood lintels and beams and a shed roof add to the design's cottagelike character; fireplaces provide additional charm. Underutilized for years, the building has returned to use as a site for intimate campus social gatherings.

Rustic charm is the dominant theme of this little example of park architecture on the UI campus.

Voxman Music Building, 1971 (razed, 2013)

ARCHITECT: MAX ABRAMOVITZ OF HARRISON AND
ABRAMOVITZ, NEW YORK, NEW YORK / NEUMANN MONSON
ARCHITECTS, IOWA CITY, IOWA

The School of Music was founded in 1906, but it suffered from a tenuous connection to the University. Instruction was in the form of private lessons, the fees for which paid the instructors' salaries. Orchestra, band, choral groups, and glee club were all supported by concert tickets. Philip Greeley Clapp was hired by President Walter A. Jessup (1916–1934) and tasked with establishing a new University department. That goal was achieved by 1921, but it would be fifty years before the School of Music had a single permanent home: Voxman Music Building (VMB), named after Clapp's successor, Himie Voxman, who led the school for twenty-six years. Voxman's namesake building gave architectural shape to the importance the School of Music plays in the instructional, academic, and cultural life of the University and state.

VMB included the Rita Benton Music Library, Voxman Hall (band/orchestra rehearsal room), Harper Hall recital room, and choral and opera rehearsal areas. Physically connected to Hancher Auditorium and Clapp Recital Hall, the Music Building also had a functional bond with these concert venues, completing the performing arts end of the Arts Campus (colorplate 11). The concrete building itself was a standardized composition with two extended rows of square office windows with prominent frames, all capped with a jutting slab roof. The shadow cast by the cornice weighs down the building and makes it seem even more horizontal and flat, a sympathetic response to the flow of the nearby river that destroyed it in 2008. The powerful geometry of the monumental projections along the river façade mark entrance stairs and provide light to the stairwells. The back of Hancher Auditorium's fly loft loomed over the entire building. Voxman Music Building's bold abstractions exemplified the New Formalism phase of Modernism championed by Abramovitz.

Repetition of simple forms and sweeping horizontals made up the formal
components of Max Abramovitz's Modernist design for Voxman Music Building.

Clapp Recital Hall, 1971 (razed, 2013)

ARCHITECT: MAX ABRAMOVITZ OF HARRISON AND
ABRAMOVITZ, NEW YORK, NEW YORK / NEUMANN MONSON
ARCHITECTS, IOWA CITY, IOWA

When Philip Greeley Clapp came to the University of Iowa in
1919, he commenced formal integration of music into the academic
life of the University, offering credit for voice and instrument classes,
organizing a symphony orchestra, and bringing national visibility to
the program. A pianist and composer as well as teacher, Clapp also
hosted a weekly radio course on music appreciation, which ran for
nearly three decades on University radio station KSUI. Musical performances at the building named in Clapp's honor ranged from individual recitals on the tracker-action Casavant organ, chamber music,
small- to medium-size instrumental and vocal group concerts to full
operas and band concerts.

The austere, Minimalist concrete and glass design of Clapp Recital
Hall harmonized with its now-vanished neighbors, Hancher Auditorium and Voxman Music Building (also designed by Max Abramovitz).
Like those structures to which it was attached (colorplate 11), Clapp
took a reductive, antiornament approach, placing a premium on formal values. In simplicity of composition, however, Clapp exceeded
the others. Glass entrance doors on the right were undifferentiated
and left uninterrupted the purity of the compositional grid. Above the
façade's glass curtain wall, a slab roof seemed to hover unsupported
by the notched cement side walls. This formal effect was repeated by
the second-floor balcony inside. The lobby staircase functioned as a
work of monumental abstract sculpture on display for the arriving
audience. The shoebox style performance hall was conceived for intimate musical events. Restraint combined with the architect's total
control of the formal elements of design were the order of the day.

The shoebox-shaped, 700-seat performance hall was conceived
for solo to mid-size musical ensemble concerts.

Hancher Auditorium, 1972 (razed, 2013)

ARCHITECT: MAX ABRAMOVITZ OF HARRISON AND
ABRAMOVITZ, NEW YORK, NEW YORK / NEUMANN MONSON
ARCHITECTS, IOWA CITY, IOWA

Although a performing arts center was included in the 1930s plan for the Arts Campus, it was not until the 1960s that funds for that purpose were obtained. The succeeding campaign led ultimately to the October 30, 1972, dedication and opening of Hancher Auditorium (colorplate 11). The first season included, among others, the Preservation Hall Jazz Band, Van Cliburn, Isaac Stern, Arthur Rubinstein, the Chicago Symphony, Alvin Ailey, Marcel Marceau, Rudolf Nureyev, and Duke Ellington. Named after Virgil Hancher, fourteenth president of the University of Iowa (1940–1964), it remained a magnet for performing artists for over 35 years. Then came the flood of 2008.

The space-frame construction of Hancher Auditorium's roof system made possible the cantilevering of the expansive façade.

UI alumnus Luther Utterback's *Untitled* (Indiana limestone blocks) of 1976, located north of the former Hancher Auditorium, was also a site for various student activities.

Max Abramovitz was famous as a designer of skyscrapers, but his buildings on the UI Arts Campus are emphatically horizontal. The broad sweep of Hancher Auditorium's façade was made possible by structural bravado and by the building's plan, with the broad base of the triangle facing the approach and the narrowing point turned toward the stage (colorplate 11). Hancher's dominant slab roof with dramatically cantilevered end sections recalled the monumentality of Main Library's south façade of a decade earlier (colorplate 6). Unlike the library's formidable brick walls and dark-tinted glass, however, Hancher featured greater and more welcoming transparency. An extensive glass-curtain wall folded back at the corners to emphasize the cantilevered wings of the roof, as if it were about to take flight.

Two massive piers, canted toward the viewer, did the muscle work to support the roof, but, in a design refinement, the top of each pier stopped short of making direct visual contact with the slab above. The actual support member was recessed in shadow, but the effect was something like levitation. Both the cantilevering and the spanning of the impressive foyer inside were made possible structurally by the

three-dimensional steel grid, known as a space frame, that covered the entire building—exposed on the interior but masked on the exterior by the slab's revetment. A secondary slab—thinner, lower, and recessed, but also visible on the exterior—corresponded inside to the foyer balcony level. With the intention to achieve a starker contrast between surface and shadow and thereby to heighten the drama of juxtaposed forms, Abramovitz added ground white quartz to the concrete of which the exterior cladding panels were made.

The ensemble's expansive curtain wall with giant support piers for the projecting roof is reminiscent of Eero Saarinen's design for the Vivian Beaumont Theater in New York (1963; now Lincoln Center Theater). Abramovitz knew it well since his Philharmonic Hall (1962; now David Geffen Hall) is its neighbor. The idea of the interior-exposed space frame elevated on piers and standing forward of the enclosing glass-curtain wall, however, seems to owe even more to Mies van der Rohe's New National Gallery in Berlin (1968).

The space frame of Hancher's performance hall, based on interlocking hexagons, was exposed inside. It floated above the accordionlike side walls, which did not reach it. The spreading plane of the balcony below also seemed independent of support.

Levitt Center for University Advancement, 1998

ARCHITECT: CHARLES GWATHMEY OF GWATHMEY SIEGEL
AND ASSOCIATES, NEW YORK, NEW YORK / BROOKS BORG
SKILES ARCHITECTURE ENGINEERING, DES MOINES, IOWA

The Levitt Center for University Advancement anchors the northern edge of the Arts Campus. From this vantage point, the site offers impressive views of the Iowa River and the University. Given its outreach-related functions and work that stretches beyond the borders of the campus, the building is well situated near the Dubuque Street exit

The Levitt Center's glass-walled rotunda acts as a lantern
for alumni, benefactors, and visitors.

142

from Interstate 80. The facility is named for Richard S. and Jeanne S. Levitt, two of the UI's most generous benefactors, and houses the University of Iowa Foundation and the University of Iowa Alumni Association, the University's primary fund-raising and alumni relations programs, respectively. Accordingly, the Levitt Center was funded with private gifts. Its outreach mandate is also reflected in the imagery of the building, which declines the guise of academic halls in favor of an aesthetic more attuned to corporate headquarters.

This look was achieved using a combination of limestone and powder-coated white metal panels for the rain-screen form of wall cladding, along with a variety of glazing—including glass block, a trademark of architect Charles Gwathmey. The use of glass adds to the building's nighttime luster, when the rotunda shines as a beacon to guests approaching the Center and visitors coming to performances at the adjacent Hancher Auditorium. During the day the solar baffles on the south façade add to the contrast between light and shade. The east-west-oriented main corridor of the rectangular block houses offices on its three middle levels, while level one of the rotunda along with the fourth level of the office block are the showplace locations for meetings, banquets, and other assemblies serving advancement activities for the entire University. The fourth-level rotunda terrace opens from a circular boardroom that crowns the rotunda. The serrated profile of the rectangular office block marks the three adjoining assembly halls from which a projecting external terrace opens up to provide vistas of the Arts Campus and beyond. One of the small twelve-inch-square windows on the fourth level perfectly enframes Frank Gehry's Iowa Advanced Technology Laboratories building in the distance, as Gwathmey acknowledges. The orientation of the building is the product of a last-minute change: the entire building was rotated 180 degrees on the chosen site late in schematic design. Rather than marking the corner of a street intersection, the rotunda came instead to signal the entrance of the original axial approach to Hancher Auditorium to the south. How fortunate was that decision, since the new Hancher—located immediately adjacent—could take the Levitt rotunda geometry as design cue, with the cylinder of one generating the cube of the other.

From the outside, the curve of the glass-block cylinder recalls the rotundas of Schaeffer and Macbride Halls, but inside it offers a towering, light-filled atrium. Le Corbusier makes his influence felt here, with superimposed pilotis forming the interior wall structure (colorplate 19). The graceful ramps and stairs with linear guard rails recall details inspired by a trip Le Corbusier took on the ocean liner *Normandie*, a ship he referred to as the paragon of the machine and the epitome of the machine aesthetic he later incorporated into many of his buildings. The sinuous quality of the atrium, with both interior balconies and the curve of the stair, reflects that source. The profile of a domeless drum rises above the rotunda. The reference here is to another architect, the eighteenth-century visionary, Etienne-Louis Boullée, whose idea is best represented in the United States by the nineteenth-century Ohio state capitol. But, in a surprising and perhaps unique design idea, the Levitt Center drum houses an inverted dome, which dramatically covers the boardroom at the top of the rotunda.

Hu Hung-Shu's stainless steel and aircraft cable sculpture, *D. Forever* (1998), hangs in the atrium space adjacent to the Levitt Center rotunda.

Hancher Auditorium, 2016

ARCHITECT: PELLI CLARKE PELLI ARCHITECTS, NEW HAVEN,

CONNECTICUT / OPN ARCHITECTS, CEDAR RAPIDS, IOWA

One of the nation's largest individual building losses to natural disaster, the Hancher-Voxman-Clapp complex (1972) received FEMA replacement approval and partial funding following the 2008 flood (colorplate 11). Recognizing that the 300,000-square-foot performing arts and School of Music complex could not be rebuilt on a single University site, FEMA approved two locations: one for the School of Music facility and one for the Hancher Auditorium. The site, while just north of the original building's placement, takes advantage of significant elevation change to protect it from future flooding. The elevated position also offers a dramatic gateway, welcoming visitors as they enter Iowa City and the University of Iowa.

Selection of Pelli Clarke Pelli was based on the international acclaim the firm has received for projects of this type and scale. César Pelli wished to honor the adjacent Levitt Center (1998), designed by his longtime friend Charles Gwathmey. The selection of exterior finishes and the initial curves of the new Hancher reflect the Levitt Center and its prominent rotunda. A notable change from the original Hancher was the building alignment. Max Abramovitz's Hancher faced northward, toward approaching visitors. Pelli's design turns his building southward, toward the campus and the fateful Iowa River Valley. Additionally, using performance arts industry current and best practices, the new Hancher has fewer seats and an auditorium volume ideal for performers and patrons alike (colorplate 10). This can be seen in the farthest row of seating from the stage, which is seventy feet closer than the last row in the now-vanished original building. Hancher Auditorium stands as a testament to the University's and Iowa City's rebound from the flood of 2008.

The parklike riverside setting of Hancher Auditorium was an inspiration to the architect, who has taken full advantage of Postmodern freedom of expression in a radically asymmetrical design. He created a curvilinear, three-sided building that responds to the river, the access drive entrance, and the street approach. The iconic view from the Hancher pedestrian bridge and the river walk shows four sweeping, horizontal, brushed-stainless-steel planes that, following the flow of the river, narrow from right to left. These gently curving convex surfaces float on pilotis masked by glass curtain walls and tilt upward, dramatically projecting toward the southwest, perhaps in homage to the now-lost lateral projections of the original Hancher (page 138). A crowning trapezoidal volume hovering over the stacked cantilevers expresses the auditorium and stage fly loft. The recessed entrance-drive façade receives arriving patrons. Here two of the planes go serpentine, sinuously weaving in and out over the main lobby as the

As seen from the south, Hancher Auditorium, reborn above the Iowa River, reaches toward the Levitt Center to form a unified composition; lancetlike cantilevers intersect with the rotunda of the earlier building (photo digitally enhanced).

entire concave composition reaches a crescendo above the auditorium and stage (colorplete 9). The sleek metal and glass exterior is softened by the introduction of wood overhangs that intersect the glass walls and become the interior ceilings. The street façade facing Park Road is actually the rear of the building, but that is not apparent, since the service entrance and loading dock are tucked away below grade. Instead, four cubic volumes attract the attention and contrast geometrically with the lyrical lines of the other two sides of the structure and with nearby Levitt Center's glass-block rotunda. The Postmodern nods to the Modern and, simultaneously, boldly abandons its restraint.

For some observers, Hancher Auditorium may suggest that a spaceship has landed on the campus lawn; for others, it is a sleek cruise liner docked along the riverbank; still others may understand it as monumental abstract sculpture. As a showpiece building it challenges the norms of architecture and, inevitably, summons imaginative responses. But this tour de force can perhaps best be described as theatrical, even symphonic, in effect.

P. Sue Beckwith, M.D., Boathouse, 2009

ARCHITECT: NEUMANN MONSON, IOWA CITY, IOWA

The Beckwith Boathouse is one of many examples of projects that display partnerships at work with the surrounding communities. Home to the largest women's intercollegiate athletics program at the UI, the rowing team, the building is sited in Iowa City's historic Terrell Mill Park. The city granted use of the land to the University, and in return, the facility helps to advance not just the UI team objectives but broader interest in rowing. Additionally, meeting and event space within the building is managed by UI Recreational Services for use by University and general public community members. The inclusion of a rowing tank training space proved to be a significant challenge during the design process. Visits to similar facilities revealed that realistic water resistance within the tank was difficult and had not been effectively achieved. The project team turned to the UI's number-one-ranked College of Engineering Hydraulics Institute. Students and faculty teamed up to create virtual models, which were expanded and constructed onsite. The resulting facility is a highlight within the

Beckwith Boathouse on the Iowa River is the home of the UI rowing team.

building and allows for year-round training. The building also represents the first campus example of "flood tolerance." The Boathouse was constructed shortly after the 2008 flood, and its building systems were elevated above flood risk elevations, and the boat storage space, which requires immediate proximity to the river, is designed to take on and then release water with little damage.

The Beckwith Boathouse occupies a prominent site in a city park at a bend in the Iowa River where it flows toward the main campus, forming a natural rowing reach. Perhaps the best example of *architecture parlante* ("speaking architecture") of any University building, it takes the shape of an object that exemplifies the building's function. The narrow floorplan and long, low horizontal lines rising on the river's edge suggest the sleek profile of a racing shell, its bow tilting dynamically downriver. The pronounced verticals of the aluminum frames of the glass curtain walls in turn allude to the shell's rigger and oars. Overhead doors provide access to the dock, a public conference room with commanding views up- and downstream projects from the center, and an ample viewing terrace extends in front of the glass pavilion housing the ergometric training room. The glazed and paneled façade facing the park repeats the racing shell motif and adds a historical note with a reference to Art Deco, the streamlined style of early twentieth-century Modernism. This theme is continued inside the rowing tank room in artist Rebecca Ekstrand's neo-Futurist *Calm Waters* mosaic. Stylistically, if not functionally, Beckwith Boathouse departs radically from the Tudor Revival half-timbers of the traditional Henley-on-Thames boathouses of rowing legend.

Kuhl House, circa 1840

ARCHITECT: ROBERT HUTCHINSON, IOWA CITY, IOWA

PREVIOUS NAME: HUTCHINSON-KUHL HOUSE

The oldest extant house in Iowa City, the Kuhl House was built around 1840 by Robert Hutchinson, a carpenter and joiner from New Hampshire. An early arrival to the Iowa Territory, Hutchinson went

Kuhl House, home of the University of Iowa Press,
is the oldest building on the UI campus.

on to help with the construction of Old Brick, a church adjacent to Main Campus North, and became Iowa City's first town marshal. His descendants sold the house to Ernest Kuhl, a professor of English at the University, in 1927. The Kuhls did extensive renovation to the original farmhouse and eventually sold it to the University in 1977. Initially used as an art studio, the building is now the home of the University of Iowa Press.

Kuhl House's limestone walls and lintels were quarried just north of the building site—the story goes that the blocks used here were rejects from the construction of Old Capitol. The original structure was a sturdy one-story frontier house, with twenty-six-inch-thick foundation walls. When the Kuhls began renovations in 1927, they replaced the original floor planking with hardwood, added a black walnut staircase, and raised the roofline. Hutchinson's original farmhouse became an elegant Colonial Revival home, with an additional six feet of height to accommodate a second story, and three dormer windows.

International Center, 1935 and 1959 (razed, 2008)

ARCHITECT: GEORGE HORNER, UNIVERSITY OF IOWA

PREVIOUS NAMES: LAW COMMONS, COLLEGE OF LAW

The Law Commons dormitory for students in the College of Law was a WPA project. When more space was needed for the college in the 1950s, a stark modern tower containing classrooms and court-rooms was added to the southwest end of the Commons. Law vacated overcrowded Gilmore Hall and moved into the new building in 1960. Earl Warren, Chief Justice of the Supreme Court of the United States, dedicated the facility. The complex was turned over to International Programs in 1986 when the new Boyd Law Building opened.

The Georgian Revival Law Commons consisted of a central three-story block with pedimented gable, modest entrance treatment, and quoining at the corners. Two lower wings set at angles from the main section formed a courtyard shaded with oak trees. The denticulated

Red brick with simple Classical detailing made an ideal architectural image for a law school dormitory.

153

The 1959 addition to the Law Commons was a major stylistic shift from the Georgian Revival of the original building. Instead of the proposed typical Modernist turquoise panel insets, the law faculty opted for judicial-robe black.

cornice provided almost the only ornamentation of the wings, whose unusual placement was a function of the narrowing of the bluff at the northern end. Design restraint and bucolic seclusion are the dominant themes. The building's east wing was anchored by a large lounge noted for the many events and gatherings it hosted. University architect George Horner's Modernist block, attached to the end of the west wing in 1959, abandoned the historicizing style of the original section for a more contemporary statement of International style Modernism. As seen from the southwest, a brick slab floating above a continuous band of windows formed the visual base for the radically asymmetrical composition of the monolithic addition's elevation. At the corner, a massive brick wall was suspended above a narrow strip of windows—a Modernist demonstration of the wall as ornament rather than structure. An oversize Brutalist concrete canopy at the main entrance in the courtyard (not shown) provided a stark contrast to the more humanistic detailing of the Georgian Revival building, which had been one of the first campus buildings designed by Horner. The Law Commons addition was one of his last. The site, which marks an important visual entrance for the campus, now hosts the University's College of Public Health Building.

Near West Campus

In 1905 during the presidency of George E. MacLean, the Olmsted brothers (John Charles and Frederick Law, Jr.), sons of Frederick Law Olmsted, recommended the expansion of the University of Iowa to the west, across the river. The first land purchases were made under President Walter A. Jessup (1916–1934), and development began in 1917 with facilities needed for training army troops. Near West Campus, like Main Campus North, is now home to a cluster of student residence halls. This campus includes the College of Law and is framed on the west by the Field House. A relatively small area along Grand Avenue, it is also one of the most impressive locations at the University of Iowa, perched on a high bluff above the Iowa River.

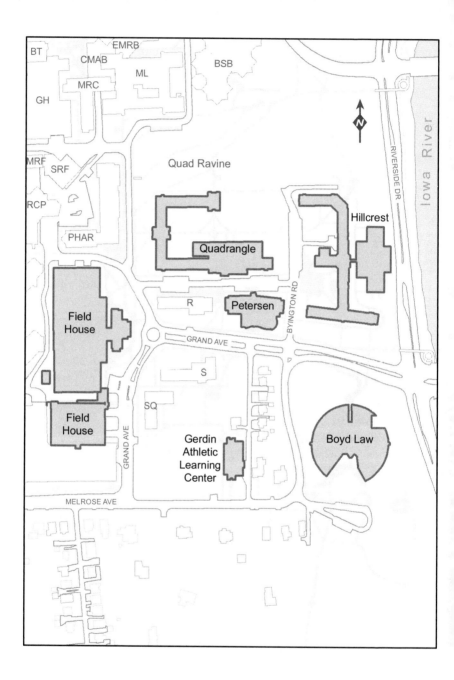

Hillcrest Residence Hall, 1939

ARCHITECT: SETH J. TEMPLE, DAVENPORT, IOWA

Built during Eugene Gilmore's presidency (1934–1940), Hillcrest Residence Hall originally housed 250 men on four floors. Expansion in years following increased the number of students it could accommodate, making Hillcrest the largest dormitory on campus until the construction of Burge Hall in 1959. The building was historically popular as a home for student-athletes because of its proximity to the

Hillcrest's stripped-down version of Collegiate Gothic verges on the rejection of ornament.

Field House. It is now the center for residence food services on the west side of campus, housing a comprehensive dining facility renovated and modernized in 2001.

Hillcrest occupies one of the highest bluffs in Iowa City, a dramatic perch from which the dormitory overlooks Main Campus across the river. The building's design emphasizes its lofty site, using ornamental spur buttresses (visible on the south wing's east façade) as vertical accents. This feature acknowledges the dominant Collegiate Gothic character of architecture on the West Campus, which is derived from the colleges at Oxford and Cambridge. The style also has as hallmarks projecting bay windows, seen on the east façade, as well as the limestone-framed windows that adorn it. Stone is used for detailing elsewhere but most extensively in this section. Above, a brick parapet disguises service elements located on the roof. Hillcrest was completed just two years before the United States entered World War II, and its mildly Gothic style was the last example of historicism in architecture to appear on the UI campus. Already by 1942 when South Quadrangle was built, the last vestige of Gothic Revival detailing had been scraped away.

Boyd Law Building, 1986

ARCHITECT: GUNNAR BIRKERTS AND ASSOCIATES,

BIRMINGHAM, MICHIGAN / WEHNER, PATTSCHULL AND

PFIFFNER, IOWA CITY, IOWA

Having first outgrown Gilmore Hall and then the Law Commons (International Center), the College of Law moved to its current home, Boyd Law Building, in 1986. Named after law professor, past provost, and past University of Iowa president Willard L. Boyd, the building contains two trial courtrooms (with jury room and judge's chambers), a 300-seat appellate courtroom also used as an auditorium, classrooms, faculty offices, and a noted Law Library that maintains more than one million volumes, both on- and off-site.

The radial plan of Boyd Law Building opens at the entrance.

Auguste Rodin's bronze, from a six-figure composition of the *Burghers of Calais* (1884–1886; cast 1987), engages themes of justice and civic virtue.

Occupying the slope of a bluff, the design hovers between Late Modernist abstraction and early Postmodern reference to local tradition. Boyd Law Building uses concrete and aluminum paneling to reflect materials and geometries reminiscent of Iowa agricultural architecture. The central dome and its cylindrical base do double duty, recollecting both grain silos and Old Capitol. The unusual radial plan (colorplate 17), unique on the UI campus and rare in modern architecture in general, is perhaps, once again, homage to the Iowa farmscape. But this design is of exceptional sophistication in its treatment of monumental ideal geometry and the more practical issues of access and light. The perimeter wall opens toward the south to provide a generous welcoming sector at the main entrance, another notch toward the slope of the bluff provides glass curtain walls, while narrow vertical breaks and the large cleft in the north façade allow natural light to descend to lower levels. The result is a building that from the exterior seems somewhat closed but which is nevertheless filled with light inside. The expression of pure geometric forms is so dominant that one commentator has seen in it a reference to the radical visionary architects of late eighteenth-century France, especially to Boullée's 1783 project for Newton's Cenotaph.

At the entrance, Rodin's sculpture represents Jean de Fiennes, the youngest of the leading citizens of Calais who offered themselves, in 1347, to the enemy in exchange for their besieged city. The piece, particularly appropriate for the College of Law context, expresses the important role of civic responsibility for the sake of the commonwealth.

Russell and Ann Gerdin
Athletic Learning Center, 2003

ARCHITECT: OPN ARCHITECTS, CEDAR RAPIDS, IOWA

The construction of the Russell and Ann Gerdin Athletic Learning Center, often called just the Athletic Learning Center, was sponsored by a gift from Russell and Ann Gerdin to the University of Iowa Foundation. The Gerdins' generosity was in response to the NCAA's Knight Commission Report identifying the need for universities to provide student-athletes with extra encouragement in their pursuit of academic achievement. The Athletic Learning Center, which houses study rooms, classrooms, and a computer lab, was one of the first facilities of its kind. Student-athletes receive tutoring and observe study hours in this freestanding unit of the Department of Athletics.

Poised at the border of Near West Campus and the Melrose Avenue neighborhood, the building responds to both neighbors, customizing its elevations depending on the direction they face. Composed of brick and stone, the building's architectural style reflects the nearby residence halls in materials, and the residential homes to the south in design. The mansard roof and dormer windows lend the building an institutional profile, while the gables break up the massing and cultivate a softer, more residential feel. This apparent hybridity is a typical Postmodern option, which allows for multiple and even contradictory references to preexisting local context. Another Postmodern touch is the deliberate violation of convention: the Athletic Learning Center's limestone rustication appears not just at the foundation but also in two bands running above the first- and second-story windows. It even interrupts the two-story, smooth-stone frontispiece of the main entrance.

The Russell and Ann Gerdin Athletic Learning Center combines elements from both academic and domestic architecture.

Field House, 1927

ARCHITECT: PROUDFOOT, RAWSON AND SOUERS,

DES MOINES, IOWA

The Field House has served more functions than nearly any other structure on campus. During the Depression years, it provided cheap accommodations for nearly 100 students who paid $1 per week to rent a cot and locker on the third floor. Built to incorporate a preexisting armory (1922) at the west end, it functioned as a barracks for the Navy Pre-Flight Training Program during World War II. Its real business, however, has always been sports; it was the home of Hawkeye basketball until 1982, a history that spanned fifty-six seasons. Today it hosts intercollegiate, intramural, and recreational activities, teams, and events.

An archival photograph of the Field House shows the façade prior to the administrative addition of 1955.

The original floor of the Field House was dirt, which made it ideal for track and field events. The building included what was then the largest indoor collegiate swimming pool in the United States, which was meant to double as a reservoir for fire fighting. The interior also contained spaces for every indoor sport or activity offered by the University. On the exterior and in keeping with its neighbors—Hillcrest and Quadrangle Residence Halls—Collegiate Gothic was used to enhance what was otherwise a rather utilitarian façade. Three sets of limestone-tipped spur buttresses project above the massive brick façade and mark the entrance-stair towers for approaching visitors. Arched windows over the portals and at the clerestory above admit generous light to the interior but also give the basilica-like building a Roman *gravitas*. Ornamental touches—including heraldic shields—are apparent in the archival photograph. Since the addition of a Modernist administrative wing against the east façade in 1955, these features are mostly obscured. The Armory was demolished in 1989 to make way for the University of Iowa Hospitals and Clinics' John Pappajohn Pavilion, but the great steel arch on the rear façade of the Field House still reveals the point at which the two structures were once joined. A second remnant was also retained: a large hawk in flight that once hovered over the original competition basketball court.

Quadrangle Residence Hall, 1920 (razed, 2016)

ARCHITECT: PROUDFOOT, BIRD AND RAWSON,

DES MOINES, IOWA

As World War I progressed, the military became increasingly short of recruits and eventually established the Student Army Training Corps to combine military and academic training of college students for the formation of officers. These student recruits swarmed to the University of Iowa, overwhelming its ability to house them. President Walter P. Jessup (1916–1934) combined funds from the War Department (intended for the construction of wooden barracks) with state money to build the Quadrangle dormitory. Students referred to the project as "Jessup's Folly" since the war ended before it could be completed. After opening, however, this facility became a model for residence life on campus. In the 1920s and 1930s it was largely self-governing, and its students often earned the highest GPAs on campus.

Quadrangle Residence Hall was an example of Collegiate Gothic, as are most of the other early buildings west of the river. Originally a closed quadrangle with four entry pavilions—one in the middle of each side—it was reduced to about two-thirds its original size when the disused northeast quadrant was razed in 1975. Each entry pavilion was topped by a crenellated parapet wall, appropriately communicating its original military function and proximity to the Armory (razed in 1989). Brick reliefs on the pavilion's side bays suggested medieval spur buttresses, and the passageways were framed in limestone. Some of the entry pavilions have heraldic shields at the top. The west pavilion, which faces the direction of the Armory, had a limestone-trimmed monumental portal and stretched limestone window lintels and sills to suggest the letter "I."

An archival aerial view shows the Quadrangle Residence Hall in its glory days in the 1920s. Crenellated entrance pavilions mark the cardinal points and lead to the enclosed courtyard. In the distance to the east on the far side of the river, the old Iowa Stadium stands are still in place. Beyond that, to the left, rise the buildings of the Pentacrest.

The castellated west entry pavilion of Quadrangle Residence Hall reflected its function and proximity to the now-vanished Armory.

Mary Louise Petersen Residence Hall, 2015

ARCHITECT: ROHRBACH ASSOCIATES, IOWA CITY, IOWA

Mary Louise Petersen Residence Hall marks the first University-built student housing project in forty-seven years. It meets the latest expectations in student housing and also addresses an over-subscribed campus housing system. Petersen Hall represents a programmatic shift by incorporating within its design the special needs of Living-Learning Communities. All campus residence halls include Living-Learning Communities, but Petersen was designed to optimize their benefits. Each floor hosts a subject of academic or personal interest, allowing the residents to immerse themselves in a community of neighbors who share common interests or academic objectives. By introducing each new student to a small, tight-knit community, this

The design of Petersen Residence Hall references both the austere planarity of its nearby Modernist predecessors and a layered wall treatment characteristic of Postmodernism.

housing arrangement not only increases classroom success but also ameliorates the sometimes daunting university setting for those who may have come from a small school or community. Petersen Hall also provides benefits to the halls surrounding it. The curvilinear projection along Grand Avenue offers social gathering, studying, and teaming space not included within the designs of its neighboring buildings. This establishes an anchor for student interactions within the neighborhood of the four residence halls.

Petersen Residence Hall is a Postmodern response to the adjacent, austere Modernist, twin red-brick towers of Rienow (1966) and Slater (1968) dorms. Those earlier vertical slabs reflect the extreme, utilitarian simplicity of modern design, whereas Petersen rejects the consistency of materials and strict symmetry seen there in favor of variety, irregularity, and visual stimulation. Brown, beige, and ocher brick and green-tinted glass provide chromatic contrasts. The serpentine façade of the projecting public spaces facing the street also adds verve to the rectilinear composition above, expressing the lively social activities of this lower part of the building. Rienow's linear, two-dimensional wall articulation gives way in Petersen to a layering effect, as seen in the setback of the end stairs and upper two floors of the eastern wing of the building. Instead of one sheer monolithic face, three surfaces recede on the right half of the street façade. In its plainness and red ocher color, the third, deepest layer seems nevertheless to nod at Modernist Rienow. Likewise, the aqua-colored panels of the glazed central section suggest the famed (infamous, to some) turquoise panels of midcentury Modernism. Retro is one of Postmodernism's many stylistic modes, and we see it here. Inside the lobby a two-story wall installation entitled *Scholastic Truth* (Eikamp Arts) is inspired by a quotation from Martin Luther King Jr.: "Intelligence plus character—that is the goal of true education."

Medical Campus

After the renowned Olmsted brothers recommended in 1905 that the University of Iowa expand westward across the Iowa River, the Medical Campus began to take shape. By the 1910s, a plan was developed to shift the hospital and medical laboratories from the Iowa Avenue Campus to the open areas on the western bluffs. Westlawn Nurses' Home, Children's Hospital, and the Psychopathic Hospital (all opened in 1919) were the first to make the leap across the river. Architecturally, this new complex would be a Gothic counterpart to the Beaux-Arts Classicism established on the Pentacrest. Today that stylistic vision has taken a Modernist and even Postmodernist turn, but the relocation of the Medical Campus is complete. Removing those buildings from the main campus not only provided room to grow for clinical, teaching, and medical research facilities, but it also freed up space along Iowa Avenue for new development in that historic campus zone.

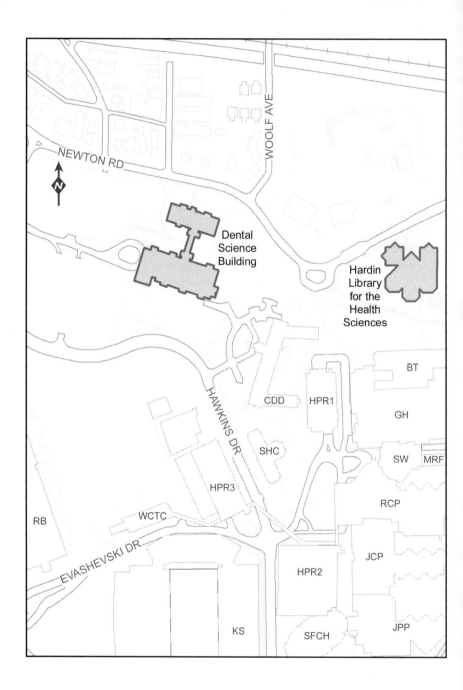

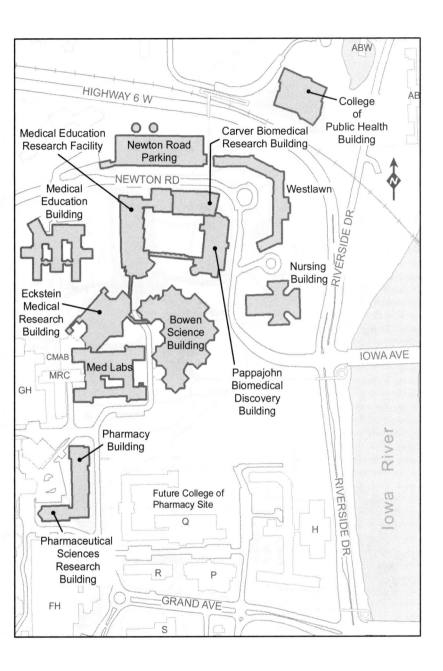

ABW

HIGHWAY 6 W

College
of
Public Health
Building

AB

Medical Education
Research Facility

Newton Road
Parking

Carver Biomedical
Research Building

NEWTON RD

Medical
Education
Building

Westlawn

Eckstein
Medical
Research
Building

Bowen
Science
Building

Nursing
Building

RIVERSIDE DR

CMAB

MRC

Med Labs

GH

Pappajohn
Biomedical
Discovery
Building

IOWA AVE

Pharmacy
Building

Iowa River

Pharmaceutical
Sciences
Research
Building

Future College of
Pharmacy Site

Q

H

RIVERSIDE DR

R

P

FH

GRAND AVE

S

175

Bowen Science Building, 1972

ARCHITECT: WALTER NETSCH OF SKIDMORE OWINGS

AND MERRILL, CHICAGO, ILLINOIS / GEORGE HORNER,

UNIVERSITY OF IOWA

PREVIOUS NAME: BASIC SCIENCES BUILDING

Howard R. Bowen's presidency (1964–1969) saw major invest-
ments in the sciences, including the construction of the Spence Laboratories of Psychology and Van Allen Hall. A new home for basic
sciences, which was later renamed after Bowen, was planned during

The ferro-concrete skeletal structure of Bowen Science Building is exposed on the
exterior as an articulated frame with brick infill.

Brutalism appears in the choice of exposed, rough-textured concrete and powerful colliding structural members that support the interior stair. The massiveness of the components engenders an emotional response from the viewer.

his administration and built under President Willard L. Boyd (1969–1981). Funding for this project included a grant of $5.1 million from the National Science Foundation as part of a project to develop Centers of Excellence across the United States. Today the building is one of the most concentrated sites of research on the campus.

Like the Lindquist Center and Hardin Library for the Health Sciences, Bowen Science Building is the work of Walter Netsch and expresses Field Theory, an experimental system developed by Netsch and used in the 1960s and 1970s to generate buildings entirely from their plans. According to Netsch, he wanted to create a "radical" building based on a series of octagons organized along an S-shaped spine and forming flexible laboratory pods. The building's articulated frame structure, highlighted by the exterior's brick infill, is spectacularly exposed at all six levels through the projecting center of the east façade. The decision to make the Bowen Science Building's structure visible extends inside where an Escher-like fantasy interior reveals the skeleton of the building. The building's siting blocks the visual axis connecting Old Capitol to Medical Laboratories and General Hospital. As if in compensation, however, its exhaust towers acknowledge the vertical accents of the hospital's venerable neo-Gothic tower.

John and Mary Pappajohn Biomedical Discovery Building, 2014

ARCHITECT: CHARLES GWATHMEY OF GWATHMEY SIEGEL

AND ASSOCIATES, NEW YORK, NEW YORK /

ROHRBACH ASSOCIATES, IOWA CITY, IOWA

By the mid-1990s the University's master plan envisioned the modernization of the health sciences research facilities comprising the Carver College of Medicine. Utility redistribution, relocation of campus roadways, and the construction of the first two buildings of the complex (MERF, 2002; CBRB, 2005) led to this capstone project, which, with the addition of a skywalk connector on the south, created a public courtyard serving all three buildings. Initially envisioned as a building that would include both health sciences research and the College of Public Health, the site proved too confined for both programs, and a location to the north was determined for the CPHB (completed, 2011). Gwathmey Siegel extended the Payette-designed motifs created by the first two buildings while attending to research objectives and a structure that would be noticeably larger than the previous phases. The ambitiousness of the project, which inspired the generous leading gift by John Pappajohn, also attracted interest from the Fraternal Order of Eagles. Their gift led to establishment of the Eagles National Diabetes Research Center, now hosted within the facility. The building site, once occupied by the Steindler Building, includes a garden named in honor of Dr. Arthur Steindler, nationally recognized for his leadership in orthopedics and pediatrics at the University of Iowa. Like Gwathmey's previous Levitt Center for University Advancement (1998), the architecture of the Pappajohn Biomedical Discovery Building contributes prominently to the University's skyline, representing the commitment to advanced research.

Pappajohn Biomedical Discovery Building holds the distinction of being Gwathmey's final major design (Charles Gwathmey died shortly after the completion of the design phase of the project). He was one of the famed New York Five group of architects, who were dedicated to the pursuit of high Modernist purity of form. They were known as the Whites, for the stark monochromatic building types they created (a good example is the Getty Museum, Los Angeles, designed by Richard Meyer). Gwathmey's Levitt Center exemplifies the classic strain of that idealistic school of the 1980s and 1990s. At PBDB, however, the architect abandoned the white panels and monumental geometry of LCUA in favor of more coloristic and articulated façades, responding to the architectural context evident in the preceding phases of this health sciences research complex. The green, preweathered (patinated) skin of the projecting volumes on the south side continues the materials used in MERF and CBRB, to which the newer building is connected. This element ruptures the purity of the white Anamosa limestone

The grandiose capstone component of the remade Medical Campus, PBDB represents an architectural and campus-planning accomplishment equaled in scale only by the Tudor Gothic research and clinical complex of the 1920s.

179

volume exposed at the building's corner, with its vertical strip window, cantilevered terrace canopy, and row of Corbusian porthole openings. Likewise, the eight vertical rows of jutting windows acknowledge the Tudor-style bay windows of Westlawn, facing it just across the street. These columnar forms rise from a gray-clad, almost Classical podium. Finally, at the northeast corner a café supported on pilotis connects to the preexisting CBRB and is expressed on the exterior in a playful serpentine flourish. At PBDB high Modernism gives way to Postmodern freedom of form and willingness to reference historical styles. The massive canopy that crowns the entire composition is illuminated at night on the underside, making a prominent linear halolike statement that can be seen from the East Campus.

College of Pharmacy Building, 1961 (to be razed, 2019), 2019 (projected), and Pharmaceutical Sciences Research Building, 1996

ARCHITECT: WOODBURN O'NEIL ARCHITECTS AND ENGINEERS, WEST DES MOINES, IOWA (1961)

BROOKS BORG SKILES ARCHITECTURE ENGINEERING: WILLIAM ANDERSON, DES MOINES, IOWA (1996)

S.L.A.M. COLLABORATIVE, BOSTON, MASSACHUSETTS / OPN ARCHITECTS, CEDAR RAPIDS, IOWA (2019)

PREVIOUS NAMES: PHARMACY HALL, WURSTER CENTER FOR PHARMACEUTICAL TECHNOLOGY

The College of Pharmacy flourished under the leadership of Dean Louis Zopf (1952–1972). Zopf not only championed the program's academic reach (including the extension of the curriculum from four to five years and mandatory continuing education for all Iowa pharmacists), but he also was instrumental in the construction of Pharmacy Hall (not illustrated), specifically dedicated to his college's needs. This original structure, built in 1961, was followed thirty-five years later by the major southward expansion, the Pharmaceutical Sciences Research Building.

The pharmaceutical research and development carried out in this laboratory building are expressed in its high-tech aesthetic. In contrast with the old brick-and-tile Pharmacy Hall and with the somewhat Modernist retro elements of the projected new building, with its metal- and concrete-clad design, the 1996 Research Building conveys a sleek, cool, technological know-how. The exposed concrete structure and reticulated metal skin add to the laboratory aura of cutting-edge efficiency, as does the decision to express vertical circulation in the form of a glazed, tubular stair tower articulated with paired aluminum

As seen from UIHC's Carver Pavilion, the Pharmaceutical Sciences Research Building, tucked away on the Medical Campus, combines futuristic architectural imagery with high-tech function.

The architect's rendering gives an idea of the projected new College of Pharmacy Building, scheduled to open in 2019 on the site of the former Quadrangle Residence Hall.

bands. A narrow channel at the top of the structure widens toward the east to accommodate venting and other climate-control units.

The College of Pharmacy existed within the original Pharmacy Hall for fifty-five years. During that time, the science and technology related to the study and training of pharmacy advanced radically. Recognizing that the original building and its systems had become obsolete, the University advanced a partnership with the state, through appropriated dollars and University and gift funding, to realize a much-needed new facility. Situated in a congested portion of the Medical Campus, the new building is to be located adjacent to the 1996 addition. The new site occupies a portion of the former Quadrangle Residence Hall. Accessibility was an important aspect of the project, and the College of Pharmacy Building includes design elements that make it a model for universal welcome. Proximity to Quad Ravine also offers future opportunities to improve campus access and interaction with the natural setting. A landscaped pharmaceutical garden is envisioned for the open space near the ravine.

The building is divided into two major masses: one to the south, hosting training and research, and, to the north, a smaller one with teaching, gathering, and administrative spaces. The building offers glimpses of the work that goes on within the college through open and glass-filled atria, welcoming students and visitors into the public spaces. The vertical columns of windows on the flank of the tower suggest a bow to nearby Rienow Residence Hall's reductive Modernism, as does the Gropius-inspired glazed element at the corner. The polychromy of variegated surface materials and the design's pronounced asymmetricality, however, are purely Postmodern.

Nursing Building, 1971

ARCHITECT: CHARLES HERBERT AND ASSOCIATES,

DES MOINES, IOWA / GEORGE HORNER, UNIVERSITY OF IOWA

The College of Nursing has a long history at the University of Iowa. Originally founded as the School of Nursing, it was organized in 1898 upon completion of University Hospital (now Seashore Hall). After attaining the status of a college in 1949, nursing was led by Myrtle Kitchell who oversaw the first matriculation of men in 1950 and the awarding of its first bachelor's degrees in 1953. The College of Nursing now offers continuing education for nurses across Iowa in addition to its regular on-campus curriculum. This broadening of its mission also saw nursing outgrow Westlawn, leading to the construction of its current home in 1971.

The monumental Nursing Building is a Brutalist concrete structure positioned on a dramatic limestone bluff above the Iowa River. The main entrance to the building is on the north flank, facing Westlawn, while a secondary entrance on the south side is below grade, leaving its commanding south façade uninterrupted. Since the street façade is also without a portal, the purity of the building's massive forms is left intact. Perhaps inspired by the prominent site, the architect sought to express the power of modern materials. Studiously avoiding any ostensible reference to nursing as an academic pursuit or profession, the architect adheres instead to Modernist abstractions. The overriding idea is an inverted, stepped pyramid of three levels resting on an immense podium, with each level separated by a thick concrete slab. The exposed vertical stair shaft of the dominant "T" configuration reveals the building's muscle. The two-story main level is contained within a darkened-glass curtain wall marked with eleven attenuated pilotis on each side. To ensure the point is well made, the curtain wall pulls back at the corners to isolate the spindly end piers even more. The result is an unusually forceful presentation of Modernist themes: exposed structure and strength of materials.

The Nursing Building makes one of the most powerful architectural statements of any building on campus—three massive concrete slabs rise from a glass curtain wall and a row of tall, slender pilotis.

Westlawn, 1919

ARCHITECT: PROUDFOOT, BIRD AND RAWSON,

DES MOINES, IOWA

PREVIOUS NAME: WESTLAWN NURSES' HOME

Westlawn has always been associated with the health sciences. Originally constructed as a dormitory for nursing students, it served that function until 1964. As a residence hall, the building was connected to the hospital by an underground tunnel. Although student nurses no longer commute below ground between the two, the functional connection remains—the building now houses the Student Health Service and University Pharmacy, the University of Iowa Hospitals and Clinics' Child Care Center, and the UI Family Planning Clinic. Westlawn also forms the eastern border of the Medical Campus green, facing the medical education and research complex to the west and giving shape to the campus space between it and the Pappajohn Biomedical Discovery Building.

The shape of Westlawn is determined by three additions to the original central section. Both wings of the building were extended in 1928 with a further extension south in 1945. In 1996 an additional projecting block was added to the east to accommodate Student Health. This section is sympathetic to Westlawn's original design though less ornamented. The Tudor Revival of the building corresponds to that of its contemporaneous neighbors, Children's Hospital (1919, razed, 1999, 2003) and the Medical Education Building (formerly Psychopathic Hospital, 1919). Each incorporated limestone detailing in the red-brick walls. At Westlawn's entrance portal, a Gothic pointed arch meets flanking pilasters, a mixing of Medieval and classical details typical of the Tudor style. Spur buttresses, three-story bay windows, and crenellated parapets create a sense of drama and evoke the perimeter wall of a castle. This visual association is made particularly strong by Westlawn's striking placement along the curving border of the bluffs overlooking the Iowa River. Viewed from the east, Westlawn commands the heights above the river valley.

Westlawn's main entrance portal is located at the intersection of its two main wings. The human scale, Tudor Revival features, and campus green in front give Westlawn its character.

College of Public Health Building, 2011

ARCHITECT: PAYETTE ASSOCIATES, BOSTON,

MASSACHUSETTS / ROHRBACH ASSOCIATES, IOWA CITY, IOWA

When it was established in 1999, the College of Public Health became the first new college at the University of Iowa in fifty years. The institutional commitment to create a physical home for the college was realized in 2011. Originally planned for a site on the Medical Campus (on the site of the Pappajohn Biomedical Discovery Building), growing program needs shifted the project to the site formerly occupied by the College of Law (1935, 1959). This location fit the thematic connection the College of Public Health provided between the health sciences and the undergraduate campus east of the river and was designed to create pedestrian pathways over the Highway 6 bridge down to the Arts Campus and across the IMU bridge. The pedestrian bridge to the Medical Campus offers an ideal vantage point for assessing the building and its surroundings. A high priority was set on designing a sustainable and energy-efficient building that

Located on one of the most prominent sites on the west side of the Iowa River, the College of Public Health Building balances with Westlawn on the opposite bluff to create an informal gateway to the UI campus.

would fit the mission of the College of Public Health. The building received certification as the first Leadership in Energy and Environmental Design (LEED) Platinum facility on the main campus.

The College of Public Health Building occupies a prominent site on the bluff where the highway and adjacent railroad curve away from the river. The doglegged south façade responds to this bend and also points to the Pentacrest on the eastern horizon. The building consists of two parallel wings conjoined by a glass atrium running the entire length and height of the structure. The limestone exterior is a design gesture to the main buildings of the nearby Medical Campus, but a small difference sets it apart. While white/buff-colored Anamosa limestone characterizes the health sciences buildings (MERF, CBRB, and PBDB), the College of Public Health Building employs a redder and earthier Mankato limestone reflecting the more bucolic site it occupies. Expansive tinted glazing maximizes the efficient use of natural light throughout the interior, while glass-enclosed projections over each of the three entrances isolate the limestone-paneled cubic volumes into quadrants. This helps relieve what would otherwise be a largely monolithic structure. To add visual interest and aid in breaking down the building's long elevations, the size and distribution of the windows vary from floor to floor. Vertically stacked panels separating the windows are mostly independent of the interior plan and progressively narrow from bottom to top, adding variety to the exterior wall composition. This is especially apparent at the corners where the wall systems meet and alternate between solid and void from bottom to top. Inside, the vast atrium with its centrally located open stair tower is designated a dialogue space, providing points of interdisciplinary contact for faculty, staff, and students from the many discrete departmental units. The atrium also reflects the intent of the south wing's cant by focusing views upon the Old Capitol across the river. Photographer Peter Feldstein's *Iowa Portraits* of larger-than-life-size, glass-paneled images displaying the citizens of small-town Iowa populate the interior and constitute an ever-present allusion to the public served by the college's curriculum and its graduates.

Newton Road Parking Ramp, 2002

ARCHITECT: HLKB ARCHITECTURE, DES MOINES, IOWA

The Newton Road Parking Ramp was designed as part of a master plan intended to increase vehicular access to the expanding Medical Campus. The ramp project created 810 new parking spaces and an associated walkway that shields pedestrians from Newton Road. Foot traffic access is also accommodated by a pedestrian bridge leading to the College of Public Health Building. The bridge, which crosses over an urban highway and a railroad line, extends the Medical Campus northward and adjacent to the Arts Campus. The multi-use parking ramp structure also includes a chilled water plant serving both the Medical and Arts Campuses.

The parking ramp's design reflects both its function and location. The use of industrial materials supports the structure's utilitarian aesthetic, though they are tailored to suit both the academic and residential areas bordering the ramp. Translucent and clear glass express different functions—the translucent panels along the walkway shield the campus from the ramp's cars, while the clear glass signals points of entry and vertical circulation. Clear glass is also used in a band along the walkway, allowing pedestrians a view of campus. A bay window–like projection breaks the long flank of the glass curtain wall, while the delicate crystalline volumes of the enclosed stairwell/elevator units at each end of the structure lend it an elegance unusual for a parking facility. On the highway side of the ramp, perforated copper cladding provides a neutral façade that blends in scale with the adjacent West-lawn. The metal panels also conceal cars and their headlights from the residential neighborhood across the highway. The tapered cooling towers, which are rendered in naturally finished precast concrete, help to alleviate the long uniform sweep of the structure's highway façade. The Newton Road Parking Ramp received a 2002 American Institute of Architects Honor Award for its creative design and was a contributing factor to HLKB's distinction as AIA national firm of the year in 2002.

The Newton Road Parking Ramp exemplifies how good design
can grace even utilitarian structures.

Medical Education and Research Facility, 2002, and Roy J. and Lucille A. Carver Biomedical Research Building, 2005

ARCHITECT: PAYETTE ASSOCIATES, BOSTON, MASSACHUSETTS /

BALDWIN WHITE ARCHITECTS, DES MOINES, IOWA (2002)

PAYETTE ASSOCIATES, BOSTON, MASSACHUSETTS / ROHRBACH

CARLSON, IOWA CITY, IOWA (2005)

The Medical Education and Research Facility and its adjacent partner, the Roy J. and Lucille A. Carver Biomedical Research Building (2005), provide classroom, laboratory, and research space for work in genetics, cardiovascular health, and respiratory diseases as well as a home for the departments of internal medicine, pediatrics, otolaryngology, and physiology. These facilities, built to operate as one, provide a significant advancement in teaching and research on the Medical Campus.

MERF commands attention with its Postmodern freedom of expression, especially in the atrium where the regularized window arrangements and austere neo-Modernist treatment of the west wing give way to an exuberant composition of cornices and sun baffles organized in ascending acute angles—all expressed in a towering ensemble of glass and prepatinated copper cladding (colorplate 20). This sheathing draws attention to the building's south end, which looks ready to take flight, penetrating and engaging the sky in the direction of General Hospital. This more fanciful component of the design is reminiscent of 1920s German Expressionist architecture, with the machine-standardized forms of the building's flank being overridden to form an image of emotive viewer-appeal. The exterior thereby expresses the energy and optimism appropriate to the advancement of medical science. It also gestures dramatically and meaningfully toward General Hospital's Gothic Tower, that grandiose architectural embodiment of the aspirations of an earlier epoch in medical science. The building

Just as the vertical profile of nearby General Hospital's Gothic Tower expressed the energy and optimism of the UI's new medical campus in the early years of the twentieth century, so do the upward-striving lines of MERF's atrium architecturally embody a similar resolve to meet the challenges of a new century.

stands as a new visual centerpiece for the Medical Campus. MERF received a 2003 Design Award from the New England Chapter of the American Institute of Architects.

The contiguous Carver Biomedical Research Building continues the combination of prepatinated copper and stone as the building form shifts to the east. This second structure creates the streetscape along Newton Road and represents the second of a three-stage creation of a large courtyard to anchor the heart of the Medical Campus.

John W. Eckstein Medical Research Building, 1989

ARCHITECT: NBBJ, SEATTLE, WASHINGTON /

HLM DESIGN, IOWA CITY, IOWA

PREVIOUS NAME: HUMAN BIOLOGY RESEARCH FACILITY

Housing research laboratories associated with the UI Roy J. and Lucille A. Carver College of Medicine, the John W. Eckstein Medical Research Building plays an important role in scientific and educational missions of the University of Iowa. Named after an alumnus of the University's medical school and residency program, a professor of internal medicine, and dean of the medical college from 1970 until 1990, the building contains research laboratories for molecular biology, immunology, and genetic engineering.

Rising above a podium created by the passageway connecting three Carver College of Medicine buildings, the Eckstein Medical Research Building is a Late Modern structure of monolithic proportions and impressive massing. Underscaled ribbon windows with horizontally reticulated panes also enhance the impression of size, as do the bands of gray- and red-glazed tiles that give the building a layered effect. To the right of the building, a gabled brick gateway leads to a courtyard linking Eckstein with the College of Medicine Administration Building. The sculpture there is one of the last created by artist Robert Arneson, who was ill with terminal cancer while working on the commission. Arneson's work forms a mirrored gateway in imitation of the brick portal leading to a passageway between Eckstein and the College of Medicine Administration Building. The artist's conception of the human figure as a pillar is echoed by the pilotis supporting the passage behind.

The John W. Eckstein Medical Research Building is characterized by a powerful massing of simple blocklike forms.

The courtyard of the Eckstein Building contains *Gateway to Self-Realization* (1992), a work by sculptor Robert Arneson.

Medical Education Building, 1919

ARCHITECT: PROUDFOOT, BIRD AND RAWSON,

DES MOINES, IOWA

PREVIOUS NAMES: PSYCHOPATHIC HOSPITAL,

PSYCHIATRIC HOSPITAL

In the original incarnation of the Medical Campus, a cluster of one- and two-story buildings provided specialized care in a quasi-domestic setting. Over the years, however, the expansion of the University of Iowa Hospitals and Clinics has largely subsumed the functions of those early buildings, and only the Medical Education Building remains today. Though it was developed as a psychiatric hospital and served that function until 1990, the building is now a unit of the UI Carver College of Medicine and houses its teaching laboratory.

Like Westlawn, the Medical Education Building is a red-brick Tudor Revival structure. The choice of style has a less institutional, more baronial, feel, with sandstone ornamentation and touches reminiscent of domestic architecture. The pointed arches at the main entrance, window surrounds, and crenellated parapets (above the bay windows) are all rendered in sandstone. The dormers and tall chimneys on the main section's roof add to Medical Education's stately air, while the low flanking wings create a sense of hominess. These wings, really passageways leading to other former wards, also provided patients with abundant cross-ventilation that was considered essential to their treatment.

The Medical Education Building's Tudor Revival style typifies the radical shift from Pentacrest Beaux-Arts Classicism to Medical Campus neo-Medievalism.

Hardin Library for the Health Sciences, 1974

ARCHITECT: WALTER NETSCH OF SKIDMORE OWINGS

AND MERRILL, CHICAGO, ILLINOIS / GEORGE HORNER,

UNIVERSITY OF IOWA

PREVIOUS NAME: HEALTH SCIENCES LIBRARY

The Hardin Library for the Health Sciences consolidated the collections of five health science libraries—medical, dental, pharmacy, nursing, and speech pathology. Its namesake, Dr. Robert C. Hardin, was dean of the College of Medicine from 1962 until 1969 and also

According to architect Walter Netsch, the abstract geometry of Hardin Library's Brutalist main entrance is intended to recall an open book.

served as the University of Iowa's vice president for health affairs under President Willard L. Boyd. Hardin also ran the Blood Transfusion Service for the European theater during the Normandy invasion of World War II. The building was renamed in his honor in 1988.

The design of the Hardin Library for the Health Sciences is based on the Field Theory (or shifted grid) method popularized by its architect, Walter Netsch. In this case a grid of squares is rotated forty-five degrees to produce a more versatile plan. The difference here is that, unlike at the Bowen Science Building or the Lindquist Center, the geometrical "field" morphs from one level to the next, moving from rotated square, to octagon, to Greek Cross. The building's façadeless elevation is nevertheless still entirely a function of the plan at each level. Diagonals and pyramidal volumes play against one another and emphasize the primacy of the plan (colorplate 13). The site performs an influential role in the design; the slope of the land allows the building a low profile as seen from the campus side to the south, with a single-story entrance that masks the bulk of the multistory building below. Hardin Library is constituted of interrupted planes of textured concrete—again, a Brutalist gesture by Netsch. Clusters of white skylights project above and dip below the roofline, creating a strong geometrical effect that also brings light into the interior. The expressive nature of Late Modernism is embodied in the architect's notion that the stepped interior pathway through the building and down to the lower level suggests walking into a book.

Dental Science Building, 1973, and South Wing addition, 2012

ARCHITECT: SMITH, HINCHMAN AND GRYLS, DETROIT, MICHIGAN /

GEORGE HORNER, UNIVERSITY OF IOWA (1973)

INVISION ARCHITECTURE, WATERLOO, IOWA (2012)

During President Willard L. Boyd's administration (1969–1981), the University of Iowa fully embraced contemporary design, leaving a progressive legacy of campus architecture particularly on the Medical Campus. The Dental Science Building, home to the College of Dentistry, is the latest of three structures erected specifically for this program, which was founded as the Department of Dentistry in 1882. Old Dental Building (1895), a Second Empire style building on the Pentacrest (razed, 1975), was the first designed expressly for dentistry, while the Beaux-Arts-inspired Trowbridge Hall (1918) housed the program until the current building was completed in 1973. A radical departure from the historicism of those earlier designs, the Dental Science Building is the most single-mindedly Brutalist building on the UI campus. Raw concrete, with traces of wooden forms still evident on the surfaces, conveys an austere aesthetic. An extension, while sensitive to the original architecture, was added to the southwestern corner of the building in 2012, and modernization of the teaching clinics within the original building was also subsequently accomplished.

Sited on a sloping topography of grassy lawns and stands of pine trees, architecture and nature reside in juxtaposition at Dental Science (colorplate 8). Approached from the north or south, the building presents a fortress-like ensemble of abstract forms, which house air vents and other utilities. Seen from the east or west, however, the building opens up, its broad axial approach revealing a bisected plane joined at the second floor by a two-story glass bridge. The north side is devoted to classrooms, administration, and research and the south to clinical activities and laboratories. Broad stairs, spanning nearly the entire space between the wings, lead under the bridge and up to the parking area to the west. In the walk along the axis of this courtyard, the glass

Monumental stairs beneath the glass bridge connect the parallel
concrete pavilions of the Dental Science Building.

curtain walls of the wings are visible, as are the more human-scaled
inner sides of the building. The courtyard also affords views of the
surrounding landscape to faculty, students, and staff working inside.
Pedestrians taking this path from the west parking area toward General Hospital witness monumental pavilions on both sides and a view
of the campus beyond.

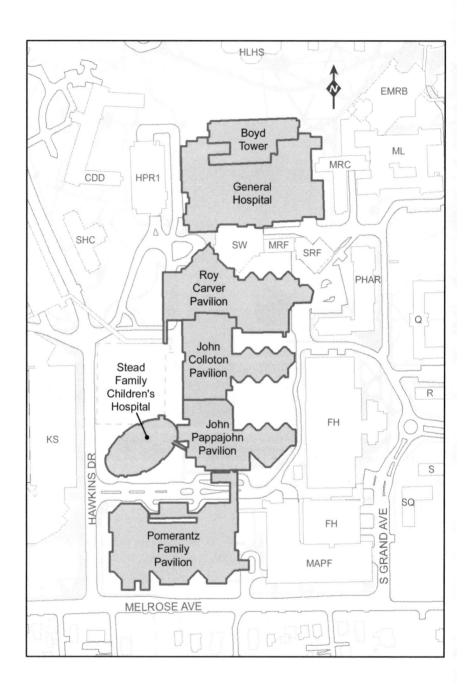

University of Iowa Hospitals and Clinics Campus

The University of Iowa Hospitals and Clinics (UIHC) forms the core of the campuses to the west of the Iowa River and a westward border to the University's main campus. As a result of the recommendation of the Olmsted brothers and of Abraham Flexner's 1910 review of the College of Medicine, President Walter Jessup (1916–1934) relocated the University's medical facilities from Iowa Avenue to the bluffs marking the western fringe of both the campus and the city. This move provided space for the construction of new University hospitals in 1919 (Psychopathic Hospital and Children's Hospital) and 1928 (General Hospital). These facilities allowed increased clinical experience for medical students and complied with two state mandates to extend health care to all poor children and adults within the state (1915, 1919). The rise of the Medical Campus and its prominent tower also set the architectural tone for the University's western presence by establishing a Gothic Revival style that contrasted with the dominant Beaux-Arts Classicism to the east. Development of the UIHC campus has been extensive over the past forty years, and now, as one of the nation's largest teaching hospitals, UIHC is virtually a city unto itself.

Medical Laboratories, 1927

ARCHITECT: PROUDFOOT, RAWSON AND SOUERS,

DES MOINES, IOWA

The Medical Laboratories building, adjacent to the General Hospital, was designed to house the medical library and State Board of Health Laboratories. Built contemporaneously with the General Hospital, the Medical Laboratories were funded along the same structure—half the monies coming from the Rockefeller Foundation and Rockefeller General Board of Education and half from the state. Both projects benefited from the advocacy of Abraham Flexner, whose damning 1910 report to the Carnegie Foundation had prompted a decade of internal reform at the hospital and medical college. Flexner and William R. Boyd, chairman of the Finance Committee of the Iowa State Board of Education, saw the University's self-scrutiny as an

Fanciful sea serpents flank the medical coat of arms
on the façade of Medical Laboratories.

ideal foundation for experiments in best practices. Their support of the College of Medicine as a potential laboratory for those efforts was instrumental in the $2,250,000 grant and further development of the transformation already under way.

Modeled on the gatehouse at Henry VIII's Hampton Court, the Medical Laboratories' east façade is a Tudor Revival composition of limestone and brick (colorplate 4). The pointed-arch portal, two-story central bay window, and flanking octagonal towers are all characteristic of this style. A medical coat of arms tops the central bay and is framed by scaly serpents—clear allusion to the serpent of Aesculapius, the Greek god of medicine. This same bay also has a panel inscribed "1925," the date recorded on the original blueprints. The slender towers are ornamented at the top with inset tracery panels and copper domes, and the balustraded parapet is topped with finials. The 1842 cornerstone of the Mechanics' Academy (razed, 1897), first hospital on the University of Iowa campus, is incorporated into the wall inside the entrance to Medical Laboratories. The crenellated polygonal stair towers along the north and south flanks of Medical Laboratories have an even greater affinity to the gatehouse at St. John's College, Cambridge. Appropriately, Oxbridge Collegiate Gothic is the preferred style here.

General Hospital, 1928

ARCHITECT: PROUDFOOT, RAWSON, SOUERS AND THOMAS,

DES MOINES, IOWA

Constructed along with the Medical Laboratories, the 900-bed General Hospital benefited from the interest of Abraham Flexner of the Rockefeller Foundation and William R. Boyd, a Cedar Rapids newspaper publisher and chair of the Finance Committee of the State of Iowa Board of Education. Their interventions produced the funding for this vast capital project, the largest in University history at that point. The 1915 and 1919 indigent care laws passed by the Iowa State Legislature had provided the impetus for the expansion. Those progressive acts of legislation mandated that the University provide health care for the entire state of Iowa, regardless of wealth—a responsibility that would have easily overwhelmed the hospital facilities then on Iowa Avenue (now Seashore Hall). Through collaboration, the state and private philanthropies not only solved questions of access and improved medical education, but also produced a new General Hospital to serve students, faculty, and the community. Upon its completion the General Hospital became one of the largest teaching hospitals in the country, a distinction that remains today.

It was predetermined that the new hospital would be designed in the Gothic style and that it would be, as recorded in early documents, "surmounted by a dome [tower], as a counterpoise to the dome in Old Capitol located directly east of it across the Iowa River." General Hospital's Collegiate Gothic Tower, designed by Amos B. Emery of Proudfoot, Rawson, Souers and Thomas, remains the best-known campus landmark—after Old Capitol—the institutional symbol of UIHC as a whole (colorplate 5). The north façade marked the original monumental entrance to the building, while the east elevation was on axis with Old Capitol and easily visible from the Pentacrest's west terrace. The

General Hospital's former main entrance is the premier example of Collegiate Gothic architecture on the UI campus.

prominence of its design not only established General Hospital as the center of the Gothic western campus, it also had important symbolic value. Just as the Pentacrest's Classicism recalled the civic virtues and high culture of Athens and the Renaissance, the Medieval style of General Hospital recalled the monastic buildings that were the first hospitals. In 1973 plans were revealed for a new seven-story block (Boyd Tower) that, while compromising a significant portion of the original Gothic entry façade, provided close-up views of the Gothic Tower base from within the new atrium. The skyline-forming Gothic Tower still hovers over the new additions and marks the hospital's origin.

As the archival photograph shows, the original structure recalled the late fifteenth-century gate tower of Magdalen College in Oxford with powerful spur buttresses to either side of the entrance and a vertical shaft that culminated in an airy, openwork superstructure. A two-story bay window rose over the entrance portal and four pointed-arch lancet windows topped the parapet. Ascending even further, leafy pinnacles capped the buttresses, and a blind gallery and horizontal band of tracery framed the lower limits of the tower's lacy upper reaches. Thankfully, this last section can still be appreciated today.

Located at the base of the tower's superstructure, a subdued St. George's dragon once greeted patients and visitors as they arrived at General Hospital's main portal. This apotropaic creature is still visible from the seventh-floor atrium of Boyd Tower.

University of Iowa Hospitals and Clinics, 1976–2005

ARCHITECT: HLM DESIGN, IOWA CITY, IOWA

What began in 1873 as a twenty-bed operation in the Mechanics' Academy on Iowa Avenue, and moved across the Iowa River in a 350-patient caravan in 1928, is now one of the largest teaching hospitals in the United States. The University of Iowa Hospitals and Clinics serves thousands of Iowans and patients from almost all states and many foreign countries each year. In fiscal year 2014, the UIHC had more than 32,000 acute inpatient admissions and 914,300 outpatient visits to its hospital- and community-based clinics. Its staff numbers more than 8,300. Comprising major clinical and research facilities, the UIHC carries on its work in a vast complex of buildings that, over the course of three decades, has engulfed the original General Hospital and extended three blocks to the south.

Boyd Tower (1976) was the first phase of this far-reaching construction project, but the main body of today's UIHC is made up of four subsequent pavilions, all developed in phases—Roy J. Carver Pavilion (1978–1988), John W. Colloton Pavilion (1980–1992), John Pappajohn Pavilion (1987–2000), and the Pomerantz Family Pavilion (1992–2005). Pomerantz, the last of these additions, includes a state-of-the-art, image-guided radiation treatment center. Compositional organization of this mammoth aggregation of structures is provided by the imposing sweep of its west façade. Consistency and coherence are achieved by the use of ribbon windows, white panel cladding, and exposed pilotis as the dominant design elements throughout. An emphatic rejection of the historicism of the General Hospital, the structure's overall effect is corporate, with an antiseptic machine aesthetic reminiscent of Mies van der Rohe's 1927 model apartment building for the German Werkbund—all capped with a busy heliport. Fully engaging the therapeutic character of art, the UIHC displays a large collection of contemporary painting, sculpture, prints, photographs, and metalsmithing in its public spaces.

The University of Iowa Hospitals and Clinics' imposing west façade
brings compositional order to the vast complex of hospital buildings.

University of Iowa Stead Family Children's Hospital, 2016

ARCHITECT: FOSTER + PARTNERS, LONDON, UK /
HEERY INTERNATIONAL, IOWA CITY, IOWA / STANLEY BEAMAN
& SEARS, ATLANTA, GEORGIA

Since the construction of the Gothic General Hospital tower in 1928, the University of Iowa Hospitals and Clinics complex has grown enormously. The majority of the growth occurred between 1976 (Boyd Tower) and 2005 (Pomerantz Pavilion). The collection of rectilinear

Kinnick Stadium stands appear to abut the rounded tower of Children's Hospital. The generous fenestration of the patient rooms allows game-day enjoyment of the action. Athletics and the healing arts come together.

buildings is the most densely populated square mile in the state of Iowa, creating a challenge for the design team, led by Norman Foster. The University of Iowa Stead Family Children's Hospital represents the first phase in a long-term, three-phase master plan for hospital growth. Two additional towers, matching the first, will stretch northward along the west face of the existing hospital. While allowing for significantly more space on the site, the design and plan also provide more breathing room between UIHC and adjacent Kinnick Stadium. Rated as one of the country's top children's hospitals, University of Iowa Stead Family Children's Hospital was the only rated children's hospital without a separate building. This project has addressed that lack and is meant to realize an even greater positive impact on children and their families in the state of Iowa. The building is named in honor of the Stead family for their generosity in making the project possible.

The compact nature of the site, its relationship with Kinnick Stadium, and the effect a building of this nature would have on its users were all primary concerns of the designers (colorplate 15). Foster had not previously designed a hospital, and he therefore relied on expertise provided by Heery and by Stanley Beaman & Sears, firms with significant hospital experience. Foster's primary realizations led to the inclusion of a four-story underground parking structure that connects to the first tower. By placing parking underground, space was created between the hospital and Kinnick Stadium. This park atop the ramp creates a primary entrance and therapeutic green space. The dramatic and elegant elliptical shape of the building emerged from Foster's goal to communicate the highest level of technology, and thus confidence, in the life-changing work that would take place in the building while attending to the need to comfort users facing stressful circumstances. The rounded façade of the building and vibrant colors of lighting and finishes inside aim to welcome those needing health care. The long-term, three-phase master plan calls for two additional, similarly designed towers that continue this theme. The layout, with the Children's Hospital canted toward the south, a north tower canted toward the north, and a larger middle tower connecting the two in a north-south alignment, is intended to create a gesture of open arms and welcome.

The Children's Hospital sharply contrasts with the Modernist rectilinear geometry of the adjacent UIHC west façade, with only the horizontal orientation of the windows visually linking the two buildings. The dominant curvilinear composition marks SFCH as a Postmodern design such as can be seen at the contemporaneous Hancher Auditorium and in the bulging glass front of the Voxman Music Building. The sweeping lines of the broad façade and the floating canopy crowning the structure also suggest a healing suaveness appropriate to the building's function. The Roman Colosseum is the progenitor of the famous elliptical buildings in the history of architecture, and perhaps the architects here were mindful of neighboring Kinnick Stadium, with its nearly ovoid (polygonal) shape, or even the interior of Carver-Hawkeye Arena. That would be appropriate, since many of the rooms and lounges in SFCH overlook the stadium and on game days provide therapeutic entertainment for the young patients. The Children's Hospital is the tallest building in Iowa City and adds a prominent feature to the skyline.

Athletics Campus

The University of Iowa's athletic facilities have expanded far beyond their early days on the east banks of the Iowa River. After the completion of the Field House in 1927, the Athletics Campus moved to more spacious quarters beyond the bluffs on the west side of the river. There the program matured over the decades, eventually outgrowing the space available in that location as well. As the Athletic Department developed and offered additional sports to its student-athletes, the border of the Athletics Campus stretched some 1.3 miles to the west. This westward advance began with the inclusion of Finkbine Golf Course and has led to the facilities now being developed beyond Mormon Trek Boulevard.

Anchored by Kinnick Stadium, the Athletics Campus includes the Hayden Fry Football Complex, the Stew and LeNore Hansen Football Performance Center, Duane Banks Baseball Stadium, and Carver-Hawkeye Arena. The gradual shift west of the Athletic Department's center of gravity reflects an increasing conflict between the need for space-intensive athletic facilities and development of academic, research, and hospital-related space. Land close to the core of the University has become still more valuable over time, and the currently developing campus to the west has allowed for continued investment in new, modern assets serving the more than 600 yearly UI student-athletes. Among the facilities being located at this western edge of the UI campus are the Roy G. Karro Building's Athletics Hall of Fame, Grant Field (the field hockey stadium named after Christine H. B. Grant, former Women's Athletics director), an amphitheater-designed soccer stadium and practice facility, the Klotz Tennis Courts and associated indoor turf buildings, and the Ashton Cross Country Course, which has become a popular recreation venue for University and community members alike. The remainder of the area is dominated by recreation fields and activities designed for UI student use.

These two areas that make up the Athletics Campus are linked by

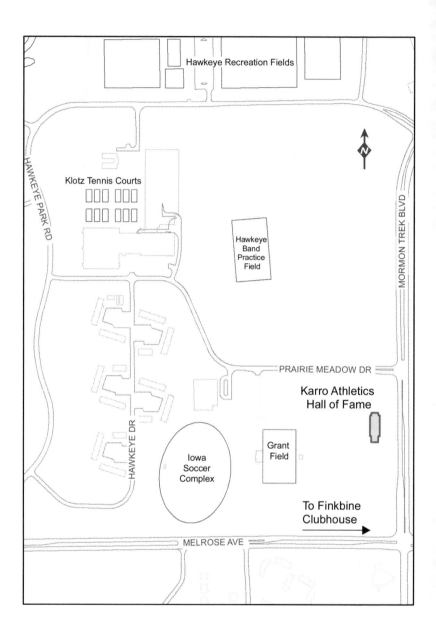

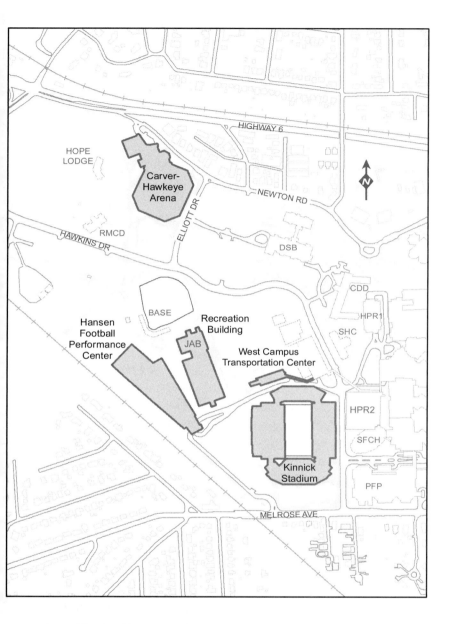

the Finkbine Golf Course and an area known as Lower Finkbine (home to a former nine-hole golf course) that hosts the Francis X. Cretzmeyer outdoor track and field venue and the Robert L. Pearl Softball Field.

Kinnick Stadium, 1929, and South Endzone Expansion and Renovation, 2006

ARCHITECT: PROUDFOOT, RAWSON, SOUERS AND THOMAS,

DES MOINES, IOWA (1929)

HNTB, KANSAS CITY, MISSOURI / NEUMANN MONSON

ARCHITECTS, IOWA CITY, IOWA (2006)

PREVIOUS NAME: IOWA STADIUM

Designed to hold 45,000 fans, Kinnick Stadium was built in less than a year on a site excavated some thirty feet below the surrounding street level. It replaced the former stadium located on the east bank of the Iowa River and was renamed in 1972 in honor of halfback Nile Kinnick, the University of Iowa's most celebrated player. Kinnick, an honors student, class president, and 1939 Heisman Trophy winner, was the backbone of the University of Iowa's legendary "Iowa Ironmen" squad. Following graduation, his life was cut tragically short when his fighter plane crashed during a training mission in World War II.

Hayden Fry, another giant in Iowa football lore, was hired as head coach in 1979. He turned around a perennially losing program and, in 1981, delivered the first winning season in nineteen years and a trip to the Rose Bowl.

Kinnick Stadium's oval plan and arcuated elevation, like that of many other football facilities from its period, reflect the Roman Colosseum. The decision to excavate the playing field below grade made possible a relatively modest and elegant external profile in harmony with the nearby residential neighborhood. Entry points are accented with monumental arches arranged in three groups of three. The dominating east and west façades are softened by ornamentation that includes Juliet-style faux balconies and arches infilled with brick. Though built with only the east and west grandstands in the beginning, Kinnick Stadium has had additions through the years that have added bleachers on the north and south and a press box, initially constructed in 1958,

The original 1929 Iowa Stadium, in a stripped-down Beaux-Arts style, was designed by the architects of the Classical buildings on the Pentacrest. The archival aerial photograph shows the old stadium when still new. In the distance are the new General Hospital with its Gothic Tower and, on the right, the Armory and Field House.

Monumental arches, Juliet balconies, and heraldic shields at the bases of the pennant poles allude both to the ancient Roman Colosseum and to medieval castles.

Sculptor Lawrence Nowlan stands on the scaffolding behind his full-scale clay model for the twelve-foot-high statue of Nile Kinnick. The completed bronze statue is located at the main entrance outside the south stands.

onto the west. Kinnick's 2006 renovation (colorplate 14) replaced the south bleachers and scoreboard. A new press box, complete with sky boxes and indoor/outdoor club seats, has replaced the original to meet contemporary standards and the needs of media technology but was also designed to respect the venerable 1929 design. The new press box has been named after former athletic director Dr. Paul W. Brechler, who oversaw construction of the first press box (affectionately known thereafter as the "Brechler Hilton"). The stadium renovations through the years have resulted in a seating capacity of nearly 70,000.

The 2006 project also included the construction of a large land-scaped approach (Krause Family Plaza) at the south end zone, providing a ceremonial entrance to the stadium and a point of welcome to the campus. New limestone panels bear the seal of the University. A colossal freestanding bronze statue of Nile Kinnick (scholar and athlete) in a pose inspired by Michelangelo's *David* greets fans entering the stadium. A life-size, high-relief bronze narrative panel just inside the colossal three-arched south entry commemorates the triumphant moment in Kinnick's career when, in the final minutes of the game, Kinnick carried the ball over the goal line to defeat mighty Notre Dame and secure the Heisman Trophy.

West Campus Transportation Center, 2012

ARCHITECT: NEUMANN MONSON, IOWA CITY, IOWA

This transportation hub was built in anticipation of the nearby Children's Hospital. It accommodates one of the nation's most utilized and efficient campus bus systems and related administrative offices. On a daily basis more than 4,000 Cambus "on-and-offs" occur at this facility. It was designed also to provide a pedestrian passageway for the many UIHC employees who use the adjacent ramp and surface parking to the north. Escalators lead to an elevated walkway, offering a climate-controlled connector above the heavy street traffic below. Given the building's immediate juxtaposition to chilled-water cooling towers, parking facilities, Kinnick Stadium, and UIHC, care was taken to create a design that fit comfortably amid close-by utilitarian, athletic, and health-care building types. Pedestrians hastening to and from work have the opportunity to experience the stark but impressive geometrical massing of architectural forms that tower above this modest but well-thought-out structure.

Elegant Minimalism characterizes the design of the West Campus Transportation Center. The yellow-and-buff-paneled floating office space shelters the recessed bus terminal below. A glass-and-steel skywalk connecting directly to UIHC joins the main body of the building at the east end, and a contrasting wood-clad maintenance facility projects correspondingly toward the west. These long, low, and sleek forms generate a sense of movement through the volumes appropriate to the function of the building. Sharp linear contours enhance the feeling of progression, and the continuous louvered windows on the south façade mask any hint of human scale, further reinforcing the abstraction of the design. WCTC's utter rejection of ornamentation and lack of even the slightest gesture to Postmodern Classicism are matched on the UI campus only by the Blank Honors Center. The sense of restraint and the absolute control of forms and surface treatments recall the achievements of Modernism in its Italian Rationalist mode of the 1930s, and in that fashion the design nods, wittily, to Modernism as a historical style. Interlocking forms and light/shade contrasts express the dynamics of a transportation hub. The curtain wall of the office level on the north side, housing the Parking and Transportation Department, appropriately surveys a vast expanse of surface parking. Inside, at the terminus of the skywalk at the head of the escalators, Susan Chrysler White's vector-filled mural, *Flash Point* (colorplate 22), gives pictorial expression to the swift movement of passersby and delights the eye all at once.

Recalling mid-twentieth-century Modernism, a small-budget utilitarian structure resulted in a controlled and elegant design for the West Campus Transportation Center, located in the shadow of Kinnick Stadium.

Recreation Building, 1970

ARCHITECT: PORTER/BRIERLY ASSOCIATES,

DES MOINES, IOWA

Best known to out-of-towners as the pregame practice venue of the University of Iowa's Marching Band, the Recreation Building serves a variety of recreation and athletic functions. Locker rooms and training facilities are located in the building's north end. The facility also contains 65,000 square feet of open track space, which is used primarily for track and field functions and intercollegiate competition. Tennis courts occupy the infield of the track.

The Recreation Building's external appearance is a function of the laminated wood beam roof structure that stretches above the open track. This distinctive structural system provides for the long spans required by the activities housed below and also adds a rich, natural glow to the building's interior. On the exterior, the thrust of the massive beams is channeled to four muscular concrete buttress piers on each long side. The meeting of roof and brick walls at ground level is mediated by an expanse of tinted glazing that fills the huge triangular configurations. A gold-colored anodized aluminum screen mounted above doors on the south façade signals the main entrance.

The shedlike profile of the Recreation Building, designed to span a vast interior space, expresses the Modernist dictum that "form follows function."

Stew and LeNore Hansen Football Performance Center, 2013

ARCHITECT: SUBSTANCE ARCHITECTURE, DES MOINES, IOWA

Gifts to the Athletics Department enabled development of a two-phase consolidation and expansion of the University of Iowa football team practice and operations facilities. The first phase was a new indoor football practice field, allowing for the aging 1984 "Hayden Fry practice bubble" to come down. The second phase created new and larger spaces for the team, coaches, and support staff, many of whom were previously housed in the single-story Jacobson Building (1995), attached to the north end of the Recreation Building (1970). Proximity to Kinnick Stadium (1929) drove the theme of the new building, and while a smaller mass, especially at the more visible south end, it was designed to reflect the feel of Kinnick. State-of-the-art facilities for

Modernist ribbon windows and Postmodern shed-canopy combine in the Hansen Football Performance Center to provide essential facilities for the football program.

game preparation, team meetings, training, and rehabilitation anchor the building's program, with a more striking and public entry aimed at recruiting and sharing past and current team successes.

The task here was to unify many distinct functions along an attenuated footprint, shaped by the site, while creating a meaningful focus to the assemblage. A projecting slab roof over the recessed dark-tinted glass curtain wall prominently marks the entrance. A deeply inset window on the south end and the wraparound ribbon window at the corner and continuing to the north—all with pronounced white enframement—add visual interest to the public entry of an otherwise mostly utilitarian structure. The red brick and detailing at the south end of the building are intended to pay homage to Kinnick Stadium. The building complex emphasizes program notoriety through labeling, in the bold IOWA FOOTBALL lettering at the entry and in the well-known Tigerhawk logo, seen on the cast-stone donor plaque and gable end of the indoor practice field rising in the background. A more interpretive version of the Tigerhawk is etched into the glass wall above the main entrance, with pixilation utilized to obscure and blend the logo into the design.

Richard O. Jacobson Athletic Building, 1995

ARCHITECT: HLKB ARCHITECTURE, DES MOINES, IOWA

The Richard O. Jacobson Athletic Building was developed to accommodate the growth of the University of Iowa football program. Named in honor of the founder of the Jacobson Companies—Richard O. Jacobson, a graduate of the Tippie College of Business and longtime supporter of the University and Hawkeye athletics—the facility was built to include weight training, sports medicine, and locker-room space serving several UI sports programs. It served as a connection from the Recreation Building, built in 1970, to the indoor football practice facility, known as the Hayden Fry Bubble. In 2013 the "bubble" was removed and replaced with surface parking. The indoor football practice field and the entire football team operations function were relocated to the adjacent Stew and LeNore Hansen Football Performance Center in 2014. The Jacobson Building will be repurposed to advance Athletic Department objectives.

The architect's design for the Jacobson Athletic Building borrows from historic athletic facilities to create a building rich with allusions to student-athletes of the past. This is especially evident in the bow-string roof trusses, which recall the geometries of armories of the past. A "battered" wall to the left of the entrance supports cantilevered protective canopies, aggressively penetrates the corrugated-aluminum façade, and runs through the entire length of the building. Inside, visitors, staff, and athletes move through spaces that use overscaled features and strong materials to demonstrate the power of the football program. Examples of this symbolic architecture are in the strength training area that features thirteen-foot-high doors, exposed-truss roof structure and tubular air ducts, and extensive mirrored walls that visually multiply the number of machines and athletes.

The Richard O. Jacobson Athletic Building expresses (in architectural form) concepts related to strength training.

Carver-Hawkeye Arena, 1983, and Practice Court and Administrative Addition, 2012

ARCHITECT: CAUDILL ROWLETT SCOTT ARCHITECTS,

HOUSTON, TEXAS / DURRANT GROUP, DUBUQUE, IOWA (1983)

HNTB CORPORATION, KANSAS CITY, MISSOURI / NEUMANN

MONSON ARCHITECTS, IOWA CITY, IOWA (2012)

Carver-Hawkeye Arena, named after Muscatine entrepreneur and philanthropist Roy J. Carver, commemorates his long-standing generosity to the University. Home to basketball, volleyball, wrestling, and the Athletic Department's administration, Carver-Hawkeye plays a role on campus that exceeds its athletic functions. Aside from shifting the center of athletics from the Field House, its 15,560-seat capacity is also used for concerts, public events, and the commencement ceremonies of the College of Liberal Arts and Sciences and the Graduate College.

Carver-Hawkeye's innovative design takes advantage of its sloping site and uses the change in elevation to visual and environmental effect. With all but the top concourse level built below grade, the structure achieves significant energy savings. The use of natural light filtering through the glass-block perimeter wall has a similar advantage, as does the exposed-truss system, space-frame roof. This design element creates a notable skyline feature while removing unoccupied structural space to outside the building's envelope and reducing the interior volume that must be heated. The tentlike central section of the roof—presaging Denver Airport—brings light into the arena during daylight hours. At night, interior light penetrates the glass-block exterior walls that function as a beacon for the approaching crowds. Inside, the building's polygonal footprint transitions into an oval amphitheater. This building received a 1984 American Institute of Architects Honor Award. In 2004 the Iowa Chapter of the AIA named Carver-Hawkeye Arena as one of the top one hundred buildings erected in the state of Iowa in the twentieth century.

230

Unlike Hancher Auditorium's interior-exposed space frame, Carver-Hawkeye Arena celebrates architectonic structure as an aesthetic component of the building's exterior profile.

Lloyd Hamrol's *Stonerise* (1983), a curving wall of monolithic blocks of Iowa limestone, refers to the traditional materials and construction techniques of the Roman Colosseum, Carver-Hawkeye Arena's ancient prototype.

This major addition to Carver-Hawkeye Arena makes a neo-Modernist statement in homage to the original award-winning sports facility.

For that reason, great care was given to the design of the major addition of 2012, which included a basketball practice court, administrative offices, and a hospitality space. Inspired by the original Caudill Rowlett Scott design, the architects made a significant neo-Modernist architectural statement, notwithstanding the utilitarian nature of the program and the irregular topography of the site—all without compromising the integrity of the main building. A sinuous three-story tinted-glass curtain wall—raised on pilotis—masks the Brutalist structure behind. The pronounced articulation of the grid pattern of the glass panes suggests a Miesian rigor but perhaps filtered through the work of his progeny at the Illinois Institute of Technology. The sweeping lower section of Chicago's famed Mies-inspired Lake Shore Tower may have been the immediate inspiration.

Karro Athletics Hall of Fame, 2002

ARCHITECT: HLKB ARCHITECTURE, DES MOINES, IOWA

Celebrating the history of University of Iowa athletics, the Roy G. Karro Building houses the University of Iowa Athletics Hall of Fame, an anchor for the Athletics Campus. Since its construction, the area around it has been further developed with the addition of a new tennis and recreation facility, a soccer stadium, and the relocated Grant Field hockey stadium. The Hall of Fame makes the achievements of University athletics accessible to the public—including Nile Kinnick's famed Heisman Trophy.

The building itself, constructed of cast-in-place concrete, exposed structural steel, and standing seam metal roofing, is formally tied to

The materials used for the construction of the Karro Athletics Hall of Fame are typical of those used in athletic venues.

the sporting facilities celebrated within. While the design is contemporary, it recalls a spectrum of athletic venues in both form and choice of materials. The three-story atrium not only orients the building toward the University's Finkbine Golf Course, but its broad expanse of glazing also accentuates the Hall of Fame's message of welcome. Approaching visitors see in and light streams out, turning the glass into a marquee by night. The building includes subgrade support and service space, a three-story atrium, meeting rooms, and two levels of display space. Topping the entire structure, an interactive area allows young fans to practice shooting baskets and kicking field goals. The rigorously geometrical façade with four square central bays, each with a smoked-glass curtain wall and crisscrossed with tie rods, gives the building much of its unpretentious appearance. Brutalist end-bay walls continue the geometry and contain the building's horizontal composition. The site, adjacent to a protected wetland, was developed with green architectural practices in mind. Runoff is controlled by a meadow wetlands pond that also maintains an ecological balance between plant and animal wildlife. Landscaping with native prairie grasses and the use of drainage swales in the parking lot also minimize the Hall of Fame's environmental impact.

University of Iowa Research Park (Oakdale)

The Oakdale Campus, now referred to as the University of Iowa Research Park, was first developed in 1904 with a state appropriation for a tuberculosis treatment center. This facility, intended to treat patients in an isolated pastoral setting, was a series of wooden cottages set among the plot's majestic oak trees. A permanent brick sanatorium was added to the site in 1917.

Since 1965 Oakdale has been administered by the University of Iowa. Now a research campus, its 250 acres border the University of Iowa Research Park, a venture aimed at incubating new research businesses and nurturing corporate relationships with the University. The passing decades have seen a dramatic increase in density in the corridor connecting Iowa City and Cedar Rapids, and this Coralville neighborhood has become home to major University and commercial research endeavors. Yet parts of this formerly isolated campus, eight miles north and west of the Main Campus, still maintain elements of the original bucolic setting.

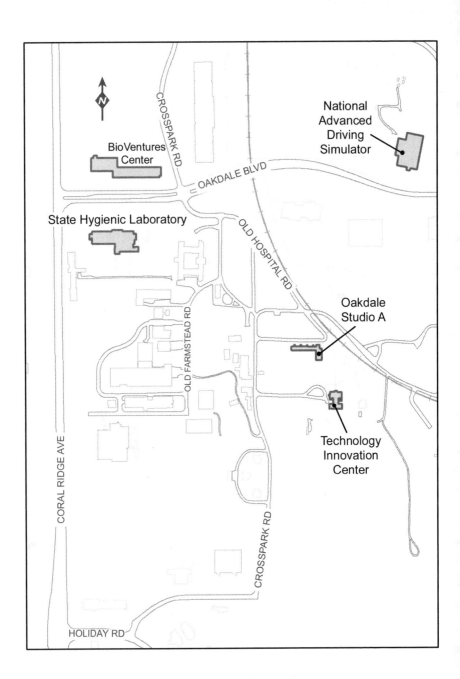

State Hygienic Laboratory at the University of Iowa, 2010

ARCHITECT: OPN ARCHITECTS, CEDAR RAPIDS, IOWA,

WITH CUH2A/HDR ARCHITECTURE

Prior to completion of the state-supported State Hygienic Laboratory, the program was housed in Oakdale Hall, originally constructed as a tuberculosis sanatorium in 1917. Outdated facilities gave way to a state-of-the-art assembly of labs and both publicly and privately supported spaces. The program serves the entire state of Iowa with active outreach and evaluation services. The site for the building was selected in tandem with the soon-to-follow BioVentures building to the north to create a gateway to the emerging University of Iowa Research Park. Additionally, the two buildings would serve as the context for future development projects in the park, setting the tone for exterior materials and massing.

A varied palette of materials—buff masonry, corrugated gray metal, white aluminum, green-tinted glazing—expresses the distinct

The many functions of the State Hygienic Laboratory are reflected in the varied geometry and material of the composition, long and low across the horizon.

functions of the interior volumes. The glass curtain wall at ground level, recessed behind concrete piers, defines the more public office space. The ribbon windows of the masonry-clad second floor indicate the secured laboratory facilities running the entire length of the building, whereas the less formal gray ribbed metal sheathing covers the circulation stairs and the mechanicals on the third floor. This is the Postmodern iteration of Louis Sullivan's dictum that form follows function. A white-paneled and asymmetrically positioned cubic space—with oversize reticulated glass panes—interrupts the horizontal sweep of the whole composition and announces the main public entrance. The low profile of the building allows it to settle harmoniously into its prairie setting.

BioVentures Center, 2010

ARCHITECT: OPN ARCHITECTS, CEDAR RAPIDS, IOWA

The University of Iowa Research Park, long known as the Oakdale Campus, is positioned near the center of the fast-developing corridor between Iowa City and Cedar Rapids. Commercial attention to this area of Coralville, which has slowly developed as a University-themed office and research campus over the decades, has recently increased. The creation of BioVentures and the State Hygienic Laboratory at the eastern intersection of Oakdale Boulevard and the bustling Highway 965 forms a gateway to the park. Both designed by the same local architect, OPN, they also establish a palette of building materials that serves to guide future development of the park. Previously, buildings added incrementally over the years had formed a checkerboard of disconnected buildings and designs. BioVentures sets forth a new con-

The BioVentures Center in the UI Research Park combines high-tech and farmstead imagery in its design.

text that will help to weave the park development together. The building itself hosts new and emerging companies that most often grow out of the University. Those companies utilize their time in the facility to hone their business, work with other adjacent start-up companies, and benefit from services offered by the Research Park staff. Many graduate from the building and expand to new facilities both in the Research Park and in the community.

The long two- and three-story composition of the BioVentures Center complements the low profile of the State Hygienic Laboratory across the street. Here the initially intended references to the rural landscape setting are even more pronounced, with the evident inspiration of the materials and scale of the vernacular architecture of the midwestern farmstead. The slatted screening of the setback west wing and the ribbed, folded-over roof of the east wing suggest the ubiquitous corncribs and equipment sheds of the agricultural scene. Simple geometry dominates, especially in the red Cor-ten steel–framed cubic opening that transverses the east wing and marks the building's main entrance. The curtain walls of this minimalist space allow a view through the building to the country landscape toward the north and the similar opening in the Hygienic Laboratory toward the south. The architects liken this to a barn with its ample doors open at each end. Curiously, notwithstanding the allusions to farmstead architecture, the building still projects a high-tech feel appropriate to its function as an incubator for emergent biotech companies.

Oakdale Hall, 1917 (razed, 2011)

ARCHITECT: UNKNOWN

PREVIOUS NAME: OAKDALE STATE TUBERCULOSIS SANATORIUM

At the height of its use as a sanatorium in the late 1940s, Oakdale Hall provided care for up to 400 inpatients each year. With the development of streptomycin in 1944, the regimen for which the sanatorium was designed radically changed, the number served gradually waned, and in 1965 the entire Oakdale Campus and its facilities

An aerial photograph best shows the many components of Oakdale Hall—at its core was the former Oakdale State Tuberculosis Sanatorium.

became part of the University of Iowa. Pulmonary and tuberculosis care was finally transferred to the University of Iowa Hospitals and Clinics in 1981. Afterward, Oakdale Hall became home to a variety of University programs, including the State Hygienic Laboratory and the Obermann Center for Advanced Studies.

Oakdale Hall was built as five red-brick blocks with the center section slightly recessed. In the archival aerial photograph taken from the southwest, those five pavilions—all in a line—are seen near the center of the aggregation of buildings. A virtually ornament-free structure, it was aimed solely at providing the care needed by the patients. The ample windows on three stories opened onto long, narrow wards where patients' beds were located for maximum direct exposure to light and air—all year round. Sunlight was deemed especially efficacious—a top-floor solarium and parallel sidewalks in the courtyard provided patient exposure. While that original plan can be appreciated in aerial views, the building's character was altered significantly by a series of additions over the decades. The 1937 administrative wing to the west is easily discerned, as it angles out of alignment with the original building. The wedge-shaped section at the center is an auditorium used to provide entertainment for the patients. The State Hygienic Laboratory later occupied the two wings to the southeast.

Oakdale Studio A, 1950

ARCHITECT: MORGAN AND GELATT, BURLINGTON, IOWA

PREVIOUS NAME: OAKDALE EMPLOYEE APARTMENT BUILDING

The Oakdale State Tuberculosis Sanatorium required housing for support personnel—physicians, nurses, medical aides, and administrative staff. Studio A was one of the ancillary residential buildings erected for employees; construction took place simultaneously with the Crosspark Road project of duplex apartments to the west, intended for the sanatorium's doctors. The original structure included twenty-four family units and twenty-six "bachelor units." An addition of the early 1960s increased its capacity by another twelve units. Today the building houses primarily faculty artist studios.

The International style Modernism of Studio A makes a fitting aesthetic match to the building's function and context; the total elimination of ornament expresses the practical considerations of a state-funded undertaking. (It would be another fifteen years before Oakdale

Oakdale Studio A holds the distinction of being the oldest Modernist building on the University of Iowa campus.

would be transferred to the University.) It also reveals the alliance between low-budget projects and stripped-down Modernism. The architect, however, has found inspiration in Walter Gropius's 1920s Bauhaus in Dessau, Germany—simple asymmetrically massed blocks reinterpreted in red brick. The building's interest lies in the variation of elemental geometries, an aesthetic option that still has architectural concerns beyond cost-effectiveness. Ferro-concrete balconies and porch canopies create projecting planes, and the grid geometry of the stone-clad stair tower's glazing provides a nodal point where the two wings of apartments join. In Oakdale Studio A, the apartment building reflects Gropius's vision of a "machine for living." Its uncompromising design predates by one year the Communications Center, the first International style building on the Main Campus, and thus holds a position of note within the history of campus architecture.

Technology Innovation Center, 1924

ARCHITECT: UNKNOWN

PREVIOUS NAME: MEDICAL ADMISSIONS BUILDING

As part of the Oakdale State Tuberculosis Sanatorium, the Medical Admissions Building processed new patients for treatment. In 1937, the construction of a new medical admissions wing on the sanatorium proper made that function obsolete, and the building was converted into a nurses' dormitory. Decades later, the 1981 incorporation of tubercular patients into the wards of the University of Iowa Hospitals and Clinics freed the building again and, since 1984, it has been home to the Technology Innovation Center. This program, the Uni-

First a medical admissions office for the nearby sanatorium, the building is now the Technology Innovation Center, the business incubator of the University of Iowa Oakdale Research Campus.

versity of Iowa's business incubator, provides laboratory space and technical support to academics and entrepreneurs working in collaboration. Their projects then continue to fruition as new commercial enterprises in the University of Iowa Research Park.

Like Oakdale Hall and its cluster of associated buildings, the Technology Innovation Center is a minimally ornamented red-brick structure. Detailing on the façade is rudimentary with a limestone keystone in the porch's arch, a gabled central dormer, and soldiering of the brick toward the top of the wall. The one exception to this minimalism is the double-armed cross inset at the corners of the main façade. This unusual embellishment is the Cross of Lorraine, sometimes known as the Patriarchal Cross. The crusader Godefroy de Bouillon, Duke of Lorraine, made it his standard after capturing Jerusalem in 1099. In 1920, the American Lung Association adopted the Cross of Lorraine as a symbol of its crusade against tuberculosis. Its incorporation into the design of this building just four years later makes this one of the earliest examples of the architectural use of this symbol.

National Advanced Driving Simulator, 1998

ARCHITECT: NEUMANN MONSON ARCHITECTS, IOWA CITY, IOWA

Built into a slope in the University of Iowa Research Park, the National Advanced Driving Simulator (NADS) is the most sophisticated facility of its kind. The starkly functionalist building accommodates a simulation chamber within which a twenty-four-foot-diameter sphere that contains the vehicle to be tested moves. This laboratory allows University of Iowa researchers, the Iowa Department of Transportation, and private entities throughout the world the opportunity to assess ground vehicles in a setting that nearly precisely approximates real driving conditions.

The advanced technology contained in the National Advanced Driving Simulator is only hinted at in the shedlike Minimalist building that houses it.

The NADS building functions as an assembly of shapes, expressing on its exterior the geometries and masses of the functional units contained within. A largely utilitarian steel-frame structure, the building uses Postmodern accents to add detail to its façade. Differing shades of the corrugated metal siding denote the diverse activities of the building's sections and create visual relationships with other nearby buildings. Small sun shades protecting the office windows also signal the distinction between areas. The clerestory-illuminated entry lobby, with an aluminum-framed glass wall and half-gable steel-frame canopy, uses its choice of forms to convey a message of no-frills welcome to visitors.

George L. Horner,
University Architect and Planner, 1906–1981

Born in Tiskilwa, Illinois, in 1906 and educated at the University of Illinois's School of Architecture, George Horner came to the University of Iowa in 1930. Working from the University architect's office on the third floor of the Old Dental Building on the Pentacrest and later from Gilmore Hall, he gave shape to an architectural and campus planning profile that embodied the aspirations of five University administrations. Walter Jessup was University president when Horner arrived on campus, and he retired almost fifty years later during Willard Boyd's administration. Jessup was the greatest builder in UI history, and Boyd was responsible (more than any other University president) for bringing cutting-edge design and nationally recognized projects to campus. Horner was a key figure in both of those noteworthy periods of University architecture, shepherding the projects of outside architects and producing designs of his own. As architect-in-residence, he was unusually active as a designer through three decades of UI architectural history. In 1946 he took a faculty appointment in the School of Fine Arts while retaining his position as University architect.

Most of Horner's own designs were built during the UI's Depression-construction boom of the 1930s and were associated with federally funded WPA initiatives. The birth of the "Iowa Idea," uniting the study and practice of the fine arts, coincided with Horner's hire and inspired the Arts Campus, which includes some of his finest work. The Art Building, the Theatre Building, and the IMU Pedestrian Bridge were all designed to nurture the arts and connect them to the greater life of campus. Horner was also responsible for that campus's rustic Lagoon Shelter House, a WPA project he collaborated on during the active prewar period.

Horner's architectural training at Illinois was still in the Beaux-Arts tradition but, like his famous classmate, Max Abramovitz, he

The Mechanical Engineering Building of 1932, probably University architect George Horner's most original design, was the first major building on campus to reject any allusion to architectural styles of the past and to have almost no ornamentation except for the minimal Art Deco moldings above the entrance. The plain treatment of the limestone exterior and the metal industrial windows adhere instead to a machine aesthetic to convey the practical discipline it houses.

would have been aware of the machine-aesthetic architecture appearing in Europe during the 1920s. This familiarity is evident in the stark plainness of one of his first UI projects, the Mechanical Engineering Building (1932), whose ornament-free walls and steel industrial windows make it his most radical work. Horner was only twenty-six at the time. When called upon to do so, he could also produce historical revival work such as the neo-Georgian Law Commons of 1935. He was most comfortable, however, with a modest version of the Art Deco or Streamline Moderne which was both frugal and progressive at the same time, as seen in the limestone-tipped brick vertical fins on the façades of Stanley Hydraulics Laboratory and the Theatre Building.

His most ambitious design, the 1936 Art Building, is both revivalist and contemporary at once. The neo-Palladian plan, with arcaded loggias linking the central block to the outlying studio pavilions, alludes to the architecture of the Italian Renaissance, while the stripped-down limestone frontispiece of the river façade looks more to the contemporary Moderne moment, as do most of the interior fixtures. In the late 1950s Horner tried his hand at International style Modernism in the Law Commons addition and the Medical Research Center, perhaps with mixed results, but those designs, too, typify his rather pragmatic and unassuming design mentality.

The importance of Horner's work extends beyond the University of Iowa. As one of the founding members of the Association of University Architects, Horner helped bring prominence to its role in campus planning, and it became the flagship professional organization of campus planners. He served as president of that organization, as well as the Iowa Association of Architects, and only retired from the University in 1979. It was not a retirement from architectural administration, however, as Horner went on to consult for numerous institutions as they set about creating university architect offices of their own. Horner died in Rancho Bernardo, California, in 1981, but his legacy is ever present in the annals of campus planning and the swath of well-designed structures he left at the University of Iowa: Music Building Rehearsal Hall, 1931; Mechanical Engineering Building, 1932; Stanley Hydraulics Laboratory addition: central block and south wing, 1933; Law Commons (later International Center), 1935; Art Building, 1936; Theatre Building, 1936; IMU Pedestrian Bridge, 1936; Motor Pool, 1937; Lagoon Shelter House, 1939; Currier Residence Hall addition: north wing, 1940; South Quadrangle, 1942; Westlawn addition: south extension, 1945; Danforth Chapel, 1952; Parklawn Residence Hall, 1955; Medical Research Center, 1957; Law Commons (later International Center) addition, 1959; and Finkbine Golf Course Clubhouse, 1963.

Buildings

Building Name	Architect / Project Architect	Year	Campus Zone
Adler Journalism Building (Philip D. Adler Journalism & Mass Communication Building)	OPN Architects, Cedar Rapids IA	2005	Main Campus South
Art Building	George Horner, University of Iowa	1936	Arts Campus
Art Building addition: printmaking (east) wing (RAZED)	Harrison & Abramovitz, New York NY/ Neumann Monson Architects, Iowa City IA	1968	Arts Campus
Art Building addition: south wing (RAZED)	Harrison & Abramovitz, New York NY/ Neumann Monson Architects, Iowa City IA	1969	Arts Campus
Art Building addition: ceramics kilns (RAZED)	Harrison & Abramovitz, New York NY/ Neumann Monson Architects, Iowa City IA	1975	Arts Campus
Art Building West	Steven Holl Architects, New York NY/ HLKB Architects, Des Moines IA	2006	Arts Campus
Duane Banks Baseball Stadium	Shive-Hattery, Iowa City IA	1975	Athletics Campus
Becker Communication Studies Building (Samuel L. Becker Communication Studies Building)	Thorson-Brom-Broshar-Snyder, Waterloo IA	1984	Main Campus South
P. Sue Beckwith, M.D., Boathouse	Neumann Monson, Iowa City IA	2009	Main Campus North
Bedell Entrepreneurship Learning Laboratory	Unknown	1929	Main Campus North
Biology Bridge	Siah Armajani, Minneapolis MN/ Brooks Borg Skiles Architecture Engineering, Des Moines IA	2000	Iowa Avenue Campus
Biology Building	Proudfoot & Bird, Des Moines IA	1905	Iowa Avenue Campus
Biology Building addition: Dubuque Street wing	Charles Richardson & Associates, Davenport IA	1965, 1971	Iowa Avenue Campus
Biology Building East	Brooks Borg Skiles Architecture Engineering: William Anderson, Des Moines IA	2000	Iowa Avenue Campus
Biomedical Research Support Facility	Heery International, Iowa City IA	2015	University of Iowa Research Park
BioVentures Center	OPN Architects, Cedar Rapids IA	2010	University of Iowa Research Park
Blank Honors Center	HLKB Architecture, Des Moines IA	2003	Main Campus North
Bowen Science Building	Skidmore Owings & Merrill: Walter Netsch, Chicago IL/ George Horner, University of Iowa	1972	Medical Campus
Bowman House	O. H. Carpenter, Iowa City IA	1921	Main Campus North
Boyd Law Building	Gunnar Birkerts & Associates, Birmingham MI/ Wehner, Pattschull & Pfiffner, Iowa City IA	1986	Near West Campus

Building Name	Architect / Project Architect	Year	Campus Zone
Boyd Tower (UIHC)	HLM Design, Iowa City IA	1976	UIHC Campus
Burge Residence Hall	Charles Altfillisch, Decorah IA	1959	Main Campus North
Burge Residence Hall renovation: dining hall	Rohrbach Carlson, Iowa City IA	2003	Main Campus North
Burge Residence Hall addition: north side	Rohrbach Associates, Iowa City IA	2010	Main Campus North
Calvin Hall	R. S. Finkbine, Des Moines IA	1885	Main Campus North
Calvin Hall addition: north side	Unknown	1927	Main Campus North
Cambus Maintenance Facility	Shive-Hattery, Iowa City IA	1972	Main Campus South
Cambus Maintenance Facility addition: south	Neumann Monson, Iowa City IA	1985	Main Campus South
Cambus Maintenance Facility addition: south side	Neumann Monson, Iowa City IA	2010	Main Campus South
Campus Recreation & Wellness Center	RDG Planning & Design, Des Moines IA	2010	Main Campus South
Carver Biomedical Research Building (Roy J. & Lucille A. Carver Biomedical Research Building)	Payette Associates, Boston MA/ Rohrbach Carlson, Iowa City IA	2005	Medical Campus
Carver-Hawkeye Arena	Caudill Rowlett Scott Architects, Houston TX/ Durrant Group, Dubuque IA	1983	Athletics Campus
Carver-Hawkeye Arena addition & renovation: north	Neumann Monson, Iowa City IA	2012	Athletics Campus
Carver Pavilion (Roy J. Carver Pavilion) (UIHC)	HLM Design, Iowa City IA	1988	UIHC Campus
Center for Disabilities & Development	Charles Richardson & Associates, Davenport IA	1954	Medical Campus
Center for Disabilities & Development addition: south	Altfillisch, Olson, Gray & Thompson Architects, Decorah IA	1965	Medical Campus
Chemistry Building	Proudfoot, Bird & Rawson, Des Moines IA	1922	Main Campus North
Chemistry Building addition: lecture hall	Brown, Healey & Bock, Cedar Rapids IA	1963	Main Campus North
Chemistry Building renovation	Brooks, Borg, Skiles, Des Moines IA	2009	Main Campus North
Chemistry Building addition	Brooks, Borg, Skiles, Des Moines IA	2009	Main Campus North
111 Church Street	Unknown	1925	Main Campus North
Clapp Recital Hall (RAZED)	Harrison & Abramovitz: Max Abramovitz, New York NY/ Neumann Monson Architects, Iowa City IA	1971	Arts Campus
College of Medicine Administration Building	NBBJ, Seattle WA/ HLM Design, Iowa City IA	1991	Medical Campus

Building Name	Architect / Project Architect	Year	Campus Zone
College of Public Health Building	Payette Associates, Boston MA/ Rohrbach Associates, Iowa City IA	2011	Medical Campus
Colloton Pavilion (John W. Colloton Pavilion) (UIHC)	HLM Design, Iowa City IA	1992	UIHC Campus
Communications Center	Brooks Borg, Architects-Engineers, Des Moines IA	1951	Main Campus South
Currier Residence Hall	Proudfoot, Bird & Rawson, Des Moines IA	1914	Main Campus North
Currier Residence Hall addition: southwest wing extension	Unknown	1928	Main Campus North
Currier Residence Hall addition: north wing	George Horner, University of Iowa	1940	Main Campus North
Currier Residence Hall addition: north wing extension	George Horner, University of Iowa	1949	Main Campus North
Currier Residence Hall renovation	George Horner, University of Iowa	1946	Main Campus North
Danforth Chapel	George Horner, University of Iowa	1952	River Valley Campus
Daum Residence Hall	Altfillisch, Olson & Gray, Decorah IA	1964	Main Campus North
Dental Science Building	Smith, Hinchman & Gryls, Detroit MI/ George Horner, University of Iowa	1973	Medical Campus
Dental Science Building addition: west	Invision Architecture, Des Moines IA	2012	Medical Campus
Dey House	Unknown	1857	Main Campus North
Dey House addition: Glenn Schaeffer Library and Archives	OPN Architects, Cedar Rapids IA	2006	Main Campus North
Eckstein Medical Research Building (John W. Eckstein Medical Research Building)	NBBJ, Seattle WA/ HLM Design, Iowa City IA	1989	Medical Campus
Engineering Research Facility	Brooks Borg & Skiles, Architects-Engineers, Des Moines IA	1986	Main Campus South
English-Philosophy Building	Sasaki, Walker & Associates, Watertown MA/Prall Architects, Des Moines IA	1966	River Valley Campus
Field House	Proudfoot, Rawson & Souers, Des Moines IA	1927	Near West Campus
Field House addition: Athletic Office Building	George Horner, University of Iowa, with Charles Altfillisch, Decorah IA	1955	Near West Campus
Field House addition & renovation: South Gym	Bussard Dikis Associates, Des Moines IA	1984	Near West Campus
Field House renovation	Unknown	1995	Near West Campus
Finkbine Golf Course Clubhouse	George Horner, University of Iowa	1963	Athletics Campus
Finkbine Golf Course Clubhouse renovation	Nowsyz & Associates, Iowa City IA	1986	Athletics Campus

Building Name	Architect / Project Architect	Year	Campus Zone
General Hospital (UIHC)	Proudfoot, Rawson, Souers & Thomas, Des Moines IA	1928	UIHC Campus
General Hospital (UIHC) addition: multiple	HLM Design, Iowa City IA	1976	UIHC Campus
Gerdin Athletic Learning Center (Russell & Ann Gerdin Athletic Learning Center)	OPN Architects, Cedar Rapids IA	2003	Near West Campus
Gilmore Hall	Proudfoot & Bird, Des Moines IA	1910	Main Campus North
Gilmore Hall addition: 3rd & 4th floors	Unknown	1961	Main Campus North
Gilmore Hall renovation	Unknown	1966	Main Campus North
Gilmore Hall renovation	Baldwin White Architects, Des Moines IA	1995	Main Campus North
Halsey Hall	Proudfoot, Bird & Rawson, Des Moines IA	1915	Main Campus North
Halsey Hall addition: west wing	Keffer & Jones, Des Moines IA	1952	Main Campus North
Hancher Auditorium (replacement)	Pelli Clarke Pelli Architects, New Haven CT/ OPN Architects, Cedar Rapids IA	2016	Arts Campus
Hancher Auditorium (RAZED)	Harrison & Abramovitz: Max Abramovitz, New York NY/ Neumann Monson Architects, Iowa City IA	1972	Arts Campus
Stew and LeNore Hansen Football Performance Center	Substance Architecture, Des Moines IA	2013	Athletics Campus
Hardin Library for the Health Sciences	Skidmore Owings & Merrill: Walter Netsch, Chicago IL/ George Horner, University of Iowa	1974	Medical Campus
Hawkeye Court Apartments (RAZED)	Emery-Prall Associates, Des Moines IA	1967	Athletics Campus
Hawkeye Drive Apartments	Dane D. Morgan & Associates, Burlington IA	1959	Athletics Campus
Hawkeye Tennis & Recreation Complex	Neumann Monson, Iowa City IA	2006	Athletics Campus
Hawkeye Tennis & Recreation Complex addition: indoor turf	Shive-Hattery, Iowa City IA	2014	Athletics Campus
Hillcrest Residence Hall	Seth J. Temple, Davenport IA	1939	Near West Campus
Hillcrest Residence Hall addition: PWA Lobby	Seth J. Temple, Davenport IA	1940	Near West Campus
Hillcrest Residence Hall addition: south	Seth J. Temple – Arthur Temple Architects, Davenport IA	1951	Near West Campus
Hillcrest Residence Hall addition: southwest	Seth J. Temple – Arthur Temple Architects, Davenport IA	1956	Near West Campus
Hillcrest Residence Hall addition: dining hall	Tinsley, Higgins, Lighter & Lyon, Des Moines IA	1961	Near West Campus

Building Name	Architect / Project Architect	Year	Campus Zone
Hoak Family Golf Complex (James M. Hoak Family Golf Complex)	Substance Architecture, Des Moines IA	2012	Athletics Campus
Hope Lodge	Plunkett Raysich Architects, Madison WI	2007	Athletics Campus
Hospital Parking Ramp 1	Brown, Healey & Bock, Cedar Rapids IA	1968	UIHC Campus
Hospital Parking Ramp 2 (replacement)	Heery International, Iowa City IA	2016	UIHC Campus
Hospital Parking Ramp 2 (RAZED)	Walker Parking, Minneapolis MN/ Brown, Healey & Bock, Cedar Rapids IA	1978	UIHC Campus
Hospital Parking Ramp 3	Neumann Monson Architects, Iowa City IA	1988	Athletics Campus
Hydraulics East Annex	Shive-Hattery, Iowa City IA	1975	Main Campus South
Hydraulics Model Annex	Shive-Hattery, Iowa City IA	1982	Main Campus South
Hydraulics Wave Basin Facility	Neumann Monson, Iowa City IA	2010	University of Iowa Research Park
Hydraulics Wind Tunnel Annex	Shive-Hattery, Iowa City IA	1984	Main Campus South
Indoor practice facility (RAZED)	University of Iowa Architect's Office	1986	Athletics Campus
Information Technology Facility	Savage-Ver Ploeg & Associates, West Des Moines IA	2011	University of Iowa Research Park
Institute for Orthopedics, Sports Medicine & Rehabilitation	Heery International, Iowa City IA	2009	Athletics Campus
Institute for Rural & Environmental Health	Unknown	1967	University of Iowa Research Park
Institute for Rural & Environmental Health addition: north	Brown, Healey & Bock, Cedar Rapids IA	1972	University of Iowa Research Park
International Center (RAZED)	George Horner, University of Iowa	1935	Arts Campus
International Center addition: south block	George Horner, University of Iowa	1959	Arts Campus
Iowa Advanced Technology Laboratories	Frank O. Gehry, Los Angeles CA/ HLKB Architecture, Des Moines IA	1992	River Valley Campus
Iowa Avenue Bridge	Proudfoot & Bird, Des Moines IA	1916	River Valley Campus
Iowa Memorial Union	Boyd & Moore, Des Moines IA	1925	River Valley Campus
Iowa Memorial Union addition	Tinsley, Higgins, Lighter & Lyon, Des Moines IA	1955	River Valley Campus
Iowa Memorial Union addition: Iowa House	Tinsley, Higgins, Lighter & Lyon, Des Moines IA	1965	River Valley Campus
Iowa Memorial Union renovation	Bussard Dikis Associates, Des Moines IA	1988	River Valley Campus
Iowa Memorial Union addition	Burt, Hill, Kosar, Rittelmann Associates, Boston MA/ OPN Architects, Cedar Rapids IA	2007	River Valley Campus
Iowa Memorial Union renovation	Rohrbach Associates, Iowa City IA	2015	River Valley Campus

Building Name	Architect / Project Architect	Year	Campus Zone
Iowa Memorial Union Parking Ramp	Tinsley, Higgins, Lighter & Lyon, Des Moines IA	1964	Main Campus North
Iowa Memorial Union Pedestrian Bridge (IMU Bridge)	George Horner, University of Iowa	1936	River Valley Campus
Jacobson Athletic Building (Richard O. Jacobson Athletic Building)	HLKB Architecture, Des Moines IA	1995	Athletics Campus
Jefferson Building	H. L. Stevens & Company, Chicago IL	1913	Main Campus North
Jessup Hall	Proudfoot, Bird & Rawson, Des Moines IA	1924	Pentacrest
Karro Athletics Hall of Fame (Roy G. Karro Building/ Athletics Hall of Fame)	HLKB Architecture, Des Moines IA	2002	Athletics Campus
Kinnick Stadium	Proudfoot, Rawson, Souers & Thomas, Des Moines IA	1929	Athletics Campus
Kinnick Stadium renovation & addition: press & sky boxes, south stands	HNTB, Kansas City MO/ Neumann Monson Architects, Iowa City IA	2006	Athletics Campus
Kuhl House	Robert Hutchinson, Iowa City IA	ca. 1840	Arts Campus
Kuhl House renovation	University of Iowa Architect's Office	1987	Arts Campus
Lagoon Shelter House	George Horner, University of Iowa	1939	Arts Campus
Levitt Center for University Advancement	Gwathmey Siegel & Associates: Charles Gwathmey, New York NY/ Brooks Borg Skiles Architecture Engineering, Des Moines IA	1998	Arts Campus
Lindquist Center	Skidmore Owings & Merrill: Walter Netsch, Chicago IL/ George Horner, University of Iowa	1973	Main Campus South
Lindquist Center addition: north building	Skidmore Owings & Merrill: Walter Netsch, Chicago IL	1980	Main Campus South
Macbride Hall	Proudfoot & Bird, Des Moines IA	1908	Pentacrest
Macbride Hall renovation: Iowa Hall	McConnell-Stevely-Anderson Architects & Planners, Cedar Rapids IA	1983	Pentacrest
MacLean Hall	Proudfoot, Bird & Rawson, Des Moines IA	1912	Pentacrest
MacLean Hall addition	Proudfoot, Bird & Rawson, Des Moines IA	1920	Pentacrest
Madison Street Residence Hall	Rohrbach Associates, Iowa City IA	2017	Main Campus North
Madison Street Services Building	OPN Architects, Cedar Rapids IA	2007	Main Campus South
Ronald McDonald House	HLM Design, Iowa City IA	1985	Athletics Campus
Ronald McDonald House addition	Neumann Monson Architects, Iowa City IA	2001	Athletics Campus

Building Name	Architect / Project Architect	Year	Campus Zone
Main Library	Keffer & Jones, Des Moines IA	1951	Main Campus South
Main Library addition: southwest	Parish & Richardson Architects, Davenport IA	1961	Main Campus South
Main Library addition: southeast	Charles Richardson & Associates, Davenport IA	1965	Main Campus South
Main Library addition: south extension	Charles Richardson & Associates, Davenport IA	1971	Main Campus South
Mayflower Residence Hall	CPMI, Des Moines IA	1968	Main Campus North
Medical Education & Research Facility	Payette Associates, Boston MA/ Baldwin White Architects, Des Moines IA	2002	Medical Campus
Medical Education & Research Facility addition: Carver Biomedical Research Building	Payette Associates, Boston MA/ Rohrbach Carlson, Iowa City IA	2005	Medical Campus
Medical Education Building	Proudfoot, Bird & Rawson, Des Moines IA	1919	Medical Campus
Medical Education Building addition: north side	George Horner, University of Iowa/ Dane D. Morgan & Associates, Burlington IA	1961	Medical Campus
Medical Laboratories	Proudfoot, Rawson & Souers, Des Moines IA	1927	UIHC Campus
Medical Research Center	George Horner, University of Iowa/ Tinsley, Higgins, Lighter & Lyon, Des Moines IA	1957	Medical Campus
Medical Research Center addition: vertical expansion	Durrant Group, Dubuque IA	1979	Medical Campus
Medical Research Facility	Dane D. Morgan & Associates, Burlington IA	1964	UIHC Campus
Melrose Avenue Parking Facility (Hospital Parking Ramp 4)	HLKB Architecture, Des Moines IA	2005	UIHC Campus
Motor Pool (RAZED)	George Horner, University of Iowa	1937	Main Campus South
Multi-Tenant Facility	HLKB Architecture, Des Moines IA	1990	University of Iowa Research Park
Multi-Tenant Facility addition: north side	HLKB Architecture, Des Moines IA	2002	University of Iowa Research Park
Museum of Art (former)	Harrison & Abramovitz: Max Abramovitz, New York NY/ Neumann Monson Architects, Iowa City IA	1969	Arts Campus
Music West – aka Museum of Art addition: Carver wing	Harrison & Abramovitz, New York NY/ Neumann Monson Architects, Iowa City IA	1975	Arts Campus
Music West – aka Museum of Art addition: Alumni Center	Abramovitz-Harris-Kingsland, New York NY/ Neumann Monson Architects, Iowa City IA	1984	Arts Campus
National Advanced Driving Simulator	Neumann Monson Architects, Iowa City IA	1998	University of Iowa Research Park

Building Name	Architect / Project Architect	Year	Campus Zone
Newton Road Parking Ramp	HLKB Architecture, Des Moines IA	2002	Medical Campus
North Campus Parking	HLKB Architecture, Des Moines IA	1990	Main Campus North
North Hall	Proudfoot, Bird & Rawson, Des Moines IA	1925	Main Campus North
Nursing Building	Charles Herbert & Associates, Des Moines IA/ George Horner, University of Iowa	1971	Medical Campus
Oakdale Hall (RAZED)	Unknown	1917	University of Iowa Research Park
Oakdale Hall addition: nurses' dormitory	Unknown	1924	University of Iowa Research Park
Oakdale Hall addition: medical administration	Unknown	1937	University of Iowa Research Park
Oakdale Hall addition: auditorium & clinic	Unknown	1951	University of Iowa Research Park
Oakdale Hall addition: patients' ward	Unknown	1954	University of Iowa Research Park
Oakdale Hall addition: kitchen & rehabilitation	Unknown	1958	University of Iowa Research Park
Oakdale Hall renovation	Unknown	1964	University of Iowa Research Park
Oakdale Studio A	Morgan & Gelatt, Burlington IA	1950	University of Iowa Research Park
Oakdale Studio A addition: 12 units	Morgan & Gelatt, Burlington IA	1963	University of Iowa Research Park
Old Capitol	John Francis Rague, Springfield IL/ Chauncey Swan, Iowa City IA	1842	Pentacrest
Old Capitol renovation	Proudfoot, Bird & Rawson, Des Moines IA	1924	Pentacrest
Old Capitol restoration	Ferry & Henderson, Springfield IL/ Viggo M. Jensen, Iowa City IA	1974	Pentacrest
Old Capitol restoration	OPN Architects, Cedar Rapids IA	2006	Pentacrest
Pappajohn Biomedical Discovery Building (John & Mary Pappajohn Biomedical Discovery Building)	Gwathmey Siegel & Associates: Charles Gwathmey, New York NY/ Rohrbach Associates, Iowa City IA	2014	Medical Campus
Pappajohn Business Building (John Pappajohn Business Building)	Architectural Resources, Cambridge MA/Neumann Monson Architects, Iowa City IA	1993	Main Campus North
Pappajohn Pavilion (UIHC)	HLM Design, Iowa City IA	2000	UIHC Campus
Parklawn Residence Hall	George Horner, University of Iowa	1955	Arts Campus
Mary Louise Petersen Residence Hall	Rohrbach Associates, Iowa City IA	2015	Near West Campus
Pharmaceutical Sciences Research Building	Brooks Borg Skiles Architecture Engineering: William Anderson, Des Moines IA	1996	Medical Campus

Building Name	Architect / Project Architect	Year	Campus Zone
Pharmacy Building	Woodburn O'Neil Architects & Engineers, West Des Moines IA	1961	Medical Campus
Pharmacy Building addition: Wurster Center for Pharmaceutical Technology	Brooks Borg Skiles Architecture Engineering: William Anderson, Des Moines IA	1996	Medical Campus
Phillips Hall	Woodburn O'Neil Architects & Engineers, West Des Moines IA	1965	Iowa Avenue Campus
Pomerantz Center	Savage-Ver Ploeg & Associates, West Des Moines IA	2005	Main Campus North
Pomerantz Family Pavilion (UIHC)	HLM Design, Iowa City IA (includes the Center for Excellence in Image-Guided Radiation Therapy)	2005	UIHC Campus
Pomerantz Family Pavilion (UIHC) addition: Ambulatory Surgery Center	Hammel, Green & Abrahamson, Minneapolis MN	2014	UIHC Campus
Power Plant	Proudfoot, Rawson & Souers, Des Moines IA	1928	River Valley Campus
Power Plant addition: central & south wings	George Horner, University of Iowa	1933	River Valley Campus
Power Plant addition: Boiler 11	Stanley Consultants, Muscatine IA	1988	River Valley Campus
Power Plant addition: east side	PRVN Consultants, North Liberty IA	2014	River Valley Campus
President's Residence	Proudfoot & Bird, Des Moines IA	1908	Main Campus North
President's Residence renovation	Durrant Group, Dubuque IA	1988	Main Campus North
President's Residence addition: garage, east extension	HLKB Architecture, Des Moines IA	2005	Main Campus North
Quadrangle Residence Hall (RAZED)	Proudfoot, Bird & Rawson, Des Moines IA	1920	Near West Campus
Quadrangle Residence Hall addition: inner ring	Proudfoot, Rawson & Souers, Des Moines IA	1925	Near West Campus
Quadrangle Residence Hall renovation	Unknown	1935	Near West Campus
Quadrangle Residence Hall addition: cafeteria	Unknown	1956	Near West Campus
Quadrangle Residence Hall renovation	Stewart Robinson Laffin	1964	Near West Campus
Recreation Building	Porter/Brierly Associates, Des Moines IA	1970	Athletics Campus
Recreation Building addition: office	Porter/Brierly Associates, Des Moines, IA	1981	Athletics Campus
Recreation Building addition: link & office	Stanley Consultants, Muscatine IA	1985	Athletics Campus
Rienow Residence Hall	Smith, Voorhees & Jensen, Des Moines IA, Sioux City IA	1966	Near West Campus
Schaeffer Hall	Proudfoot & Bird, Des Moines IA	1902	Pentacrest
Schaeffer Hall renovation	HLKB Architecture, Des Moines IA	1998	Pentacrest

Building Name	Architect / Project Architect	Year	Campus Zone
Sciences Library (name change)	Proudfoot & Bird, Des Moines IA	1902	Iowa Avenue Campus
Sciences Library renovation	Brooks Borg Skiles Architecture Engineering, Des Moines IA	2004	Iowa Avenue Campus
Seamans Center for the Engineering Arts & Sciences	Proudfoot & Bird, Des Moines IA	1905	Main Campus South
Seamans Center for the Engineering Arts & Sciences addition: materials testing lab	UI Mechanical Engineering Professor B. P. Fleming	1907	Main Campus South
Seamans Center for the Engineering Arts & Sciences addition: Mechanical Engineering Building	George Horner, University of Iowa	1932	Main Campus South
Seamans Center for the Engineering Arts & Sciences addition: radio	George Horner, University of Iowa	1939	Main Campus South
Seamans Center for the Engineering Arts & Sciences addition: electrical engineering	N. Clifford Prall, Des Moines IA	1964	Main Campus South
Seamans Center for the Engineering Arts & Sciences addition: south wing	Anshen + Allen, Los Angeles CA/ Neumann Monson Architects, Iowa City IA	2001	Main Campus South
Seamans Center for the Engineering Arts & Sciences addition: south annex	BNIM, Des Moines IA	2018	Main Campus South
Seashore Hall	Josselyn & Taylor, Cedar Rapids IA	1899	Iowa Avenue Campus
Seashore Hall addition: east wing, porch, main entrance	Proudfoot & Bird, Des Moines IA	1908	Iowa Avenue Campus
Seashore Hall addition: north pavilions	Proudfoot, Bird & Rawson, Des Moines IA	1915	Iowa Avenue Campus
Shambaugh House	O. H. Carpenter, Iowa City IA	1900	Main Campus North
Slater Residence Hall	Smith, Voorhees & Jensen, Des Moines IA/Sioux City IA	1968	Near West Campus
South Quadrangle	George Horner, University of Iowa	1942	Near West Campus
Spence Laboratories of Psychology	Louis C. Kingston, Davenport IA	1968	Iowa Avenue Campus
Stadium at Robert L. Pearl Softball Field	HLM Design, Iowa City IA	1999	Athletics Campus

Building Name	Architect / Project Architect	Year	Campus Zone
Stanley Hydraulics Laboratory (C. Maxwell Stanley Hydraulics Laboratory)	Proudfoot, Rawson & Souers, Des Moines IA	1928	River Valley Campus
Stanley Hydraulics Laboratory addition: central & south wings	George Horner, University of Iowa	1933	River Valley Campus
Stanley Hydraulics Laboratory renovation	OPN Architects, Cedar Rapids IA	2002	River Valley Campus
Stanley Residence Hall & Ecklund Lounge	Altfillisch, Olson, Gray & Thompson, Decorah IA	1966	Main Campus North
State Hygienic Laboratory at the University of Iowa	OPN Architects, Cedar Rapids IA, with CUH2A/HDR Architecture	2010	University of Iowa Research Park
Stuit Hall (Old Music Building) (name change)	Proudfoot, Bird & Rawson, Des Moines IA	1918	Iowa Avenue Campus
Stuit Hall addition: rehearsal hall (RAZED)	George Horner, University of Iowa	1931	Iowa Avenue Campus
Stuit Hall renovation	BNIM, Des Moines IA	2010	Iowa Avenue Campus
Technology Innovation Center	Unknown	1924	University of Iowa Research Park
Theatre Building	George Horner, University of Iowa	1936	Arts Campus
Theatre Building addition: David L. Thayer Theatre & Theatre B	Abramovitz-Harris-Kingsland: Max Abramovitz, New York NY/ Neumann Monson Architects, Iowa City IA	1985	Arts Campus
Theatre Building addition: flood recovery	Neumann Monson, Iowa City IA	2015	Arts Campus
Trowbridge Hall	Proudfoot, Bird & Rawson, Des Moines IA	1918	Main Campus North
University Capitol Centre	Unknown	1981	Main Campus South
University Capitol Centre addition: School of Music	Neumann Monson, Iowa City IA	2010	Main Campus South
University of Iowa Stead Family Children's Hospital	Foster + Partners, UK/Heery International, Iowa City IA/Stanley Beaman & Sears, Atlanta GA	2016	UIHC Campus
University Services Building	OPN Architects, Cedar Rapids IA	1999	Main Campus South
Van Allen Hall	Durrant Group, Dubuque IA	1964	Iowa Avenue Campus
Van Allen Hall addition: east extension	Durrant Group, Dubuque IA	1970	Iowa Avenue Campus
Visual Arts Building	Steven Holl Architects, New York NY/ BNIM, Des Moines IA	2016	Arts Campus
Voxman Music Building (replacement)	LMN Architects, Seattle WA/ Neumann Monson, Iowa City IA	2016	Main Campus South
Voxman Music Building (RAZED)	Harrison & Abramovitz: Max Abramovitz, New York NY/ Neumann Monson Architects, Iowa City IA	1971	Arts Campus
Water Plant	Stanley Engineering, Muscatine IA	1963	River Valley Campus
Wendell Johnson Speech & Hearing Center	Woodburn O'Neil Architects & Engineers, West Des Moines IA	1967	Medical Campus

263

Building Name	Architect / Project Architect	Year	Campus Zone
West Campus Transportation Center	Neumann Monson, Iowa City IA	2012	Athletics Campus
Westlawn	Proudfoot, Bird & Rawson, Des Moines IA	1919	Medical Campus
Westlawn renovation	Proudfoot, Rawson & Souers, Des Moines IA	1928	Medical Campus
Westlawn addition: south extension	George Horner, University of Iowa	1945	Medical Campus
Westlawn addition: Student Health expansion	Baldwin White Architects, Des Moines IA	1996	Medical Campus

Architects

Architect / Project Architect	Building Name	Year	Campus Zone
Abramovitz-Harris-Kingsland, New York NY/ Neumann Monson Architects, Iowa City IA	Music West – aka Museum of Art addition: Alumni Center	1984	Arts Campus
Abramovitz-Harris-Kingsland: Max Abramovitz, New York NY/ Neumann Monson Architects, Iowa City IA	Theatre Building addition: David L. Thayer Theatre & Theatre B	1985	Arts Campus
Altfillisch, Olson, Gray & Thompson, Decorah IA	Stanley Residence Hall & Ecklund Lounge	1966	Main Campus North
Altfillisch, Olson, & Gray, Decorah IA	Daum Residence Hall	1964	Main Campus North
Altfillisch, Olson, Gray & Thompson Architects, Decorah IA	Center for Disabilities & Development addition: south	1965	Medical Campus
Anshen + Allen, Los Angeles CA/ Neumann Monson Architects, Iowa City IA	Seamans Center for the Engineering Arts & Sciences addition: south wing	2001	Main Campus South
Architectural Resources, Cambridge MA/ Neumann Monson Architects, Iowa City IA	Pappajohn Business Building (John Pappajohn Business Building)	1993	Main Campus North
Baldwin White Architects, Des Moines IA	Gilmore Hall renovation	1995	Main Campus North
Baldwin White Architects, Des Moines IA	Westlawn addition: Student Health expansion	1996	Medical Campus
BNIM, Des Moines IA	Stuit Hall renovation	2010	Iowa Avenue Campus
BNIM, Des Moines IA	Seamans Center for the Engineering Arts & Sciences addition: south annex	2018	Main Campus South
Boyd & Moore, Des Moines IA	Iowa Memorial Union	1925	River Valley Campus
Brooks Borg & Skiles, Architects-Engineers, Des Moines IA	Engineering Research Facility	1986	Main Campus South
Brooks Borg Skiles Architecture Engineering, Des Moines IA	Sciences Library renovation	2004	Iowa Avenue Campus
Brooks Borg Skiles Architecture Engineering: William Anderson, Des Moines IA	Pharmaceutical Sciences Research Building	1996	Medical Campus
Brooks Borg Skiles Architecture Engineering: William Anderson, Des Moines IA	Biology Building East	2000	Iowa Avenue Campus

Architect / Project Architect	Building Name	Year	Campus Zone
Brooks Borg, Architects-Engineers, Des Moines IA	Communications Center	1951	Main Campus South
Brooks, Borg, Skiles, Des Moines IA	Chemistry Building renovation	2009	Main Campus North
Brooks, Borg, Skiles, Des Moines IA	Chemistry Building addition	2009	Main Campus North
Brown, Healey & Bock, Cedar Rapids IA	Institute for Rural & Environmental Health addition: north	1972	University of Iowa Research Park
Brown, Healey & Bock, Cedar Rapids IA	Hospital Parking Ramp 1	1968	UIHC Campus
Brown, Healey & Bock, Cedar Rapids IA	Chemistry Building addition: lecture hall	1963	Main Campus North
Burt, Hill, Kosar, Rittelmann Associates, Boston MA/ OPN Architects, Cedar Rapids IA	Iowa Memorial Union addition	2007	River Valley Campus
Bussard Dikis Associates, Des Moines IA	Field House addition & renovation: South Gym	1984	Near West Campus
Bussard Dikis Associates, Des Moines IA	Iowa Memorial Union renovation	1988	River Valley Campus
Caudill Rowlett Scott Architects, Houston TX/ Durrant Group, Dubuque IA	Carver-Hawkeye Arena	1983	Athletics Campus
Charles Altfillisch, Decorah IA	Burge Residence Hall	1959	Main Campus North
Charles Herbert & Associates, Des Moines IA/ George Horner, University of Iowa	Nursing Building	1971	Medical Campus
Charles Richardson & Associates, Davenport IA	Biology Building addition: Dubuque Street wing	1965, 1971	Iowa Avenue Campus
Charles Richardson & Associates, Davenport IA	Center for Disabilities & Development	1954	Medical Campus
Charles Richardson & Associates, Davenport IA	Main Library addition: southeast	1965	Main Campus South
Charles Richardson & Associates, Davenport IA	Main Library addition: south extension	1971	Main Campus South
CPMI, Des Moines IA	Mayflower Residence Hall	1968	Main Campus North
Dane D. Morgan & Associates, Burlington IA	Hawkeye Drive Apartments	1959	Athletics Campus
Dane D. Morgan & Associates, Burlington IA	Medical Research Facility	1964	UIHC Campus
Durrant Group, Dubuque IA	President's Residence renovation	1988	Main Campus North
Durrant Group, Dubuque IA	Van Allen Hall	1964	Iowa Avenue Campus
Durrant Group, Dubuque IA	Van Allen Hall addition: east extension	1970	Iowa Avenue Campus
Durrant Group, Dubuque IA	Medical Research Center addition: vertical expansion	1979	Medical Campus
Emery-Prall Associates, Des Moines IA	Hawkeye Court Apartments (RAZED)	1967	Athletics Campus

266

Architect / Project Architect	Building Name	Year	Campus Zone
Ferry & Henderson, Springfield IL/ Viggo M. Jensen, Iowa City IA	Old Capitol restoration	1974	Pentacrest
Foster + Partners, UK/ Heery International, Iowa City IA/ Stanley Beaman & Sears, Atlanta GA	University of Iowa Stead Family Children's Hospital	2016	UIHC Campus
Frank O. Gehry, Los Angeles CA/ HLKB Architecture, Des Moines IA	Iowa Advanced Technology Laboratories	1992	River Valley Campus
George Horner, University of Iowa	Currier Residence Hall addition: north wing	1940	Main Campus North
George Horner, University of Iowa	Finkbine Golf Course Clubhouse	1963	Athletics Campus
George Horner, University of Iowa	International Center (RAZED)	1935	Arts Campus
George Horner, University of Iowa	International Center addition: south block (RAZED)	1959	Arts Campus
George Horner, University of Iowa	Iowa Memorial Union Pedestrian Bridge (IMU Bridge)	1936	River Valley Campus
George Horner, University of Iowa	Lagoon Shelter House	1939	Arts Campus
George Horner, University of Iowa	Motor Pool (RAZED)	1937	Main Campus South
George Horner, University of Iowa	Parklawn Residence Hall	1955	Arts Campus
George Horner, University of Iowa	Power Plant addition: central & south wings	1933	River Valley Campus
George Horner, University of Iowa	Seamans Center for the Engineering Arts & Sciences addition: Mechanical Engineering Building	1932	Main Campus South
George Horner, University of Iowa	Seamans Center for the Engineering Arts & Sciences addition: radio	1939	Main Campus South
George Horner, University of Iowa	South Quadrangle	1942	Near West Campus
George Horner, University of Iowa	Stanley Hydraulics Laboratory addition: central & south wings	1933	River Valley Campus
George Horner, University of Iowa	Stuit Hall addition: rehearsal hall (RAZED)	1931	Iowa Avenue Campus
George Horner, University of Iowa	Theatre Building	1936	Arts Campus
George Horner, University of Iowa	Westlawn addition: south extension	1945	Medical Campus
George Horner, University of Iowa	Art Building	1936	Arts Campus
George Horner, University of Iowa	Currier Residence Hall addition: north wing extension	1949	Main Campus North

Architect / Project Architect	Building Name	Year	Campus Zone
George Horner, University of Iowa	Currier Residence Hall renovation	1946	Main Campus North
George Horner, University of Iowa	Danforth Chapel	1952	River Valley Campus
George Horner, University of Iowa, with Charles Altfillisch, Decorah IA	Field House addition: Athletic Office Building	1955	Near West Campus
George Horner, University of Iowa/Dane D. Morgan & Associates, Burlington IA	Medical Education Building addition: north side	1961	Medical Campus
George Horner, University of Iowa/ Tinsley, Higgins, Lighter & Lyon, Des Moines IA	Medical Research Center	1957	Medical Campus
Gunnar Birkerts & Associates, Birmingham MI/ Wehner, Pattschull & Pfiffner, Iowa City IA	Boyd Law Building	1986	Near West Campus
Gwathmey Siegel & Associates: Charles Gwathmey, New York NY/ Brooks Borg Skiles Architecture Engineering, Des Moines IA	Levitt Center for University Advancement	1998	Arts Campus
Gwathmey Siegel & Associates: Charles Gwathmey, New York NY/ Rohrbach Associates, Iowa City IA	Pappajohn Biomedical Discovery Building (John & Mary Pappajohn Biomedical Discovery Building)	2014	Medical Campus
H. L. Stevens & Company, Chicago IL	Jefferson Building	1913	Main Campus North
Hammel, Green & Abrahamson, Minneapolis MN	Pomerantz Family Pavilion (UIHC) addition: Ambulatory Surgery Center	2014	UIHC Campus
Harrison & Abramovitz: Max Abramovitz, New York NY/ Neumann Monson Architects, Iowa City IA	Music West – aka Museum of Art (name change)	1969	Arts Campus
Harrison & Abramovitz, New York NY/ Neumann Monson Architects, Iowa City IA	Art Building addition: printmaking (east) wing (RAZED)	1968	Arts Campus
Harrison & Abramovitz, New York NY/ Neumann Monson Architects, Iowa City IA	Art Building addition: south wing (RAZED)	1969	Arts Campus
Harrison & Abramovitz, New York NY/ Neumann Monson Architects, Iowa City IA	Art Building addition: ceramics kilns (RAZED)	1975	Arts Campus

Architect / Project Architect	Building Name	Year	Campus Zone
Harrison & Abramovitz, New York NY/ Neumann Monson Architects, Iowa City IA	Former Museum of Art addition: Carver wing	1975	Arts Campus
Harrison & Abramovitz: Max Abramovitz, New York NY/ Neumann Monson Architects, Iowa City IA	Clapp Recital Hall (RAZED)	1971	Arts Campus
Harrison & Abramovitz: Max Abramovitz, New York NY/ Neumann Monson Architects, Iowa City IA	Hancher Auditorium (RAZED)	1972	Arts Campus
Harrison & Abramovitz: Max Abramovitz, New York NY/ Neumann Monson Architects, Iowa City IA	Voxman Music Building (RAZED)	1971	Arts Campus
Heery International, Iowa City IA	Biomedical Research Support Facility	2015	University of Iowa Research Park
Heery International, Iowa City IA	Hospital Parking Ramp 2 (replacement)	2016	UIHC Campus
Heery International, Iowa City IA	Institute for Orthopedics, Sports Medicine & Rehabilitation	2009	Athletics Campus
HLKB Architecture, Des Moines IA	Blank Honors Center	2003	Main Campus North
HLKB Architecture, Des Moines IA	Jacobson Athletic Building (Richard O. Jacobson Athletic Building)	1995	Athletics Campus
HLKB Architecture, Des Moines IA	Karro Athletics Hall of Fame (Roy G. Karro Building/ Athletics Hall of Fame)	2002	Athletics Campus
HLKB Architecture, Des Moines IA	Melrose Avenue Parking Facility (Hospital Parking Ramp 4)	2005	UIHC Campus
HLKB Architecture, Des Moines IA	Newton Road Parking Ramp	2002	Medical Campus
HLKB Architecture, Des Moines IA	North Campus Parking	1990	Main Campus North
HLKB Architecture, Des Moines IA	President's Residence addition: garage, east extension	2005	Main Campus North
HLKB Architecture, Des Moines IA	Schaeffer Hall renovation	1998	Pentacrest
HLKB Architecture, Des Moines IA	Multi-Tenant Facility	1990	University of Iowa Research Park
HLKB Architecture, Des Moines IA	Multi-Tenant Facility addition: north side	2002	University of Iowa Research Park
HLM Design, Iowa City IA	General Hospital (UIHC) addition: multiple	1976	UIHC Campus
HLM Design, Iowa City IA	Pappajohn Pavilion (UIHC)	2000	UIHC Campus

Architect / Project Architect	Building Name	Year	Campus Zone
HLM Design, Iowa City IA	Ronald McDonald House	1985	Athletics Campus
HLM Design, Iowa City IA	Stadium at Robert L. Pearl Softball Field	1999	Athletics Campus
HLM Design, Iowa City IA	Boyd Tower (UIHC)	1976	UIHC Campus
HLM Design, Iowa City IA	Carver Pavilion (Roy J. Carver Pavilion) (UIHC)	1988	UIHC Campus
HLM Design, Iowa City IA	Colloton Pavilion (John W. Colloton Pavilion) (UIHC)	1992	UIHC Campus
HLM Design, Iowa City IA (includes the Center for Excellence in Image-Guided Radiation Therapy)	Pomerantz Family Pavilion (UIHC)	2005	UIHC Campus
HNTB, Kansas City MO/ Neumann Monson Architects, Iowa City IA	Kinnick Stadium renovation & addition: press & sky boxes, south stands	2006	Athletics Campus
Invision Architecture, Des Moines IA	Dental Science Building addition: west	2012	Medical Campus
John Francis Rague, Springfield IL/ Chauncey Swan, Iowa City IA	Old Capitol	1842	Pentacrest
Josselyn & Taylor, Cedar Rapids IA	Seashore Hall	1899	Iowa Avenue Campus
Keffer & Jones, Des Moines IA	Halsey Hall addition: west wing	1952	Main Campus North
Keffer & Jones, Des Moines IA	Main Library	1951	Main Campus South
LMN Architects, Seattle WA/ Neumann Monson, Iowa City IA	Voxman Music Building (replacement)	2016	Main Campus South
Louis C. Kingston, Davenport IA	Spence Laboratories of Psychology	1968	Iowa Avenue Campus
McConnell-Stevely-Anderson Architects & Planners, Cedar Rapids IA	Macbride Hall renovation: Iowa Hall	1983	Pentacrest
Morgan & Gelatt, Burlington IA	Oakdale Studio A	1950	University of Iowa Research Park
Morgan & Gelatt, Burlington IA	Oakdale Studio A addition: 12 units	1963	University of Iowa Research Park
N. Clifford Prall, Des Moines IA	Seamans Center for the Engineering Arts & Sciences addition: electrical engineering	1964	Main Campus South
NBBJ, Seattle WA/ HLM Design, Iowa City IA	College of Medicine Administration Building	1991	Medical Campus
NBBJ, Seattle WA/ HLM Design, Iowa City IA	Eckstein Medical Research Building (John W. Eckstein Medical Research Building)	1989	Medical Campus
Neumann Monson Architects, Iowa City IA	Hospital Parking Ramp 3	1988	Athletics Campus

Architect / Project Architect	Building Name	Year	Campus Zone
Neumann Monson Architects, Iowa City IA	National Advanced Driving Simulator	1998	University of Iowa Research Park
Neumann Monson Architects, Iowa City IA	Ronald McDonald House addition	2001	Athletics Campus
Neumann Monson, Iowa City IA	Carver-Hawkeye Arena addition & renovation: north	2012	Athletics Campus
Neumann Monson, Iowa City IA	Theatre Building addition: flood recovery	2015	Arts Campus
Neumann Monson, Iowa City IA	University Capitol Centre addition: School of Music	2010	Main Campus South
Neumann Monson, Iowa City IA	West Campus Transportation Center	2012	Athletics Campus
Neumann Monson, Iowa City IA	P. Sue Beckwith, M.D., Boathouse	2009	Main Campus North
Neumann Monson, Iowa City IA	Cambus Maintenance Facility addition: south	1985	Main Campus South
Neumann Monson, Iowa City IA	Cambus Maintenance Facility addition: south side	2010	Main Campus South
Neumann Monson, Iowa City IA	Hawkeye Tennis & Recreation Complex	2006	Athletics Campus
Neumann Monson, Iowa City IA	Hydraulics Wave Basin Facility	2010	University of Iowa Research Park
Nowsyz & Associates, Iowa City IA	Finkbine Golf Course Clubhouse renovation	1986	Athletics Campus
O. H. Carpenter, Iowa City IA	Shambaugh House	1900	Main Campus North
O. H. Carpenter, Iowa City IA	Bowman House	1921	Main Campus North
OPN Architects, Cedar Rapids IA	Stanley Hydraulics Laboratory renovation	2002	River Valley Campus
OPN Architects, Cedar Rapids IA	Gerdin Athletic Learning Center (Russell & Ann Gerdin Athletic Learning Center)	2003	Near West Campus
OPN Architects, Cedar Rapids IA	Madison Street Services Building	2007	Main Campus South
OPN Architects, Cedar Rapids IA	Dey House addition: Glenn Schaeffer Library and Archives	2006	Main Campus North
OPN Architects, Cedar Rapids IA	Old Capitol restoration	2006	Pentacrest
OPN Architects, Cedar Rapids IA	BioVentures Center	2010	University of Iowa Research Park
OPN Architects, Cedar Rapids IA, with CUH2A/HDR Architecture	State Hygienic Laboratory at the University of Iowa	2010	University of Iowa Research Park
OPN Architects, Cedar Rapids IA	University Services Building	1999	Main Campus South
OPN Architects, Cedar Rapids IA	Adler Journalism Building (Philip D. Adler Journalism & Mass Communication Building)	2005	Main Campus South
Parish & Richardson Architects, Davenport IA	Main Library addition: southwest	1961	Main Campus South

Architect / Project Architect	Building Name	Year	Campus Zone
Payette Associates, Boston MA/Baldwin White Architects, Des Moines IA	Medical Education & Research Facility	2002	Medical Campus
Payette Associates, Boston MA/ Rohrbach Carlson, Iowa City IA	Medical Education & Research Facility addition: Carver Biomedical Research Building	2005	Medical Campus
Payette Associates, Boston MA/ Rohrbach Carlson, Iowa City IA	Carver Biomedical Research Building (Roy J. & Lucille A. Carver Biomedical Research Building)	2005	Medical Campus
Payette Associates, Boston MA/ Rohrbach Associates, Iowa City IA	College of Public Health Building	2011	Medical Campus
Pelli Clarke Pelli Architects, New Haven CT/ OPN Architects, Cedar Rapids IA	Hancher Auditorium	2016	Arts Campus
Plunkett Raysich Architects, Madison WI	Hope Lodge	2007	Athletics Campus
Porter/Brierly Associates, Des Moines IA	Recreation Building	1970	Athletics Campus
Porter/Brierly Associates, Des Moines IA	Recreation Building addition: office	1981	Athletics Campus
Proudfoot & Bird, Des Moines IA	Gilmore Hall	1910	Main Campus North
Proudfoot & Bird, Des Moines IA	Iowa Avenue Bridge	1916	River Valley Campus
Proudfoot & Bird, Des Moines IA	Macbride Hall	1908	Pentacrest
Proudfoot & Bird, Des Moines IA	President's Residence	1908	Main Campus North
Proudfoot & Bird, Des Moines IA	Schaeffer Hall	1902	Pentacrest
Proudfoot & Bird, Des Moines IA	Seamans Center for the Engineering Arts & Sciences	1905	Main Campus South
Proudfoot & Bird, Des Moines IA	Seashore Hall addition: east wing, porch, main entrance	1908	Iowa Avenue Campus
Proudfoot & Bird, Des Moines IA	Biology Building	1905	Iowa Avenue Campus
Proudfoot & Bird, Des Moines IA	Sciences Library	1902	Iowa Avenue Campus
Proudfoot, Bird & Rawson, Des Moines IA	Halsey Hall	1915	Main Campus North
Proudfoot, Bird & Rawson, Des Moines IA	Jessup Hall	1924	Pentacrest
Proudfoot, Bird & Rawson, Des Moines IA	North Hall	1925	Main Campus North
Proudfoot, Bird & Rawson, Des Moines IA	Old Capitol renovation	1924	Pentacrest

Architect / Project Architect	Building Name	Year	Campus Zone
Proudfoot, Bird & Rawson, Des Moines IA	Quadrangle Residence Hall (RAZED)	1920	Near West Campus
Proudfoot, Bird & Rawson, Des Moines IA	Seashore Hall addition: north pavilions	1915	Iowa Avenue Campus
Proudfoot, Bird & Rawson, Des Moines IA	Stuit Hall (Old Music Building)	1918	Iowa Avenue Campus
Proudfoot, Bird & Rawson, Des Moines IA	Trowbridge Hall	1918	Main Campus North
Proudfoot, Bird & Rawson, Des Moines IA	Westlawn	1919	Medical Campus
Proudfoot, Bird & Rawson, Des Moines IA	Chemistry Building	1922	Main Campus North
Proudfoot, Bird & Rawson, Des Moines IA	Currier Residence Hall	1914	Main Campus North
Proudfoot, Bird & Rawson, Des Moines IA	MacLean Hall	1912	Pentacrest
Proudfoot, Bird & Rawson, Des Moines IA	MacLean Hall addition	1920	Pentacrest
Proudfoot, Bird & Rawson, Des Moines IA	Medical Education Building	1919	Medical Campus
Proudfoot, Rawson & Souers, Des Moines IA	Field House	1927	Near West Campus
Proudfoot, Rawson & Souers, Des Moines IA	Power Plant	1928	River Valley Campus
Proudfoot, Rawson & Souers, Des Moines IA	Quadrangle Residence Hall addition: inner ring (RAZED)	1925	Near West Campus
Proudfoot, Rawson & Souers, Des Moines IA	Stanley Hydraulics Laboratory (C. Maxwell Stanley Hydraulics Laboratory)	1928	River Valley Campus
Proudfoot, Rawson & Souers, Des Moines IA	Westlawn renovation	1928	Medical Campus
Proudfoot, Rawson & Souers, Des Moines IA	Medical Laboratories	1927	UIHC Campus
Proudfoot, Rawson, Souers & Thomas, Des Moines IA	Kinnick Stadium	1929	Athletics Campus
Proudfoot, Rawson, Souers & Thomas, Des Moines IA	General Hospital (UIHC)	1928	UIHC Campus
PRVN Consultants, North Liberty IA	Power Plant addition: east side	2014	River Valley Campus
R. S. Finkbine, Des Moines IA	Calvin Hall	1885	Main Campus North
RDG Planning & Design, Des Moines IA	Campus Recreation & Wellness Center	2010	Main Campus South
Robert Hutchinson, Iowa City IA	Kuhl House	ca. 1840	Arts Campus
Rohrbach Associates, Iowa City IA	Burge Residence Hall addition: north side	2010	Main Campus North
Rohrbach Associates, Iowa City IA	Iowa Memorial Union renovation	2015	River Valley Campus
Rohrbach Associates, Iowa City IA	Madison Street Residence Hall	2017	Main Campus North

273

Architect / Project Architect	Building Name	Year	Campus Zone
Rohrbach Associates, Iowa City IA	Mary Louise Petersen Residence Hall	2015	Near West Campus
Rohrbach Carlson, Iowa City IA	Burge Residence Hall renovation: dining hall	2003	Main Campus North
Sasaki, Walker & Associates, Watertown MA/ Prall Architects, Des Moines IA	English-Philosophy Building	1966	River Valley Campus
Savage-Ver Ploeg & Associates, West Des Moines IA	Information Technology Facility	2011	University of Iowa Research Park
Savage-Ver Ploeg & Associates, West Des Moines IA	Pomerantz Center	2005	Main Campus North
Seth J. Temple – Arthur Temple Architects, Davenport IA	Hillcrest Residence Hall addition: south	1951	Near West Campus
Seth J. Temple – Arthur Temple Architects, Davenport IA	Hillcrest Residence Hall addition: southwest	1956	Near West Campus
Seth J. Temple, Davenport IA	Hillcrest Residence Hall	1939	Near West Campus
Seth J. Temple, Davenport IA	Hillcrest Residence Hall addition: PWA Lobby	1940	Near West Campus
Shive-Hattery, Iowa City IA	Cambus Maintenance Facility	1972	Main Campus South
Shive-Hattery, Iowa City IA	Duane Banks Baseball Stadium	1975	Athletics Campus
Shive-Hattery, Iowa City IA	Hawkeye Tennis & Recreation Complex addition: indoor turf	2014	Athletics Campus
Shive-Hattery, Iowa City IA	Hydraulics East Annex	1975	Main Campus South
Shive-Hattery, Iowa City IA	Hydraulics Model Annex	1982	Main Campus South
Shive-Hattery, Iowa City IA	Hydraulics Wind Tunnel Annex	1984	Main Campus South
Siah Armajani, Minneapolis MN/ Brooks Borg Skiles Architecture Engineering, Des Moines IA	Biology Bridge	2000	Iowa Avenue Campus
Skidmore Owings & Merrill: Walter Netsch, Chicago IL	Lindquist Center addition: north building	1980	Main Campus South
Skidmore Owings & Merrill: Walter Netsch, Chicago IL/ George Horner, University of Iowa	Hardin Library for the Health Sciences	1974	Medical Campus
Skidmore Owings & Merrill: Walter Netsch, Chicago IL/ George Horner, University of Iowa	Lindquist Center	1973	Main Campus South
Skidmore Owings & Merrill: Walter Netsch, Chicago IL/ George Horner, University of Iowa	Bowen Science Building	1972	Medical Campus

Architect / Project Architect	Building Name	Year	Campus Zone
Smith, Hinchman & Gryls, Detroit MI/George Horner, University of Iowa	Dental Science Building	1973	Medical Campus
Smith, Voorhees & Jensen, Des Moines IA, Sioux City IA	Rienow Residence Hall	1966	Near West Campus
Smith, Voorhees & Jensen, Des Moines IA, Sioux City IA	Slater Residence Hall	1968	Near West Campus
Stanley Consultants, Muscatine IA	Recreation Building addition: link & office	1985	Athletics Campus
Stanley Consultants, Muscatine IA	Power Plant addition: Boiler 11	1988	River Valley Campus
Stanley Engineering, Muscatine IA	Water Plant	1963	River Valley Campus
Steven Holl Architects, New York NY/ BNIM, Des Moines IA	Visual Arts Building	2016	Arts Campus
Steven Holl Architects, New York NY/ HLKB Architects, Des Moines IA	Art Building West	2006	Arts Campus
Stewart Robinson Laffin	Quadrangle Residence Hall renovation	1964	Near West Campus
Substance Architecture, Des Moines IA	Stew & LeNore Hansen Football Performance Center	2013	Athletics Campus
Substance Architecture, Des Moines IA	Hoak Family Golf Complex (James M. Hoak Family Golf Complex)	2012	Athletics Campus
Thorson-Brom-Broshar-Snyder, Waterloo IA	Becker Communication Studies Building (Samuel L. Becker Communication Studies Building)	1984	Main Campus South
Tinsley, Higgins, Lighter & Lyon, Des Moines IA	Hillcrest Residence Hall addition: dining hall	1961	Near West Campus
Tinsley, Higgins, Lighter & Lyon, Des Moines IA	Iowa Memorial Union addition	1955	River Valley Campus
Tinsley, Higgins, Lighter & Lyon, Des Moines IA	Iowa Memorial Union addition: Iowa House	1965	River Valley Campus
Tinsley, Higgins, Lighter & Lyon, Des Moines IA	Iowa Memorial Union Parking Ramp	1964	Main Campus North
UI Mechanical Engineering Professor B. P. Fleming	Seamans Center for the Engineering Arts & Sciences addition: materials testing lab	1907	Main Campus South
University of Iowa Architect's Office	Indoor practice facility (RAZED)	1986	Athletics Campus
Unknown	Bedell Entrepreneurship Learning Laboratory	1929	Main Campus North
Unknown	Calvin Hall addition: north side	1927	Main Campus North
Unknown	111 Church Street	1925	Main Campus North
Unknown	Currier Residence Hall addition: southwest wing extension	1928	Main Campus North

Architect / Project Architect	Building Name	Year	Campus Zone
Unknown	Field House renovation	1995	Near West Campus
Unknown	Gilmore Hall addition: 3rd & 4th floors	1961	Main Campus North
Unknown	Gilmore Hall renovation	1966	Main Campus North
Unknown	Institute for Rural & Environmental Health	1967	University of Iowa Research Park
Unknown	Oakdale Hall (RAZED)	1917	University of Iowa Research Park
Unknown	Oakdale Hall addition: nurses' dormitory	1924	University of Iowa Research Park
Unknown	Oakdale Hall addition: medical administration	1937	University of Iowa Research Park
Unknown	Oakdale Hall addition: auditorium & clinic	1951	University of Iowa Research Park
Unknown	Oakdale Hall addition: patients' ward	1954	University of Iowa Research Park
Unknown	Oakdale Hall addition: kitchen & rehabilitation	1958	University of Iowa Research Park
Unknown	Oakdale Hall renovation	1964	University of Iowa Research Park
Unknown	Quadrangle Residence Hall renovation	1935	Near West Campus
Unknown	Quadrangle Residence Hall addition: cafeteria (RAZED)	1956	Near West Campus
Unknown	Technology Innovation Center	1924	University of Iowa Research Park
Unknown	University Capitol Centre	1981	Main Campus South
Unknown	Dey House	1857	Main Campus North
Walker Parking, Minneapolis MN/Brown, Healey & Bock, Cedar Rapids IA	Hospital Parking Ramp 2 (RAZED)	1978	UIHC Campus
Woodburn O'Neil Architects & Engineers, West Des Moines IA	Wendell Johnson Speech & Hearing Center	1967	Medical Campus
Woodburn O'Neil Architects & Engineers, West Des Moines IA	Pharmacy Building	1961	Medical Campus
Woodburn O'Neil Architects & Engineers, West Des Moines IA	Phillips Hall	1965	Iowa Avenue Campus

Chronology of Building Completion / Occupancy Dates

Year	Building Name	Architect / Project Architect
ca. 1840	Kuhl House	Robert Hutchinson, Iowa City IA
1842	Old Capitol	John Francis Rague, Springfield IL/ Chauncey Swan, Iowa City IA
1857	Dey House	Unknown
1885	Calvin Hall	R. S. Finkbine, Des Moines IA
1899	Seashore Hall	Josselyn & Taylor, Cedar Rapids IA
1900	Shambaugh House	O. H. Carpenter, Iowa City IA
1902	Schaeffer Hall	Proudfoot & Bird, Des Moines IA
1902	Sciences Library	Proudfoot & Bird, Des Moines IA
1905	Seamans Center for the Engineering Arts & Sciences	Proudfoot & Bird, Des Moines IA
1905	Biology Building	Proudfoot & Bird, Des Moines IA
1907	Seamans Center for the Engineering Arts & Sciences addition: materials testing lab	UI Mechanical Engineering Professor B. P. Fleming
1908	Macbride Hall	Proudfoot & Bird, Des Moines IA
1908	President's Residence	Proudfoot & Bird, Des Moines IA
1908	Seashore Hall addition: east wing, porch, main entrance	Proudfoot & Bird, Des Moines IA
1910	Gilmore Hall	Proudfoot & Bird, Des Moines IA
1912	MacLean Hall	Proudfoot, Bird & Rawson, Des Moines IA
1913	Jefferson Building	H. L. Stevens & Company, Chicago IL
1914	Currier Residence Hall	Proudfoot, Bird & Rawson, Des Moines IA
1915	Halsey Hall	Proudfoot, Bird & Rawson, Des Moines IA
1915	Seashore Hall addition: north pavilions	Proudfoot, Bird & Rawson, Des Moines IA
1916	Iowa Avenue Bridge	Proudfoot & Bird, Des Moines IA
1917	Oakdale Hall (RAZED)	Unknown
1918	Stuit Hall (Old Music Building)	Proudfoot, Bird & Rawson, Des Moines IA
1918	Trowbridge Hall	Proudfoot, Bird & Rawson, Des Moines IA
1919	Westlawn	Proudfoot, Bird & Rawson, Des Moines IA
1919	Medical Education Building	Proudfoot, Bird & Rawson, Des Moines IA
1920	Quadrangle Residence Hall (RAZED)	Proudfoot, Bird & Rawson, Des Moines IA
1920	MacLean Hall addition	Proudfoot, Bird & Rawson, Des Moines IA
1921	Bowman House	O. H. Carpenter, Iowa City IA
1922	Chemistry Building	Proudfoot, Bird & Rawson, Des Moines IA
1924	Jessup Hall	Proudfoot, Bird & Rawson, Des Moines IA
1924	Old Capitol renovation	Proudfoot, Bird & Rawson, Des Moines IA
1924	Oakdale Hall addition: nurses' dormitory (RAZED)	Unknown
1924	Technology Innovation Center	Unknown
1925	Iowa Memorial Union	Boyd & Moore, Des Moines IA
1925	North Hall	Proudfoot, Bird & Rawson, Des Moines IA
1925	Quadrangle Residence Hall addition: inner ring	Proudfoot, Rawson & Souers, Des Moines IA
1925	111 Church Street	Unknown

Year	Building Name	Architect / Project Architect
1927	Field House	Proudfoot, Rawson & Souers, Des Moines IA
1927	Medical Laboratories	Proudfoot, Rawson & Souers, Des Moines IA
1927	Calvin Hall addition: north side	Unknown
1928	Power Plant	Proudfoot, Rawson & Souers, Des Moines IA
1928	Stanley Hydraulics Laboratory (C. Maxwell Stanley Hydraulics Laboratory)	Proudfoot, Rawson & Souers, Des Moines IA
1928	Westlawn renovation	Proudfoot, Rawson & Souers, Des Moines IA
1928	Currier Residence Hall addition: southwest wing extension	Unknown
1928	General Hospital (UIHC)	Proudfoot, Rawson, Souers & Thomas, Des Moines IA
1929	Kinnick Stadium	Proudfoot, Rawson, Souers & Thomas, Des Moines IA
1929	Bedell Entrepreneurship Learning Laboratory	Unknown
1931	Stuit Hall addition: rehearsal hall (RAZED)	George Horner, University of Iowa
1932	Seamans Center for the Engineering Arts & Sciences addition: Mechanical Engineering Building	George Horner, University of Iowa
1933	Power Plant addition: central & south wings	George Horner, University of Iowa
1933	Stanley Hydraulics Laboratory addition: central & south wings	George Horner, University of Iowa
1935	International Center (RAZED)	George Horner, University of Iowa
1935	Quadrangle Residence Hall renovation	Unknown
1936	Iowa Memorial Union Pedestrian Bridge (IMU Bridge)	George Horner, University of Iowa
1936	Theatre Building	George Horner, University of Iowa
1936	Art Building	George Horner, University of Iowa
1937	Motor Pool (RAZED)	George Horner, University of Iowa
1937	Oakdale Hall addition: medical administration (RAZED)	Unknown
1939	Lagoon Shelter House	George Horner, University of Iowa
1939	Seamans Center for the Engineering Arts & Sciences addition: radio	George Horner, University of Iowa
1939	Hillcrest Residence Hall	Seth J. Temple, Davenport IA
1940	Currier Residence Hall addition: north wing	George Horner, University of Iowa
1940	Hillcrest Residence Hall addition: PWA Lobby	Seth J. Temple, Davenport IA
1942	South Quadrangle	George Horner, University of Iowa
1945	Westlawn addition: south extension	George Horner, University of Iowa
1946	Currier Residence Hall renovation	George Horner, University of Iowa
1949	Currier Residence Hall addition: north wing extension	George Horner, University of Iowa
1950	Oakdale Studio A	Morgan & Gelatt, Burlington IA
1951	Communications Center	Brooks Borg, Architects-Engineers, Des Moines IA
1951	Main Library	Keffer & Jones, Des Moines IA

Year	Building Name	Architect / Project Architect
1951	Hillcrest Residence Hall addition: south	Seth J. Temple – Arthur Temple Architects, Davenport IA
1951	Oakdale Hall addition: auditorium & clinic (RAZED)	Unknown
1952	Danforth Chapel	George Horner, University of Iowa
1952	Halsey Hall addition: west wing	Keffer & Jones, Des Moines IA
1954	Center for Disabilities & Development	Charles Richardson & Associates, Davenport IA
1954	Oakdale Hall addition: patients' ward (RAZED)	Unknown
1955	Parklawn Residence Hall	George Horner, University of Iowa
1955	Field House addition: Athletic Office Building	George Horner, University of Iowa, with Charles Altfillisch, Decorah IA
1955	Iowa Memorial Union addition	Tinsley, Higgins, Lighter & Lyon, Des Moines IA
1956	Hillcrest Residence Hall addition: southwest	Seth J. Temple – Arthur Temple Architects, Davenport IA
1956	Quadrangle Residence Hall addition: cafeteria	Unknown
1957	Medical Research Center	George Horner, University of Iowa/ Tinsley, Higgins, Lighter & Lyon, Des Moines IA
1958	Oakdale Hall addition: kitchen & rehabilitation (RAZED)	Unknown
1959	Burge Residence Hall	Charles Altfillisch, Decorah IA
1959	Hawkeye Drive Apartments	Dane D. Morgan & Associates, Burlington IA
1959	International Center addition: south block (RAZED)	George Horner, University of Iowa
1961	Medical Education Building addition: north side	George Horner, University of Iowa/ Dane D. Morgan & Associates, Burlington IA
1961	Main Library addition: southwest	Parish & Richardson Architects, Davenport IA
1961	Hillcrest Residence Hall addition: dining hall	Tinsley, Higgins, Lighter & Lyon, Des Moines IA
1961	Gilmore Hall addition: 3rd & 4th floors	Unknown
1961	Pharmacy Building	Woodburn O'Neil Architects & Engineers, West Des Moines IA
1963	Chemistry Building addition: lecture hall	Brown, Healey & Bock, Cedar Rapids IA
1963	Finkbine Golf Course Clubhouse	George Horner, University of Iowa
1963	Oakdale Studio A addition: 12 units	Morgan & Gelatt, Burlington IA
1963	Water Plant	Stanley Engineering, Muscatine IA
1964	Daum Residence Hall	Altfillisch, Olson, & Gray, Decorah IA
1964	Medical Research Facility	Dane D. Morgan & Associates, Burlington IA
1964	Van Allen Hall	Durrant Group, Dubuque IA
1964	Seamans Center for the Engineering Arts & Sciences addition: electrical engineering	N. Clifford Prall, Des Moines IA
1964	Quadrangle Residence Hall renovation	Stewart Robinson Laffin
1964	Iowa Memorial Union Parking Ramp	Tinsley, Higgins, Lighter & Lyon, Des Moines IA

Year	Building Name	Architect / Project Architect
1964	Oakdale Hall renovation (RAZED)	Unknown
1965	Biology Building addition: Dubuque Street wing	Charles Richardson & Associates, Davenport IA
1965	Center for Disabilities & Development addition: south	Altfillisch, Olson, Gray & Thompson Architects, Decorah IA
1965	Main Library addition: southeast	Charles Richardson & Associates, Davenport IA
1965	Iowa Memorial Union addition: Iowa House	Tinsley, Higgins, Lighter & Lyon, Des Moines IA
1965	Phillips Hall	Woodburn O'Neil Architects & Engineers, West Des Moines IA
1966	Stanley Residence Hall & Ecklund Lounge	Altfillisch, Olson, Gray & Thompson, Decorah IA
1966	English-Philosophy Building	Sasaki, Walker & Associates, Watertown MA/ Prall Architects, Des Moines IA
1966	Rienow Residence Hall	Smith, Voorhees & Jensen, Des Moines IA, Sioux City IA
1966	Gilmore Hall renovation	Unknown
1967	Hawkeye Court Apartments (RAZED)	Emery-Prall Associates, Des Moines IA
1967	Institute for Rural & Environmental Health	Unknown
1967	Wendell Johnson Speech & Hearing Center	Woodburn O'Neil Architects & Engineers, West Des Moines IA
1968	Hospital Parking Ramp 1	Brown, Healey & Bock, Cedar Rapids IA
1968	Mayflower Residence Hall	CPMI, Des Moines IA
1968	Art Building addition: printmaking (east) wing (RAZED)	Harrison & Abramovitz, New York NY/ Neumann Monson Architects, Iowa City IA
1968	Spence Laboratories of Psychology	Louis C. Kingston, Davenport IA
1968	Slater Residence Hall	Smith, Voorhees & Jensen, Des Moines IA, Sioux City IA
1969	Former Museum of Art	Harrison & Abramovitz: Max Abramovitz, New York NY/ Neumann Monson Architects, Iowa City IA
1969	Art Building addition: south wing (RAZED)	Harrison & Abramovitz, New York NY/ Neumann Monson Architects, Iowa City IA
1970	Van Allen Hall addition: east extension	Durrant Group, Dubuque IA
1970	Recreation Building	Porter/Brierly Associates, Des Moines IA
1971	Biology Building addition: Dubuque Street wing	Charles Richardson & Associates, Davenport IA
1971	Nursing Building	Charles Herbert & Associates, Des Moines IA/ George Horner, University of Iowa
1971	Main Library addition: south extension	Charles Richardson & Associates, Davenport IA
1971	Clapp Recital Hall (RAZED)	Harrison & Abramovitz: Max Abramovitz, New York NY/ Neumann Monson Architects, Iowa City IA
1971	Voxman Music Building (RAZED)	Harrison & Abramovitz: Max Abramovitz, New York NY/ Neumann Monson Architects, Iowa City IA
1972	Institute for Rural & Environmental Health addition: north	Brown, Healey & Bock, Cedar Rapids IA
1972	Hancher Auditorium (RAZED)	Harrison & Abramovitz: Max Abramovitz, New York NY/ Neumann Monson Architects, Iowa City IA
1972	Cambus Maintenance Facility	Shive-Hattery, Iowa City IA

Year	Building Name	Architect / Project Architect
1972	Bowen Science Building	Skidmore Owings & Merrill: Walter Netsch, Chicago IL/ George Horner, University of Iowa
1973	Lindquist Center	Skidmore Owings & Merrill: Walter Netsch, Chicago IL/ George Horner, University of Iowa
1973	Dental Science Building	Smith, Hinchman & Gryls, Detroit MI/ George Horner, University of Iowa
1974	Old Capitol restoration	Ferry & Henderson, Springfield IL/ Viggo M. Jensen, Iowa City IA
1974	Hardin Library for the Health Sciences	Skidmore Owings & Merrill: Walter Netsch, Chicago IL/ George Horner, University of Iowa
1975	Art Building addition: ceramics kilns (RAZED)	Harrison & Abramovitz, New York NY/ Neumann Monson Architects, Iowa City IA
1975	Music West – aka Museum of Art addition: Carver wing	Harrison & Abramovitz, New York NY/ Neumann Monson Architects, Iowa City IA
1975	Duane Banks Baseball Stadium	Shive-Hattery, Iowa City IA
1975	Hydraulics East Annex	Shive-Hattery, Iowa City IA
1976	Boyd Tower (UIHC)	HLM Design, Iowa City IA
1976	General Hospital (UIHC) addition: multiple	HLM Design, Iowa City IA
1978	Hospital Parking Ramp 2 (RAZED)	Walker Parking, Minneapolis MN/ Brown, Healey & Bock, Cedar Rapids IA
1979	Medical Research Center addition: vertical expansion	Durrant Group, Dubuque IA
1980	Lindquist Center addition: north building	Skidmore Owings & Merrill: Walter Netsch, Chicago IL
1981	Recreation Building addition: office	Porter/Brierly Associates, Des Moines IA
1981	University Capitol Centre	Unknown
1982	Hydraulics Model Annex	Shive-Hattery, Iowa City IA
1983	Carver-Hawkeye Arena	Caudill Rowlett Scott Architects, Houston TX/ Durrant Group, Dubuque IA
1983	Macbride Hall renovation: Iowa Hall	McConnell-Stevely-Anderson Architects & Planners, Cedar Rapids IA
1984	Former Museum of Art addition: Alumni Center	Abramovitz-Harris-Kingsland, New York NY/ Neumann Monson Architects, Iowa City IA
1984	Field House addition & renovation: South Gym	Bussard Dikis Associates, Des Moines IA
1984	Hydraulics Wind Tunnel Annex	Shive-Hattery, Iowa City IA
1984	Becker Communication Studies Building (Samuel L. Becker Communication Studies Building)	Thorson-Brom-Broshar-Snyder, Waterloo IA
1985	Theatre Building addition: David L. Thayer Theatre & Theatre B	Abramovitz-Harris-Kingsland: Max Abramovitz, New York NY/Neumann Monson Architects, Iowa City IA
1985	Ronald McDonald House	HLM Design, Iowa City IA
1985	Cambus Maintenance Facility addition: south	Neumann Monson, Iowa City IA
1985	Recreation Building addition: link & office	Stanley Consultants, Muscatine IA
1986	Engineering Research Facility	Brooks Borg & Skiles, Architects-Engineers, Des Moines IA

Year	Building Name	Architect / Project Architect
1986	Boyd Law Building	Gunnar Birkerts & Associates, Birmingham MI/ Wehner, Pattschull & Pfiffner, Iowa City IA
1986	Finkbine Golf Course Clubhouse renovation	Nowsyz & Associates, Iowa City IA
1986	Indoor practice facility (RAZED)	University of Iowa Architect's Office
1987	Kuhl House renovation	University of Iowa Architect's Office
1988	Iowa Memorial Union renovation	Bussard Dikis Associates, Des Moines IA
1988	President's Residence renovation	Durrant Group, Dubuque IA
1988	Carver Pavilion (Roy J. Carver Pavilion) (UIHC)	HLM Design, Iowa City IA
1988	Hospital Parking Ramp 3	Neumann Monson Architects, Iowa City IA
1988	Power Plant addition: Boiler 11	Stanley Consultants, Muscatine IA
1989	Eckstein Medical Research Building (John W. Eckstein Medical Research Building)	NBBJ, Seattle WA/ HLM Design, Iowa City IA
1990	North Campus Parking	HLKB Architecture, Des Moines IA
1990	Multi-Tenant Facility	HLKB Architecture, Des Moines IA
1991	College of Medicine Administration Building	NBBJ, Seattle WA/HLM Design, Iowa City IA
1992	Iowa Advanced Technology Laboratories	Frank O. Gehry, Los Angeles CA/ HLKB Architecture, Des Moines IA
1992	Colloton Pavilion (John W. Colloton Pavilion) (UIHC)	HLM Design, Iowa City IA
1993	Pappajohn Business Building (John Pappajohn Business Building)	Architectural Resources, Cambridge MA/ Neumann Monson Architects, Iowa City IA
1995	Gilmore Hall renovation	Baldwin White Architects, Des Moines IA
1995	Jacobson Athletic Building (Richard O. Jacobson Athletic Building)	HLKB Architecture, Des Moines IA
1995	Field House renovation	Unknown
1996	Westlawn addition: Student Health expansion	Baldwin White Architects, Des Moines IA
1996	Pharmaceutical Sciences Research Building	Brooks Borg Skiles Architecture Engineering, Des Moines IA
1996	Pharmacy Building addition: Wurster Center	Brooks Borg Skiles Architecture Engineering: William Anderson, Des Moines IA
1998	Levitt Center for University Advancement	Gwathmey Siegel & Associates: Charles Gwathmey, New York NY/ Brooks Borg Skiles Architecture Engineering, Des Moines IA
1998	Schaeffer Hall renovation	HLKB Architecture, Des Moines IA
1998	National Advanced Driving Simulator	Neumann Monson Architects, Iowa City IA
1999	Stadium at Robert L. Pearl Softball Field	HLM Design, Iowa City IA
1999	University Services Building	OPN Architects, Cedar Rapids IA
2000	Biology Building East	Brooks Borg Skiles Architecture Engineering: William Anderson, Des Moines IA
2000	Pappajohn Pavilion (UIHC)	HLM Design, Iowa City IA

Year	Building Name	Architect / Project Architect
2000	Biology Bridge	Siah Armajani, Minneapolis MN/ Brooks Borg Skiles Architecture Engineering, Des Moines IA
2001	Seamans Center for the Engineering Arts & Sciences addition: south wing	Anshen + Allen, Los Angeles CA/ Neumann Monson Architects, Iowa City IA
2001	Ronald McDonald House addition	Neumann Monson Architects, Iowa City IA
2002	Karro Athletics Hall of Fame (Roy G. Karro Building/Athletics Hall of Fame)	HLKB Architecture, Des Moines IA
2002	Newton Road Parking Ramp	HLKB Architecture, Des Moines IA
2002	Multi-Tenant Facility addition: north side	HLKB Architecture, Des Moines IA
2002	Stanley Hydraulics Laboratory renovation	OPN Architects, Cedar Rapids IA
2002	Medical Education & Research Facility	Payette Associates, Boston MA/ Baldwin White Architects, Des Moines IA
2003	Blank Honors Center	HLKB Architecture, Des Moines IA
2003	Gerdin Athletic Learning Center (Russell & Ann Gerdin Athletic Learning Center)	OPN Architects, Cedar Rapids IA
2003	Burge Residence Hall renovation: dining hall	Rohrbach Carlson, Iowa City IA
2004	Sciences Library renovation	Brooks Borg Skiles Architecture Engineering, Des Moines IA
2005	Melrose Avenue Parking Facility (Hospital Parking Ramp 4)	HLKB Architecture, Des Moines IA
2005	President's Residence extension: garage, east	HLKB Architecture, Des Moines IA
2005	Pomerantz Family Pavilion (UIHC)	HLM Design, Iowa City IA (includes the Center for Excellence in Image-Guided Radiation Therapy)
2005	Adler Journalism Building (Philip D. Adler Journalism & Mass Communication Building)	OPN Architects, Cedar Rapids IA
2005	Medical Education & Research Facility addition: Carver Biomedical Research Building	Payette Associates, Boston MA/ Rohrbach Carlson, Iowa City IA
2005	Carver Biomedical Research Building (Roy J. & Lucille A. Carver Biomedical Research Building)	Payette Associates, Boston MA/ Rohrbach Carlson, Iowa City IA
2005	Pomerantz Center	Savage-Ver Ploeg & Associates, West Des Moines IA
2006	Kinnick Stadium renovation & addition: press & sky boxes, south stands	HNTB, Kansas City MO/Neumann Monson Architects, Iowa City IA
2006	Hawkeye Tennis & Recreation Complex	Neumann Monson, Iowa City IA
2006	Dey House addition: Glenn Schaeffer Library and Archives	OPN Architects, Cedar Rapids IA
2006	Old Capitol restoration	OPN Architects, Cedar Rapids IA

Year	Building Name	Architect / Project Architect
2006	Art Building West	Steven Holl Architects, New York NY/ HLKB Architects, Des Moines IA
2007	Iowa Memorial Union addition	Burt, Hill, Kosar, Rittelmann Associates, Boston MA/ OPN Architects, Cedar Rapids IA
2007	Madison Street Services Building	OPN Architects, Cedar Rapids IA
2007	Hope Lodge	Plunkett Raysich Architects, Madison WI
2009	Chemistry Building renovation	Brooks, Borg, Skiles, Des Moines IA
2009	Chemistry Building addition	Brooks, Borg, Skiles, Des Moines IA
2009	Institute for Orthopaedics, Sports Medicine & Rehabilitation	Heery International, Iowa City IA
2009	P. Sue Beckwith, M.D., Boathouse	Neumann Monson, Iowa City IA
2010	Stuit Hall renovation	BNIM, Des Moines IA
2010	University Capitol Centre addition: School of Music	Neumann Monson, Iowa City IA
2010	Cambus Maintenance Facility addition: south side	Neumann Monson, Iowa City IA
2010	Hydraulics Wave Basin Facility	Neumann Monson, Iowa City IA
2010	BioVentures Center	OPN Architects, Cedar Rapids IA
2010	State Hygienic Laboratory at the University of Iowa	OPN Architects, Cedar Rapids IA, with CUH2A/HDR Architecture
2010	Campus Recreation & Wellness Center	RDG Planning & Design, Des Moines IA
2010	Burge Residence Hall addition: north side	Rohrbach Associates, Iowa City IA
2011	College of Public Health Building	Payette Associates, Boston MA/ Rohrbach Associates, Iowa City IA
2011	Information Technology Facility	Savage-Ver Ploeg & Associates, West Des Moines IA
2012	Dental Science Building addition: west	Invision Architecture, Des Moines IA
2012	Carver-Hawkeye Arena addition & renovation: north	Neumann Monson, Iowa City IA
2012	West Campus Transportation Center	Neumann Monson, Iowa City IA
2012	Hoak Family Golf Complex (James M. Hoak Family Golf Complex)	Substance Architecture, Des Moines IA
2013	Stew & LeNore Hansen Football Performance Center	Substance Architecture, Des Moines IA
2014	Pomerantz Family Pavilion (UIHC) addition: Ambulatory Surgery Center	Hammel, Green & Abrahamson, Minneapolis MN
2014	Power Plant addition: east side	PRVN Consultants, North Liberty IA
2014	Pappajohn Biomedical Discovery Building (John & Mary Pappajohn Biomedical Discovery Building)	Gwathmey Siegel & Associates: Charles Gwathmey, New York NY/Rohrbach Associates, Iowa City IA
2014	Hawkeye Tennis & Recreation Complex addition: indoor turf	Shive-Hattery, Iowa City IA
2015	Biomedical Research Support Facility	Heery International, Iowa City IA
2015	Theatre Building addition: flood recovery	Neumann Monson, Iowa City IA

Sculptures

Building	Artist	Title	Date	Medium	Location
Adler Journalism & Mass Communication Building	James Sanborn	Iacto	2004	metallic cylinder	south plaza
Art Building	John Orth	The Agrarian	1981	cast iron	southeast river front
Art Building West	Richard Artschwager	Sitting	2006	galvalume, 55% aluminum-zinc alloy coated sheet metal	quarry pond deck
Art Building West	Douglas Hansen	Were One	1971	ceramic and steel	south of quarry pond
Art Building West	David Luck	Shared Rhythms	1984	copper, brass, other metals	room 150
Becker Communication Studies Building	**David Middlebrook**	**Small World**	**1986**	**bronze, Italian marble, clay**	**auditorium atrium**
Beckwith Boathouse	Kenneth Snelson	Four Module Piece: Form 2	1968	aluminum, stainless steel	Terrell Mill Park
Beckwith Boathouse	Rebecca Ekstrand & Thomas Rosborough Studios	Calm Waters	2010	glass-tile mosaic	rowing tank room
Biology Building East	**Siah Armajani**	**Bridge for Iowa**	**2000**	**steel, glass**	**Dubuque Street**
Blank Honors Center	Lawrence Weiner	In Line With A Thing In Itself	2005	vinyl letters	west side of building
Bowen Science Building	Chunghi Choo	Orb in Cradle	1998	aluminum	2nd floor main foyer
Bowen Science Building	Pol Bury	Kinetic Fountain	1969	stainless steel	atrium
Boyd Law Building	**Hu Hung-shu**	**For All Seasons**	**1987**	**stainless steel, aircraft cable**	**interior**
Boyd Law Building	**Auguste Rodin**	**Jean de Fiennes, from Burghers of Calais**	**1884–1886**	**bronze**	**south courtyard**
Campus Recreation & Wellness Center	Lawrence J. Nowlan	Swimmer	2009	bronze high relief	2nd floor
Campus Recreation & Wellness Center	Gary Drostle	Movement & Vitality	2010	cut glass mosaic	1st floor main entrance

*Entries in **bold** are described more fully in the text*

Building	Artist	Title	Date	Medium	Location
Campus Recreation & Wellness Center	**Gary Drostle**	**River of Life**	**2010**	**cut glass mosaic**	**1st floor main foyer**
Carver-Hawkeye Arena	**Lloyd Hamrol**	**Stonerise**	**1983**	**Iowa limestone**	**south side**
Carver-Hawkeye Arena	David Lawton	Hawk	1990	stainless steel	south side, Hawkins Drive
Carver-Hawkeye Arena	Lawrence J. Nowlan	Dan Gable	2012	bronze	exterior to building
Chemistry Building	Max Whitby & Element Collections	Interactive Periodic Table	2009	mixed media	east main entrance foyer
College of Public Health Building	Peter Feldstein	Iowa Portraits	2012	photo etched images on glass	floors 1–3
Dental Science Building	Robert Schefman	Untitled	1982	Cor-ten steel	east lawn
Eckstein Medical Research Building	**Robert Arneson**	**Gateway to Self-Realization**	**1992**	**painted bronze, stainless steel**	**west courtyard**
English-Philosophy Building	Paul Slepak	Untitled	1978	Cor-ten steel	north entrance patio
General Hospital (Boyd Tower)	Ronda Reinke	To Cleve's Creamery from Grandpa's Farm	1980	cast iron	northwest corner
Hancher Auditorium (new)	El Anatsui	Anonymous Creature	2009	aluminum, copper wire	2nd floor above ascending stairs
Hancher Auditorium (new)	**Francesca Bettridge**	**Untitled**	**2016**	**LED lighting**	**auditorium**
Hancher Auditorium (new)	Anita Jung	Untitled	2016	acrylic, collage on panel	interior main level
Hancher Auditorium (former)	Ernest Trova	Profile Canto II	1973	Cor-ten steel	relocated
Hancher Auditorium (former)	**Luther Utterback**	**Untitled**	**1976**	**Indiana limestone**	**relocated**
Iowa Advanced Technology Laboratories	Sol Lewitt	2–3–1–1	1994	aluminum, white paint	river façade
Iowa Memorial Union	Harry E. Stinson	Armed Services	1933	limestone	Main Lounge entrance
Iowa Memorial Union	Elizabeth Catlett	Stepping Out	2000	bronze	lobby

288

Building	Artist	Title	Date	Medium	Location
Kinnick Stadium	Lawrence J. Nowlan	Nile Kinnick	2006	bronze	Kraus Family Pavilion south side of building
Kinnick Stadium	Lawrence J. Nowlan	Ironmen	2006	bronze high relief	south side of building in concourse
Levitt Center	**Hu Hung-shu**	**D. Forever**	**1998**	**stainless steel, aircraft cable**	**atrium**
Levitt Center	Shirley Wyrick	Building a Foundation	1998	bronze	atrium
Library (main)	Isabel Barbuzza	01_D_ cataloged	2014	cut and folded books, glue, plywood, steel, fabric leather	Madison Street foyer
Library (main)	Isabel Barbuzza	02_D_ cataloged	2014	cut and folded books, glue, plywood, steel, fabric leather	Madison Street foyer
Library (main)	Jim Shrosbree	CHROMO (magia) redux	2014	aluminum, auto enamel	south 1st floor foyer
Lindquist Center	Fletcher Benton	Folded Circle, 2 Squares	1977	polished bronze, granite	interior
Lindquist Center	Alfred Lee Burns	Untitled	1975	steel, concrete, cable	northwest side of south building
Lindquist Center	Takaski Naraha	Sculpture 79–9	1979	black Swedish granite	interior
Lindquist Center	**Louise Nevelson**	**Voyage**	**1975**	**Cor-ten steel painted black**	**courtyard**
Lindquist Center	Melvin Schuler	Geometric Abstraction No. 2	1979	copper over redwood	interior
Lindquist Center	Barry Tinsley	Those Hills Again	1979	steel	interior
Medical Education & Research Facility	John F. Simon Jr.	Channels	2002	plasma screens, paint	west corridor
Museum of Art (former)	Mark di Suvero	Untitled	1971	painted steel	relocated
Museum of Art (former)	David Jokinen	Untitled	1989	red concrete, iron, stone, earth	river façade
Museum of Art (former)	Beverly Pepper	Omega	1974	Cor-ten steel	relocated

Building	Artist	Title	Date	Medium	Location
Museum of Art (former)	Lila Katsen	Oracle	1974	Cor-ten and stainless steel	river side
Museum of Art (former)	George Rickey	Four Rectangles Oblique: Variation II	1972–1975	stainless steel	relocated
Museum of Art (former)	George Rickey	Two Lines Oblique	1967–1969	stainless steel	relocated
National Advanced Driving Simulator	Joe Nelson	Gemini	1994	cast iron	University of Iowa Research Park
Petersen Residence Hall	Eikamp Arts	Scholastic Truth	2015	wood, resin	main foyer
Phillips Hall	**Gregg LeFevre**	**Literary Walk**	**2001**	**bronze**	**Iowa Avenue**
Pomerantz Center	**Unknown**	**Bird T. Baldwin**	**1928**	**bronze**	**Market Street**
Pomerantz Center	**Peter Randall-Page**	**Ridge and Furrow**	**2011**	**Cornwall boulder**	**Cleary Walkway**
Riverside Dr./Iowa Ave. Ped Bridge	Brian M. Fritz	Untitled	1997	stainless steel	spiral ramp
Schaeffer Hall	William Carlson	Reticulated Aperture	1999	cast glass panels	north stairs
State Hygienic Laboratory	Norie Sato	Study Circles	2010	hand-painted, silkscreened, sandblasted glass panels	north foyer
UIHC	Fletcher Benton	Folded Square Alphabet D	1980	painted steel plate, red	relocated
UIHC	Julius Schmidt	Untitled	1985	bronze	Carver Pavilion courtyard
UIHC	Susan Chrysler White	Giardini	2007	Plexiglas, acrylic paint	Pomerantz Family Pavilion
Visual Arts Building	Rebecca Thompson	The Guardians	2015	stone, stainless steel	southeast corner
Visual Arts Building	Mike Metz	Stone Motorcycles	2016	stone	east façade
Voxman Music Building	Dale Chihuly	Forest, Amber & Gilded Chandelier (04.219.ch)	1996–2003	blown glass	atrium
West Campus Transportation Center	**Susan Chrysler White**	**Flash Point**	**2012**	**acrylic on aluminum**	**Sky Link escalators**

Glossary

arcade—A series of consecutive arches supported by piers or columns

arch, blind—An arch without an opening; applied as a decorative treatment to a flat surface

arch, pointed—Characteristic of Gothic architecture, this arch culminates with a point instead of the conventional semicircular curve

architrave—An element of classical architecture comprising the lowest portion of the entablature; the component below the frieze

Art Deco—A style derived from the 1925 Paris Exposition of Decorative Arts; characterized by repetition of sleek, curvilinear forms in imitation of machine-made objects

Art Moderne—Design popular in the 1920s to 1940s incorporating motifs suggestive of machine-made objects; see also Art Deco

articulated frame—The external expression of the internal structure of a building

atrium—A large reception room or open courtyard, usually the first space entered, which provides a transitional space to other parts of a building

axial relationships—The relation of buildings, streets, or other design elements to one another along a center line

balustrade—Composed of short posts (balusters) that support a horizontal rail; this can be used as a decorative feature, to enclose a space, or as a handrail

basilica—For ancient Romans, a large open meeting hall; became the predominant plan for Christian churches

bas-relief—A sculpture that projects only slightly from the surrounding surface; also called low relief

bay—One of a series of upright wall sections defined by flanking columns, pilasters, piers, buttresses, or other vertical elements

Beaux-Arts Classicism—A style of architecture popular in the nineteenth and twentieth centuries influenced by the principles of the École des Beaux-Arts in Paris and using motifs from Roman architecture

bracket—A small, ornamental architectural piece protruding from a wall and used to support another element above it

Brutalism—A mid-twentieth-century style emphasizing the aesthetic of exposed concrete, especially with the surface texture of the wooden forms

cantilever—A projecting horizontal element that is seemingly unsupported, like a balcony

capital—The upper, decorative component of a column

casement window—A side-hinged window having a vertical sash

castellated—Containing parts of a medieval castle, such as crenellations

Chicago window—A large, oblong window flanked by two narrow sash windows

Civilian Conservation Corps—A New Deal program (1933–1941) designed to provide employment for men between the ages of eighteen and twenty-five on flood control jobs and other environmental projects

cladding—A protective covering applied to the external surface of a structure

Classical, Classicism—A style used in, or reflecting qualities and motifs of, Greek and Roman art and architecture; characterized by symmetry and rationality

Classical Revival—A later return to Greco-Roman visual arts; see also neo-Classical or Beaux-Arts Classicism

clerestory—A row of windows along the upper part of a wall

Collegiate Gothic—A secular version of Gothic architecture revived for nineteenth-century university campuses

Colonial—Eighteenth-century American domestic architecture, primarily brick and clapboard

Colonial Revival—A historicizing trend in the nineteenth and twentieth centuries of domestic architecture that references eighteenth-century forms of the American colonies

colonnette—A slender, shorter form of a column, usually for decoration

column—A freestanding vertical element comprised of a base, shaft, and capital

column, engaged—A column embedded into a wall

console—An ornamental bracket, often an S-curve shape, supporting or buttressing a structural element above or behind

Constructivism—An art movement originating in Russia in the early twentieth century; in architecture it emphasized the structure and the industrial materials of a building

corbels—A projecting element supporting an upper structure, as under a balcony

Corinthian—An order of classical architecture characterized by capitals with acanthus-leaf ornamentation

cornice—The uppermost portion of an entablature; a projecting molding that runs along the top of a building

crenellation/crenellated—Notches cut into a parapet surrounding a platform or roof; most notably the battlements on top of a castle tower offering protection to archers

curtain wall—A non-load-bearing section of a wall; using one material, usually glass, that gives a uniform appearance

denticulation—A series of small, toothlike squares (dentils) running horizontally under a cornice

Doric—An order of classical architecture characterized by a simple, cushion capital and containing triglyphs and metopes in the frieze of the entablature

dormer—A window projecting from the sloping side of a roof

English Gothic—The medieval architecture of the thirteenth and fourteenth centuries typical of England

entablature—The horizontal feature above columns in classical architecture that is divided into three parts: cornice (uppermost element), frieze (inscription or sculptural relief), and architrave

façade—Exterior surface or front of an edifice

Field Theory—A design methodology of the 1970s employing multiples of a geometrical unit ("field") for the generation of building floor plans

finials—A series of crowning vertical ornaments extending above the primary massing of a building

Flemish Bond brickwork—Alternating short and long bricks along each horizontal course

fluting—Consecutive concave grooves running along the length of a column shaft or pilaster

frieze—A horizontal band between the cornice and architrave in a classical entablature, sometimes containing an inscription

frontispiece—An element designating the main entrance or primary façade of a building

gable—The triangular (or variant) shape formed by the end of a pitched roof

gallery, blind—A continuous arcade of closed arches serving to decorate a wall

gambrel roof—A roof where each gable is composed of one gradually inclining plane and one steep, nearly vertical plane; similar to a mansard roof

Georgian Revival—The nineteenth-century return to visual forms of the Georgian period

Georgian style—An architectural and decorative program employing elements of Renaissance Classicism; associated with the tastes of England's kings George I–IV (1714–1830) and typical of the American colonies and early U.S. republic

German Expressionism—In architecture, a style developed in Germany in the 1920s aimed at emotional appeal

glazing—An opening covered by glass; a wall of glass

Gothic—The dominant architectural style in Europe from the twelfth to the fifteenth century, having pointed arches, masonry rib vaulting, and extensive stained-glass windows

Gothic Revival—A stylistic trend employing characteristics of Gothic architecture beginning in the mid eighteenth century in Europe and extending into the early twentieth century in the U.S.

Greek Revival—A neo-Classical style that aimed to recreate the characteristics of Greek, as opposed to Roman, architecture; characterized by simplified forms

headers and stretchers—A header is a brick laid with its short end showing on the exterior of a wall; a stretcher is laid with its long side showing

hip roof—A roof where the gables, instead of extending vertically, slope back toward the ridge

incising—A process by which a design is cut into a material

International—An architectural style appearing first in Europe in 1920–1930; characterized by a machine aesthetic and historical allusions

International style Modernism—See International

Ionic—An order of classical architecture characterized by a capital comprised of two volute scrolls

Italian Baroque—A style popular from the late sixteenth century to the early eighteenth century; a synthesis of architecture, painting, and sculpture characterized by elliptical forms, dynamic compositions, and an emphasis on highlights and shadow

Italian Renaissance—The period of the late fourteenth to sixteenth centuries marked by a revival of classical ideals and motifs

Italianate—A style of architecture popular in the nineteenth century recalling Italian Renaissance architectural and decorative forms

keystone—The stone at the pinnacle of an arch

lancet window—A slim, vertically arched window with a pointed, spearlike top

lantern—A small round or polygonal crowning structure with narrow windows admitting light to an interior space

lintel—A horizontal element supported by two vertical posts and forming an open space such as a doorway or window

loggia—A roofed, open gallery featuring an arcade or colonnade along the side of a building

Lombard band—A prominent horizontal decorative line composed of small blind arches and running along the top of a wall or other structural element; a characteristic feature of Romanesque architecture

lunette—A flat, semicircular surface, often over a door, used as a space for murals, mosaics, sculpture, or as a decorative treatment in itself

machine aesthetic—An emphasis on the machine-made and industrial, with mass-produced elements in structural and surface treatments

mansard roof—A roof where all four sides have a double slope, the lower one being more severe

massing—The exterior assemblage or orientation of a building's spatial volumes

Medieval—Architectural styles characteristic of the Middle Ages, primarily Romanesque and Gothic

Medieval Revival—Nineteenth- and early twentieth-century styles employing Romanesque and Gothic motifs

metope—The square space between triglyphs on a Doric frieze

Minimalism—A style aimed at simplifying forms to essential geometric elements; lacking decoration

Modern—A general stylistic orientation of the twentieth century that rejected historical motifs in favor of machine aesthetics and the utilization of new materials and structural systems

Moderne—A style popular in the 1920s through 1940s and based on a machine aesthetic, often with streamlined effects

Modernism—In architecture, a style that rejected all reference to historical or past styles

modular—A method of building design where proportions of space and structure are determined by the geometric ratios between part and whole

monolithic—Created from a single piece of material (e.g., stone); a monolithic column shaft cut from the quarry as one piece, not made up of assembled cut drums

mullion—A thin, vertical pier separating the openings of adjacent windows or doors

mutule—One of a series of projecting rectangular blocks supporting a cornice

neo-Classical—An eighteenth-century revival of ancient Greek and Roman architecture

neo-Gothic—Any post-medieval use of Gothic forms or motifs; see also Gothic Revival

neo-Miesian—Architecture influenced by Ludwig Mies van der Rohe (1886–1969)

New Formalism—A modernist style (since the 1960s) characterized by symmetry and stylized classical composition

oculus—A small circular opening or "eye" at the top of a dome or in a wall

pagoda—A stepped tower of multiple roof structures; often associated with Buddhist temples

Palladianism—An architectural style inspired by sixteenth-century Italian architect Palladio adapting elements from Roman architecture to contemporary building types

palmette—A decorative element resembling a palm leaf

parapet—A protective wall creating a barrier against a severe drop

pavilion—A vertically projecting exterior volume of a larger building

pediment—A triangular-shaped gable crowning a portico, door, or window

pier—A freestanding vertical element, usually rectangular in form, supporting a structure above

pilaster—An engaged pier that seems embedded into the wall, similar to an engaged column, used for decorative purposes

piloti—An exposed, usually round pillar in front of a recessed first-story wall and supporting the second floor of a building

podium—A platform providing a base for a building

portico—A structure that covers the area before the entrance to a building; usually takes the shape of a temple façade with a pediment, entablature, and columns

Postmodernism—A variety of late twentieth-century styles that reacted to Modernism and moved toward more diverse, individual styles, sometimes introducing ornament and motifs from earlier styles

Prairie—An architectural style with its roots in the American Midwest (Frank Lloyd Wright); emphasized the relationship of a building to its site, focused on the use of natural materials, and stressed horizontality

punched window—A window deeply inset into a wall and often without enframement

PWA—The Public Works Administration (1933–1947) was a Roosevelt-era federally funded program for infrastructure development

Queen Anne—An architectural style influenced by the tastes of England's Queen Anne (early sixteenth century), developed in the U.S. in the late nineteenth century; characterized by multiple gables and asymmetry

quoins, quoining—Distinctively cut stones at the corner of a wall, usually to emphasize or decorate

relief—An image carved into a flat surface so that the forms project from, but remain attached to, the background

revetment—External cladding of fine material, such as marble or other high-quality stone, over an otherwise structural surface

ribbon window—One of a series of horizontal windows, separated only by mullions, that forms a band across the exterior wall of a building

Rococo—A style of the late Baroque characterized by elegant curvilinear forms and pastel colors

Romanesque—An architectural style of the Middle Ages characterized by the use of round arches and weighty masonry construction

Romanesque Revival—A nineteenth-century emulation of Romanesque architecture, usually emphasizing round arches and heavy masonry

rotunda—A building or room, circular in plan, usually topped by a dome

Russian Constructivism—See Constructivism

rustication—Masonry made to look as if cut from large stone blocks, usually left with a rough surface texture

scroll—A decorative spiral form

Second Empire—A French style popular in the second half of the nineteenth century, during the reign of Napoleon III, showing a profusion of ornament

slab roof—A flat roof, often of a simple slab of concrete or stone

solarium—A sun terrace

space-frame construction—Interconnected truss-framework roof structure that can cover large spaces

Spanish Colonial Revival—The reuse of forms and motifs from the Spanish Colonial occupation in North America; stuccoed surfaces, terra-cotta tile roofs, and curvilinear elements are characteristic

spur buttress—In masonry construction, a sloping pier built against a wall to help strengthen the wall and alleviate the outward thrust of the weight from above

Streamline Moderne—Popular in the 1930s and 1940s; characterized by aerodynamic forms like rounded corners and horizontal bands

swag—A carved ornament in the form of a garland or cloth draped over two supports

terra-cotta—An unglazed fired clay often used for architectural decoration or as a building material

terrazzo—A flooring made from marble chips and cement that is polished after drying

tracery—Ornamental stonework carved in graceful, organic patterns

transept—The lateral space crossing a longitudinal space; in ecclesiastical architecture, it is the arm of the cross-shaped church plan

triglyph—Part of a frieze in the Doric order; an element of Classical architecture made to resemble the end of a wooden beam

truss—A framework of timbers that supports the roof

Tudor Revival—A nineteenth-century revival of a mixture of English Gothic and Renaissance architecture

volute—Spiral scroll, appearing in a pair, comprising an Ionic capital

Werkbund—An association of German designers of the first half of the twentieth century; in the late 1920s its leaders, Mies van der Rohe among them, rejected traditional styles in favor of the strong advocacy of Modern architecture

Westwerk—The west end of a church (Carolingian or Romanesque) that opens to the nave and is usually crowned by a tower

widow's walk—A balustraded or otherwise railed rooftop platform

WPA—The Works Projects Administration (1935–1943) was a federally funded building program aimed at reemploying an idled workforce in the construction of public buildings, many of which were of Moderne style

Zigzag Moderne—See Art Deco

Bibliography

Eckhardt, Patricia. "Proudfoot and Bird, Campus Architects: Building Facilities for Professional Education at the University of Iowa, 1898–1910." Ph.D. dissertation, University of Iowa, 1990.

Gebhard, David, and Gerald Mansheim. *Buildings of Iowa*. New York: Oxford University Press, 1993.

Gerber, John C. *A Pictorial History of the University of Iowa*. Iowa City: University of Iowa Press, 1988.

Horner, George L. *Architectural Design of the Architect's Office*. Cedar Rapids, Iowa: French-Stamats Company, 1939.

"Iowa's Fields." *Progressive Architecture* 54 (1973): 82–91.

Keyes, Margaret N. *Old Capitol: Portrait of an Iowa Landmark*. Iowa City: University of Iowa Press, 1988.

———. *Nineteenth Century Home Architecture of Iowa City*. Iowa City: University of Iowa Press, 1993.

Lafore, Laurence. *American Classic*. Iowa City: Iowa State Historical Department, 1975.

Levey, Samuel. *The Rise of a University Teaching Hospital, a Leadership Perspective: The University of Iowa Hospitals and Clinics*. Chicago: Health Administration Press, 1997.

Mansheim, Gerald. *Iowa City: An Illustrated History*. Norfolk, Virginia: Donning Company, 1989.

Persons, Stow. *The University of Iowa in the Twentieth Century: An Institutional History*. Iowa City: University of Iowa Press, 1990.

Svendsen, Marlys. *Iowa City Historic Preservation Plan and Appendices*. Iowa City, 2008.

Weber, Irving B. *Historical Stories about Iowa City*. 2 vols. Iowa City: Iowa City Lions Club, 1976–1979.

Index